THE FIRST TIME
INVESTOR

The McGraw·Hill Companies

Copyright © 2004 by Larry Chambers and Dale Rogers. All rights reserved. Printed in the United States of America. Except as permitted under the United States Copyright Act of 1976, no part of this publication may be reproduced or distributed in any form or by any means, or stored in a database or retrieval system, without the prior written permission of the publisher.

1 2 3 4 5 6 7 8 9 0   AGM/AGM   0 9 8 7 6 5 4

ISBN 0-07-142037-1

This publication is designed to provide accurate and authoritative information in regard to the subject matter covered. It is sold with the understanding that neither the author nor the publisher is engaged in rendering legal, accounting, futures/securities trading, or other professional service. If legal advice or other expert assistance is required, the services of a competent professional person should be sought.
> —*From a Declaration of Principles jointly adopted by a Committee of the American Bar Association and a Committee of Publishers*

McGraw-Hill books are available at special quantity discounts to use as premiums and sales promotions, or for use in corporate training programs. For more information, please write to the Director of Special Sales, Professional Publishing, McGraw-Hill, Two Penn Plaza, New York, NY 10121-2298. Or contact your local bookstore.

 This book is printed on recycled, acid-free paper containing a minimum of 50% recycled, de-inked fiber.

Library of Congress Cataloging-in-Publication Data
Chambers, Larry.
  The first time investor : how to start safe, invest smart, and sleep well / by Larry Chambers and Dale Rogers.
    p. cm.
  ISBN 0-07-142037-1 (alk. paper)
  1. Investments.   2. Finance, Personal.   I. Rogers, Dale.   II. Title.

HG4521.C4513 2004
332.6—dc22

                                    2003021907

THE FIRST TIME INVESTOR

How to Start Safe, Invest Smart, and Sleep Well

Larry Chambers
Dale Rogers

Third Edition

McGraw-Hill
New York • Chicago • San Francisco • Lisbon • London • Madrid •
Mexico City • Milan • New Delhi • San Juan • Seoul • Singapore •
Sydney • Toronto

CONTENTS

PART FOUR

PART FIVE

ACKNOWLEDGMENTS

OUR AMERICAN LABOR UNIONS

Ten years ago, the Department of Labor proposed to take 15 percent of all the pension and 401(k) money in the United States and put it into economically targeted investments as a way of funding a rebuilding plan for inner cities plus additional welfare programs. Our government even ignored its own ERISA rules *against* the diversion of plan assets in the effort to use private retirement fund assets to support these social programs.

But the proposal was rolled back and went away—and not because of anything any conservatives or business owners did. The proposal was dropped because of the rebellion in the *labor unions*. The labor union members reacted exactly the way every capitalist does when someone reaches for their chips, and said, "You're not using *my* retirement money for your federal programs." We owe them a tremendous note of thanks for saving our retirement system.

INTRODUCTION

The purpose of this book is twofold. First, it's to help you to become a successful investor. Second, and just as important, it's to get you to take the necessary steps to avoid becoming an investment victim!

You cannot continue performing the same old actions and expect to get a different result!

It was over a decade ago that I first wrote *The First Time Investor: How to Start Safe, Invest Smart, and Sleep Well.* The United States had just finished a war with Iraq; communism was crumbling; and the Berlin Wall had come down. In the financial news, the real estate market was in a slump; there were insider-trading scandals; and the junk bond market had collapsed. Ironic, isn't it?

A wave of pessimism spread over America. Prophets of doom and gloom were *New York Times* bestselling authors. The biggest expert was Dr. Robbie Batra. His book announced the coming economic depression and peddled his version of investment advice. The advice in *The First Time Investor* was contrary to both Dr. Batra's and Wall Street's predictions— but you would have made money had you followed it.

A year ago Kelli Christiansen, my editor at McGraw-Hill, asked me to do a revision of this book. It was about the same time that I met an investment advisor by the name of Dale Rogers. Dale had a lot to say, because for the last three decades, he had been successfully and carefully managing 55,000 participants in over 300 retirement plans across the country. With that much business, Dale doesn't have time for sugar-coating anything or telling you what you want to hear. In fact, he's more of an in-your-face-with-the-truth kind of guy. What you decide after that is up to you; you've at least been told the hard, cold facts!

My earlier books, like most I've read, simply contained definitions of mutual funds and stocks, with no relationship to the various theories of investing—including Modern Portfolio Theory and efficient market theory (which we will be explaining in this book). Since these are the very principles upon which the markets work, I thought everyone understood these theories. But I found out that active management firms have been marketing under the terminology without actually employing the academic discipline. For most of the 1990s while the market was just going straight up, it almost didn't matter. But, from 1999 forward, it became apparent that all Wall Street had been doing was selling products unchallenged by research and a lot more was necessary if an investment portfolio was to withstand a three-year downturn, which was almost as bad as any we've ever experienced.

It wasn't until after many lengthy discussions with Dale Rogers that I really understood what the investing public has been sold. It jolted me. It's hard to accept that the best and brightest on Wall Street, the highest-paid salespeople and marketing teams, have taken the concept of modern investment theory and manipulated it simply in order to sell different types of products and funds. In fact, in 2002, the number of stock and bond mutual funds surpassed the number of stocks listed on all three exchanges combined. (See Figure I.1.)

It's buyer beware!

The more I read and write about the world of investing, the more I find there are mountains of evidence from the academic side warning you and explaining to you why buying and selling alone aren't enough to build wealth—that most investments are chosen the same way you would buy a new car: from emotion. Past performance is no indication of future success.

One of the magazines I have written for is a broker's trade magazine called *Registered Rep*. Recently, an article explained the results of an experiment at Wake Forest University where a psychology professor and 600 students were given a choice of investing with two different stockbrokers who would recommend the same stock. One stockbroker took a cautious approach, explaining the risks involved as well as the potential rewards, while the other broker didn't mention risk—he just gave very confident recommendations. Students overwhelmingly said that they would invest with the broker who told them nothing of the risks. Professor Eric Stone explained to *Registered Rep* that people are overly impressed with confidence. When people feel out of their league, they prefer to rely on an expert who acts confidently.

Meanwhile, hundreds of millions of dollars are spent annually on advertising to convince you that brokerage firms have specialized knowledge that is of value to you, without any data to support its claims. We've simply been conditioned to believe that investment management is a complex and arcane subject best left to the self-proclaimed experts.

The good news is that Dale Rogers is a credible expert with real clients and a real track record, and I'm proud to have coauthored this book with

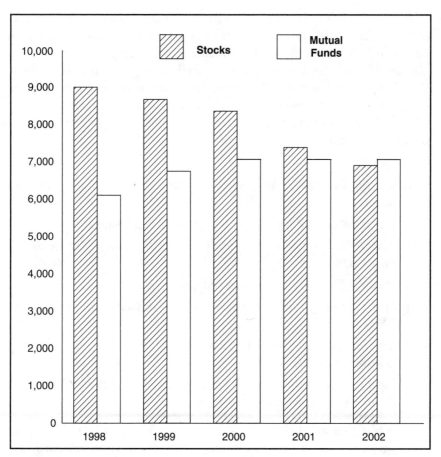

FIGURE I.1
Number of Stock and Bond Mutual Funds versus the Number of Stocks, 1998–2003
Source: Investment Company Institute.

him. We both feel passionately about our generation of baby boomers who are suffering financially and who will continue to suffer, mostly because of the misleading advice in financial books and the media. That's where this book is going. We want to explain to you how to avoid the nonsense and the miscommunication, the investment pornography that's out there, and make the right moves that position you for a chance of investment success.

But don't take my word on this; just check what today's leading experts of investment advice are saying. *Consumer Reports* (CR) rated seven of the best-selling finance books in the September 2003 issue. After reviewing a number of best-seller lists and recommended reading lists on Amazon.com, they decided to judge the following seven finance titles. *Consumer Reports* had each subject reviewed by experts as well as having finance experts review all seven books in their entirety. The reviewers' responses resulted in the following ranking:

1. *Making the Most of Your Money* by Jane Bryant Quinn (Simon & Schuster, 1997)
2. *The Road to Wealth* by Suze Orman (Riverhead Books, 2001)
3. *The Nine Steps to Financial Freedom* by Suze Orman (Three Rivers Press, 2000)
4. *Personal Finance for Dummies* (3d ed.) by Eric Tyson (Wiley, 2000)
5. *Smart Women Finish Rich* (rev. ed.) by David Bach (Smart Workbook, 2002)
6. *The Motley Fool Personal Financial Workbook* by David and Tom Gardner (Fireside, 2003)
7. *Pay Yourself First: The African American Guide to Financial Success and Security* by Jesse Brown (John Wiley, 2001)

Dale and I added *Rich Dad's Guide to Investing* by Robert T. Kiyosaki and Sharon L. Lechter (Warner Books, 2000), which is prominently featured in most any bookstore you enter.

You will notice that any discussion of the underpinnings of how the markets actually work is blatantly missing. None of the top consumer investment books mention Modern Portfolio Theory, efficient market theory, or any other factors that can account for 96 percent of all stock returns. Without this basic information, there is no value for the unsuspecting reader, who has been given marketing definitions presented as factual information.

Suze Orman tours the country promoting not only her books, but also the two financial services companies she represents. The authors of *Rich Dad's Guide to Investing* tell the reader on page 3 that their book "isn't about investing." What? The rest of the book is on how to invest and get into a business. Eric Tyson's book, *Personal Finance for Dummies*, is really about how to pick and buy mutual funds and how to avoid the fund investing pit-falls. But he never goes out on a limb other than to choose some big-name mutual funds.

Smart Women Finish Rich by David Bach is more a motivation builder—how to get out of debt. He does recommend index funds, but he doesn't explain why index funds work. He also recommends how to use the phone book to find top-level nationally recognized brokerage firms—among them are Paine Webber and Morgan Stanley. Let's see now—Paine Webber was the top advisor to Enron, and Morgan Stanley announced it is required to pay a settlement of $25 million and disgorgement of an additional $25 million in penalties. Merrill Lynch in May 2003 agreed to pay $100 million to settle allegations of tainted research. Merrill Lynch is part of a "global" settlement in which Merrill and other top Wall Street firms pledged to pay $1.4 billion to settle federal and state charges that they had put their interests ahead of their investors. Before you go running to your phone book, you may want to see how much each firm will pay as part of the $1.4 billion civil settlement, which includes $900 million in penalties, as reported in the *Washington Post* and *Wall Street Journal* (December 23, 2002):

Citigroup/Salomon Smith Barney	$400 million
Credit Suisse First Boston	$200 million
Merrill Lynch	$200 million
Morgan Stanley	$125 million
Goldman Sachs Group	$110 million
Lehman Brothers Holdings	$80 million
J.P. Morgan Chase	$80 million
Bear Stearns	$80 million
UBS Warburg	$80 million
U.S. Bancorp Piper Jaffray	$32.5 million

If you're buying this book just to get another look at definitions, you might as well close it and go away. This book is about how to make money in the stock market, and also how to avoid losing it. So I'm warning you up front—this is not going to be a Pollyanna-ish defining of investment terms or a don't-you-worry, every-little-thing-is-gonna-be-alright kind of book. What you read here may evoke some strong reactions and may put everything you believe about investing in question. But, at the very least, it will get you thinking; and that's the first step to avoiding becoming an investment victim!

HOW TO USE THIS BOOK

I recommend first skimming the entire book to get a general sense of where Dale and I are headed. Then you'll want to read the chapters in the order presented, since each chapter builds on the previous ones. Follow it straight through and you'll do fine. The first part explains the academic theory behind what we're setting out to accomplish. The theory gives you a deeper sense of how things work. If you're already familiar with how asset class investing, markets, and Modern Portfolio Theory work, and you're eager to get going right away, you may want to jump to Part Two, the action steps, which take you step-by-step through the process of building your own portfolio. Don't forget to come back to earlier chapters, however, since they will refresh your knowledge of the fundamentals.

WHAT IT TAKES

The text is really a course designed to make a short trip out of what can otherwise be an endless journey, but it does require you to put in some time to learn these lessons and steps. What you'll be learning is technique. Technique is neutral. With proper technique, whatever your investment goals are, they can be shaped into your own investment program. The deeper your understanding, the more wisely you'll invest.

Larry Chambers

THE FIRST TIME INVESTOR

PART ONE
GETTING STARTED: INVESTING THE SUCCESSFUL WAY

Whether you are a first time investor or a sixth time investor who keeps learning the hard way, or even if you've been in debt a long time and are still searching for a way to become an investor, you are in the right place. This book will change your attitude as well as your approach to investing. It will dramatically alter the way you think about how the stock market works and how you should invest your own hard-earned money. In fact, you just might find these ideas may change your life.

Wall Street is not going to be thrilled with this book. Why? Because our message is that traditional Wall Street investment strategies—primarily stock picking and market timing—do not work.

We will reveal to you how to be a successful investor by not playing the investment "marketing" game. You will end up reaping far more benefits with a lot less effort and risk. The best part is you will also learn how to evaluate investment advice you receive the correct way—you will never again fall prey to the misguided recommendation of an uninformed broker or well-meaning friends.

If you are new to investing, don't worry. If you are an experienced investor, you will find our ideas refreshing, exciting, and new.

The difference between investors who reach their goals and those who never do is not how much time they spend hunting for the right mutual fund, but how much time they waste in the wrong asset classes. This book will teach you the principles of asset class investing. Asset class investing takes advantage of the best and the brightest and designs portfolios that use this knowledge successfully. It is a strategic, long-term investment philosophy that allows you to step into the world of rational thought backed by empirical evidence—and away from the world of emotional decision making.

CHAPTER 1

WE WANT YOU TO BECOME RICH!

"Good morning, my name is Dale Rogers." It was 100 degrees inside the break room of a small Dallas manufacturing company, and I was surrounded by about 20 folded-arm skeptics intended to guard against being "sold" anything. This was a tough-looking crowd; even their tattoos had tattoos!

"Your employer has put an investment plan in place as a benefit for you, and I'm here to explain how you can retire with some money rather than work this hard the rest of your lives," I continued, expecting they were going to toss me off the premises at any minute for just wearing a suit. I explained how each and every employee is a profit center and has a responsibility to do something every day that will make their employer a buck—or at least save the employer a buck.

"It's the sum total of that effort that makes a company profitable. It is then your employer's responsibility to share that profit with you (its employees) in the form of increased employer matching contributions to the plan. That's basic free enterprise. You make your employer's business so profitable that he (the employer) has to decide whether to give the money to Uncle Sam or to you, the employees. Even a selfish employer would rather give money to the employees than pay more taxes."

It wasn't until I added, "Don't hold your breath waiting for the government to take care of your retirement," that I got their attention. What really had them leaning forward was when I showed them that they had been performing the very actions required to accumulate a fortune for themselves. The same contributions they'd made over the years to Social Security could have made them millionaires. "You can't change that system, but you can use the same concept to fund your own retirement plan, and this company will help you do it."

Later that afternoon back in my office, I got a phone call from the company's owner. "You're not going to believe what happened after you left," he

3

began, laughing. "Two of my top guys came into my office after lunch and an-nounced, 'We're here to tell you we did a citizen's firing of old Joe.'

"I said, 'You did what?'

"'Yeah, we loaded Joe's tools into his pickup and told him never to come back. You see, Joe had been seeing his girlfriend during installation jobs and taking company tools every once in a while. It irked us, but frankly, we'd thought it was none of our business. Then today when that 'feller' in the suit said how each of us is part of what this company makes, we realized that Joe was just taking money out of all our pockets. So, we ran him off.'"

Twenty years later, that company is at the top of its industry. Those em-ployees took the concept to heart. They saved and invested money in their re-tirement plan and changed their lives. For many, it broke a family financial pattern that had persisted for generations.

WE WANT YOU TO BECOME A CAPITALIST!

We have a not-so-hidden agenda to make a capitalist of every rank-and-file worker we come in contact with. A capitalist is every businessperson, first time investor, and rank-and-file employee who understands what it takes to make a profit. Why is this important? Because if you have money, it doesn't just affect the future of your family; the future of this country is going to be totally different if huge segments of our population don't have money.

We equate capitalism with freedom—they go hand in hand. The op-portunity for an individual to create wealth is based on free enterprise and personal initiative. A person who starts working at age 20 and never earns above minimum wage can retire a millionaire. It's not just possible; it's easy to do. If that worker invested only 6 to 10 percent of what he or she made, and the company provided a 50 percent match, the worker would become a millionaire by retirement.

When you start to accumulate money, your thinking process is altered. You say, "I can have what I want, but I may not want that right now." Your choices become different and you may want to do good for humanity rather than just for yourself. You are now able to give to your church, synagogue, or favorite charity. You're able to help with specific needs. Money will open doors to the finest schools and the best health care. But you have to start somewhere.

You Must Become an Investor

Saving money is hard to do; sometimes, even painful. You have to make a commitment to your goal. It may require sacrifice while, in the meantime, you're bombarded every day to buy something you can't afford. And, let's say you hate your job. If you knew that you were creating wealth, it might change your attitude. Most people would stand on their heads every day if they thought it would create personal wealth!

Saving should be taught to first graders—how to put their pennies, nickels, and dimes into a jar, where they soon add up to a dollar. Then show them what they can do with a dollar. After a couple of years, teach them the power of compounding and the Rule of 72.

The Rule of 72 is simply a shorthand method for figuring out how your money will compound. You can take any interest rate at which you're accumulating money—let's use the current rate banks are paying on savings accounts—2 percent—and divide that number into 72. The answer is 36. What does that mean? At 2 percent, it takes 36 years to double your money. The answer will always be the number of years it takes to double your money at a given percentage.

Saver versus investor

You could open a savings account at the bank and, right now, earn a safe 2 percent. At least that will keep you above the poverty line. But, if you walk into the bank to borrow money, it's going to charge you maybe 8 percent. Who gets the money in between? The bank. It's *investing* over long periods of time with the capital (savings accounts) you're providing.

So why shouldn't you, with the same effort and the same savings, become the investor rather than keeping the bank rich? What if you knew that the historical average annual return of the stock market is 12 percent? Investing in the stock market could double your money in 6 years, compared to 36 years with your savings account.

Is it because you're afraid to *risk* your hard-earned principal in the stock market or another investment you know nothing about? That's what the financial institutions are "banking on"! They don't share that fear of investing because they know that volatility is an integral function of producing higher returns. They know how to invest without *speculating*.

Investor versus speculator

Speculators are always rolling the dice—betting on a short-term high return. You never hear about their losses—only their gains.

When people don't understand investing, they think making money through investing is just luck. No one wants to risk principal on a lucky bet. But, doubling your investment every 6 years is no crapshoot. Unfortunately, most people make emotional rather than informed decisions that amount to no more than guessing or betting.

Being informed is the key to all of this. It's not magic, or a secret, or insider information, or a hot tip. Academics have figured this out through research, and the knowledge is available to everyone who will take the time to learn it. That is why you must have a long-term investment strategy that will protect you when markets are bad and grow when markets move up. This book will teach you how to build an efficiently diversified portfolio so that you're not worried about market volatility. Success is guaranteed over long periods of time.

CREATE MAXIMUM WEALTH

If you don't focus on allowing your investments to compound over the long term, you're missing the point. It's not a simple arithmetic progression; it's a geometric progression. Would you believe a one-time deposit of $10,000 compounding at 12 percent could be worth $20 million by retirement?

Here's an example. Give a one-time gift of $10,000 to your grandchild at birth. Set up an account the way we will show you, put $10,000 in pure stocks, and, if the $10,000 averages a 12 percent return, this is what occurs: By age 6, the $10,000 has grown to $20,000; at age 12, it's $40,000; and at age 18, it's $80,000. Every 6 years, it's doubling. By age 42, it's $1,280,000; at age 48, only 6 years later, it's $2,560,000. At age 54, another 6 years later, it's $5,120,000. At age 60, it's $10,240,000; and by age 65, it's just under $20,000,000!

Almost anything that is allowed to accumulate steadily will grow in terms of simple square numbers. Imagine a pond in your garden with a floating lily pad that doubles in size every day. Say it takes 80 days for the lilies to entirely cover the pond. On which day is half the pond still uncovered, open to the sun and air? It's the 79th day!

Capitalists are created at all levels—you can start at any age and your wealth doesn't have to reach $1 million. It's not the dollar amount; it's the difference in hope and possibility. You can go out and work for *your money* or have your money work for *you*. You've already been trained to do this with your automatic FICA contributions that you don't touch until retirement. By the time you've finished reading this book, you're going to say, "Why settle for Social Security? I don't have to depend on the government to do this for me—I can do it for myself." Just think, if you accumulate a million dollars by retirement and you're fortunate enough to earn 8 percent on your investment, you would have an income of $80,000 a year! Or would you rather just get the $13,200 a year from Social Security?

SUMMARY

- Saving and investing are two different things and, more importantly, provide two entirely different results. Investing is necessary to actually put your money to work creating wealth.
- Volatility is a necessary and integral function of the market. Develop an investment philosophy to manage it to produce higher returns without speculating.
- Wealth is accumulated through compounding over time.
- Being a capitalist simply means taking the initiative to create your own wealth in our free enterprise system.

In the next chapter, we will begin to show you how to move from being a saver to being a successful investor.

CHAPTER 2

GOING FROM A SAVER TO AN INVESTOR

Americans have to be the most optimistic people in the history of the world because we believe that, in some magical way, everything is going to turn out okay. But we're here to tell you it doesn't always turn out okay without your own intentional effort.

Retirements are always paid for—one way or the other.

I remember this extremely cold January morning almost 20 years ago when I was driving to my office. I'd spotted a small figure wrapped tightly in a winter coat, barely trudging along, kind of stooped over against this blowing wind. The sun wasn't even up yet, but I recognized the woman as one of the ladies who worked in the school cafeteria. I was the president of the School District Board of Trustees and had met this lady at one of our events. I stopped, opened the door, and called to her, "Mrs. Miller, where are you headed?" She strained to reply, "To the school, Mr. Rogers."

"Well, would you like a ride? I'm going right by there and can drop you off," I offered, although it was actually out of my way. She was a little reluctant at first, but then got into the car, "Oh, that would be very kind, Mr. Rogers, thank you." She shivered for several minutes before the heater finally warmed her.

We chatted a little for the next mile until I pulled up as close as I could to the cafeteria door; she thanked me profusely. I watched as this almost 80-year-old lady went through the heavy door to work in the school cafeteria. Her husband had died some years back, but he had never accumulated anything. She had taken the cafeteria job rather than public assistance.

Now, do you think this lady was working in a school cafeteria under these grueling conditions, at nearly 80 years of age, having to lift heavy kettles of food, just because she loved the children so much? No! She was too proud to take assistance, and because her husband had died without providing any sort of retirement for either of them, she had to continue to work.

Why tell you this terrible story? Because we want you to truly understand that you will either pay for your retirement now with tiny little sacrifices of money while you're young, healthy, and energetic, or you will pay a very painful price later on. *You* do not want to be that little old lady in 30 years!

HOW DO YOU START?

Become a Saver

You can start small, really small, but be consistent. You'll be encouraged by how quickly your weekly or monthly contributions add up. Challenge yourself to increase the amount. Pay yourself a bonus.

Saving that is automatic is a far more successful method than just hoping to have some money left over at the end of every month. You'll soon forget that it's even being deducted. Whether your goal is to save for higher education for a child, for a new home, or a comfortable retirement, *paying yourself first* is a prudent layaway plan for your future.

Every financial expert seems to recommend saving at least 10 percent of your yearly gross income toward your goal. That's nice, but for some people who are just beginning to save, 10 percent is considerably more than they can afford, so they get discouraged and don't save anything. People do need some individual help to get started.

A high school biology teacher showed his class this little experiment. First, he boiled a pot of water on the Bunsen burner. He took a frog and put it into the pot (this was in the days before animal rights); the frog instantly hopped out unharmed. He repeated the action with the same result. Then the teacher removed the pot of boiling water and replaced it with a pot of cold water. He dropped the frog into this water, and we watched the frog settle comfortably on the bottom. Gradually, the water heated up and got warmer and warmer until the frog was cooked without making any effort to escape.

If you've never saved a dime and we instruct you to save 10 percent of your pay today, we've essentially thrown you into that pot of boiling water—you'll abandon the plan in an instant. Any chance for saving and investing is gone. But if we help you begin at 1 percent, and we coach you to raise that to 2 percent, and so forth until, by small degrees as you are comfortable, you get to saving 6 to 10 percent of your pay, you'll have a better chance of staying with the program.

Initially, the dollar figure involved isn't nearly as important as the fact that you have made a commitment to the "pay yourself first" philosophy. It's all about prioritizing your life so that a financially secure future is your top financial goal.

If you aren't saving anything now, and you're overwhelmed at the thought of a 10 percent savings rate, start your personal savings program by setting a more realistic goal. Start by contributing just 1 percent of your gross annual income to your 401(k) plan. To frame this savings goal in terms of real dollars, calculate 1 percent of your gross yearly income and then divide by 12. If 1 percent is more than you are able to save right now, reduce it by half. Next, designate the proper dollar amount to be withdrawn from your paycheck, and your 401(k) plan will make an automatic investment in your future every time you get paid. Although a few dollars every month might not seem like much at first, over the long haul, every little bit adds up.

By dedicating a percentage of your income toward saving for the future, you have made a conscious decision that your future is important. You have made a commitment that an investment in yourself comes before your membership at the health club, a day at the spa, or a night on the town. You have made a decision that saving for the future is more important than spending money on recreation today.

When your financial situation improves and circumstances permit, gradually increase the amount of money earmarked for your 401(k) plan and your savings will hit that 10 percent mark more quickly than you might think. Once you get to 10 percent, there's no reason to stop there. If you can afford to increase your contribution percentage beyond 10 percent, you may be able to retire early. If you choose to keep working to full retirement age, your 401(k) balance will be that much better off for every extra dollar that you saved. Rest assured that when you're relaxing on the beach somewhere 20 years from now, you won't be complaining that you have too much money in your 401(k) plan.

Become an Investor

You begin by saving, but true wealth creation is built through investing. A *saver* is someone who saves money regularly and does not want to *risk* it by investing. An *investor* is someone who has an expectation of return through appreciation in the capital value. Risk is not synonymous with gambling or get-rich-quick schemes; it can be calculated and modulated to methodically build investment success.

Investment success doesn't come in a grand moment; it comes from doing many tasks—often boring, seemingly irrelevant tasks—one at a time, in a quiet, systematic method. The four action ingredients for saving and investing are:

1. Determine what you want.
2. Decide what you're willing to eliminate in order to get what you want.
3. Associate with people who will help you get what you want.
4. Have a plan (process) that works and then work the plan.

Determine what you want

Be absolutely clear about what you want out of your life before you decide what you're willing to put into it. Why is it so important? Because getting clear about your future creates focus, energy, and passion. That creates *purposeful living* and becomes a compass that gives you your heading when you get lost in the fog of emotion. In any life endeavor, there are going to be moments when you experience fatigue, frustration, and doubt. In those moments, you are acutely aware of what you are doing, how exacting it is, and how much easier it would be to just quit—to take the easy way out. You need that clarity of purpose to provide the perspective and perseverance when the road gets rough.

What do you want to get out of life? What would make the hard work worth it? What would make you take the extra hours to learn as much as you could about it? We suggest that you take the time right now and write down what you want.

Be as specific and vital and real as you can. Write down the things you want out of life. Make several copies. One copy is for you to carry at all times. That way you can answer the question when your inner voice demands to know: Why am I doing this? Send a second copy to someone who can gently remind you that this is very important and real and you have excellent reasons for staying with it. If the reasons are strong enough to get you started, they're probably strong enough to keep you going.

Decide what you're willing to eliminate in order to get what you want

Reschedule your life to start doing the things that build your future. Stop making excuses and start making it happen. Yes, this is a lot easier said than done. It's a huge mental transaction to move from chasing dreams to learning to make decisions based on facts.

We get blinded into believing there are no alternatives. Take a step out of your life and look around. Is there really no one doing *it* any differently than you? You may have to be creative, even inventive, and especially courageous to find ways to do what it is you say you want to do. It may upset those closest to you that you're breaking the old patterns, but eventually, those who care for you will see the evidence of your actions. They may even be inspired to take charge of their own futures!

Associate with people who will help you get what you want

Many people worry about what others think. And when you operate like this, you've just given your power over to others. People frequently make major decisions about their own lives based on assumptions about what their friends or family might think. Unknowingly, they've appointed these people as the designated drivers of their lives.

Have you ever been around people who have expectant, positive, and unshakable attitudes? Such attitudes are like airborne viruses—they're extremely contagious—you can't be with these people for any extended period of time without catching some of what they have. Their infectious excitement, joy, hope, and wisdom are like a hurricane impacting people wherever they go. But unlike a hurricane, it's a positive impact.

On the other hand, there are people whose beliefs and attitudes expose their doubts and disbeliefs, cynicisms, and criticisms about life in general. These people have one way of doing things—their way or the highway—and their knowledge of living is usually misguided.

You need grounded people to keep you focused, people who are able to ignore their discomfort and to work harder than ever before—to push beyond their old limits of strength. These people are needed to help others do what they will not do on their own.

Before we go to the last ingredient, stop and think about something with me. When some people walk into a room, they stimulate joy, while others eliminate it; some invite laughter, while others extinguish it. Our question to you is this: What emotions do you arrive with when you think about investing? If you feel anxiety, fear, and anger, that's going to affect whether you can ever be a successful investor. It's truly all in your attitude.

Have a plan that works and then work the plan

Remember the Y2K scare and how people spent enormous amounts of time planning, anticipating, and scheduling where they were going to be and what was going to happen? In the end, it seemed like we'd spent four years planning for that one night, and it was over in a nanosecond. Yet, most people don't spend even one evening planning for their futures!

When you understand this fourth ingredient for success, you will find yourself wonderfully prepared for life. Have a plan that works. Why is this simple ingredient so important? Planning is knowing where you're at today and where you want to be tomorrow. And you do this by breaking your dreams down into components and phases. You set realistic goals that reflect the component parts or the phase. These goals are the signposts that will tell you where you are and what to do next.

This is neither new advice nor complicated advice. To build a house, you have a blueprint and work backward from the finished product. It's precisely the same way successful people build any business: just one step at a time. Unfortunately, people get caught in a pattern of avoidance, false starts, and failed finishes. An unanticipated obstacle arises and they abandon the entire plan. They listen to old tapes of fear of failure playing in their minds. It usually does not occur to people to challenge their own thinking. They've lived with these beliefs for so long, they no longer even question them. It doesn't matter whether their beliefs are true, reasonable, or accurate. They're familiar and comfortable.

Maybe your mother used to tell you stories about growing up during the Depression and passed on her worries. We have catchphrases that reveal our belief systems about money and wealth: "Well, I'll never be a millionaire." "I'm not smart enough." "If I get into the stock market, it's time to get *out.*" "I'm too much in debt." "I would like to, but . . ." If you pay attention, you will hear the self-limiting and self-dismissing beliefs other people have. What are yours?

Do this exercise with us: Identify your investment beliefs. Ask yourself who told you that. Try to identify how you came to believe that. Values are made up and then perpetuated for safety. Do your thoughts fan the fires of confidence or do they squelch motivation and courage? Do they inspire your belief in yourself to attempt new challenges or do they talk you out of things before you get involved in anything that's outside your comfort zone?

You have to be mentally tough to be an investor, because initially, you will have no tangible proof that what you're doing will work. This is why you must understand how markets work, but you will need to manage the self-talk that influences your response to setbacks and failures and plays a role in how you handle success. In short, no aspect of your life is exempt from the power of self-talk. You need the ability to stay focused, on task, and not let anything deter you no matter what happens around you, to persevere and stay tethered to your dreams and objectives. That requires having a well-thought-out plan . . . and sticking to it!

SUMMARY

Start being responsible by becoming a saver. The steps you take now will lay the groundwork for the lifestyle you will enjoy later. If you want to enjoy a future that is free from financial worries, your first step is to start saving today. You can start small, really small, but be consistent. You'll be encouraged by how quickly your weekly or monthly contributions add up. Challenge yourself to increase the amount.

When you "find" more money, invest it! Once you've done everything you can do to live within your means, and hopefully well below, you need to remain constantly on the lookout for additional opportunities to increase the amount you save. Any time you get a raise or earn a bonus is a prime opportunity to increase your savings. Since you were able to get by on your former salary, the additional income is "found" money. Adding this money to your monthly investment should be completely painless.

Investment success doesn't come in a grand moment. It comes from doing many tasks—often boring, seemingly irrelevant tasks—one at time, in a quiet, systematic method. The five action ingredients for saving and investing are:

1. Determine what you want and establish a clear focus you feel passionate about.

2. Decide what you're willing to eliminate in order to get what you want.

3. Accept responsibility for your own thinking and associate with people who will help you get what you want.

4. Have a plan (process) that works and then work the plan.

5. Take the time to understand how markets work. (This is the subject of our next chapter.)

CHAPTER 3

NOISE, CLUTTER, AND NONSENSE

Most first time investors have never heard of Modern Investment Theory or care what *asset allocation* or *diversification* mean. (We will discuss both of these strategies in detail later.) The information they get about investing comes from television, newspapers, magazines, and conversations with coworkers or friends. Most of this "noise" is misguided, sensationalized, and lacks any theoretical foundation. In fact, many false ideas are so widespread that the public, for the most part, simply accepts them as fact. It's kind of like the old saying, "If you tell a lie loud enough and long enough, it becomes the truth."

The media is providing us with up-to-the-minute news, live streaming price quotes, current company information, all couched as information that will aid in individual stock selection and market timing. What most investors don't realize is that chasing the best-performing mutual fund and attempting to time the market swings are strategies that are costly to implement and have an extremely low probability of success. Meanwhile, in a much-quoted study by Brinson, Hood, and Beebower,[1] asset allocation accounted for 94 percent of the total variation in returns. That means that less than 6 percent of a portfolio's performance was due to the specific choice of individual stocks, market timing, lower transaction costs, or other miscellaneous influences. Determining the correct asset allocation is the single most important determinant of the long-term success of any investment portfolio.

So, why isn't the media constantly talking about asset allocation? Because of their agenda to sell ad space and increase audience. They would

---

[1] Gary P. Brinson, L. Randolph Hood, and Gilbert L. Beebower, "Determinants of Portfolio Performance," *Financial Analysts Journal*, 42:4 (July–August 1986), pp. 39–44.

lose their audience if they quoted academics whose advice might be to turn off those TV sets and check back in 20 years, as Eugene Fama—a professor of finance at The University of Chicago who introduced the efficient market theory to the investment community—once told an audience. Passive investing works; it just doesn't sell. What gets ratings and sells publications are fast price movements, exciting stock predictions, and strong emotional content. That's a perfect fit with Wall Street's agenda: to create more buy and sell transactions, without which Wall Street, in its present form, simply could not exist. Academics don't care what the outcomes are when they are conducting research.

You may recall those flashy ads touting triple-digit returns that most of the major mutual fund companies had placed in nearly every investment publication in the late 1990s and early 2000. Then came the market's downturn, and the fund companies switched from selling performance to selling their image. With that switch, the focus of the ads changed from attracting new assets to retaining existing ones. Now, it appears they may be about to shift back again. In 2002, the mutual fund companies told you to think long term, but by late 2003, thanks to the stock market's recent climb, they were saying that the short term is what's really important, and they were all touting their funds' one-year or year-to-date performance. Confusing, isn't it?

This is not intended to demonize the media; the media is just a mirror of what we want. Our decisions are mostly made by the right side, or emotional part, of our brain, which wants what it knows. And, when some information or concept is unfamiliar—something we don't know—we get overloaded, tune out, and look for something, or someone, familiar. That someone may be the newscaster we see every day on TV, or a recognizable long-standing financial publication, or a rich celebrity or financial guru, an expert. What we are really looking for is someone to protect us and make our decisions for us; but these experts aren't looking out for our best interests—they're just selling books, tapes, and TV shows. Chances are, they don't know any more than you do about what investment path you should take. Ninety percent of all financial gurus are just another version of Suze Orman with a different hairdo. You have to learn the difference.

Charles Ellis wrote a great book a few years ago called *Winning the Loser's Game.* Charley did a fabulous job of putting Wall Street and investing in perspective. He tells you straight out that people do not understand the way this game is played. The emphasis and the power are given to marketing departments to devise products that look wonderful, make the company a lot of money, and sell very well. Their tactic is to give you a beautiful and expensive color brochure with a picture of a couple playing tennis or sailing—you're supposed to visualize yourself doing those things—and several inserts with detailed performance records demonstrating the company's prowess in the marketplace. But where do you fit in that picture? I'll tell you: Any assets that you invest with that company add to their bottom line to prove that they are the best at attracting additional assets—not necessarily the best at managing your investments or at helping you accumulate wealth or at meeting your specific investing needs. They are the best at gathering assets, which is why they are in business!

WE ARE DRIVEN BY OUR EMOTIONS

So, why would a relatively intelligent person invest based on mutual fund ads in the back of *Money* magazine? Because most people want to believe that someone else is in control and knows and can predict what will happen in the future.

This is one of the strongest psychological needs we all share. We cannot handle the seemingly random nature of our own existence, let alone the random nature of our institutions such as the stock market. We will give up food, sex, and money to live in a predictable world—only we don't!

Psychologists say that, in the broadest sense, you can reduce all human behavior to fear and greed as the two competing emotions that drive us. In investing, fear can be paralyzing and greed doesn't know when to quit. Both leave us vulnerable. What we want most is validation for what we already believe. We seek out people and information (factual or otherwise) that support conclusions we've already reached.

Everyone is entitled to his or her own opinion. The damage occurs when someone who is highly regarded or has otherwise achieved recognition rides that elevator to the status of guru and biases the attitudes and decisions of his or her admirers. Gurus might even succumb to the same thin air from which they pulled their predictions and ignore or abandon facts and logic in their evangelistic fervor. Not to worry; by the time the "chips fall," a new guru will have arisen.

Howard Ruff—an author whose words shook the country in 1979 with his best-selling book, *How to Prosper During the Coming Bad Years*—predicted a depression throughout the 1980s and 1990s because of the massive U.S. debt. His advice was, "Buy gold, silver and diamonds before it's too late!" Any followers of that advice missed the greatest bull market our economy has ever experienced.

Another example of the guru mentality is found in the book *Rich Dad's Prophecy: Why the Biggest Stock Market Crash in History Is Still Coming* by Robert Kiyosaki. He's also the author of *Rich Dad, Poor Dad,* which has sold over 10 million copies. In his latest book, he predicts the collapse of the stock market in 12 years as the baby boomers pull their money out of the 401(k) plans.

At first glance it sounds rational and may even have some validity, but when you examine his logic, obvious flaws arise. First, money, like energy, operates inside a closed system. And, like energy, it doesn't disappear; it simply takes on a different form. If all the baby boomers sold their mutual funds at the same time and left the market, the proceeds would either get reinvested or be converted into purchasing power. Either way, some companies are going to be making a profit. And profits equate to higher earnings; higher earnings drive up stock prices—just the opposite result from Kiyosaki's prediction.

Behavioral finance researchers tell us that sensational media evokes a strong emotional response, frequently influencing investors to make irrational decisions. When investors react emotionally, they frequently move in the wrong direction and do the wrong thing at the wrong time.

Paul Andreassen, a psychologist at Harvard, researched the relationship between the news media and investing by separating people into two groups: The first group bought and sold stocks based solely on recent price data. The second group traded after being given the price data plus news headlines that explained the changes. When stock prices were volatile, he found that the group that had access to the news headlines earned less than half as much per share traded as the group that received only price data.

Andreassen theorized that people tend to consider news reports as accurate predictions. When a jump in a stock's price is accompanied by news that seems to support the price movement, we take that as a sign that the trend will continue. As a result, we're likely to buy, buy, buy when the news is good (and the market is *high*). Conversely, when the news is pessimistic (and the market is *low*), we tend to sell, sell, sell. With thousands of investors reacting this way, stocks can be artificially driven to unrealistically high—or low—levels. An excellent example of this would be the tech stocks.

Your guess is as good as mine! During 1990, there were endless stories depicting consumer confidence being at a multiperiod low; the media mantra was "Don't own stocks." Hedge fund experts were telling us that it was time to be shorting the market. As bankruptcies reached record numbers, a frequently heard prediction was that the decade would see a depression for the rich.

In 1997, the media forewarned of a worldwide meltdown in the U.S. economy. Even Federal Reserve Chairman Alan Greenspan was quoted as saying, "The U.S. can't remain an island of prosperity." And who's going to contradict him? Yet by 1999, that story was forgotten and the refrain had become, "Everyone is getting rich buying high-tech offerings!" But the people who jumped on that bandwagon still haven't recovered from their losses and many never will.

It's one thing to be down 10 percent in any one year. It only takes a bit more than 10 percent to get back to even. But if you lose 75 percent, you're going to have to make 300 percent to get back to even. (For example, say you start with $100 invested. You lose $75 and now have $25. You'd have to make 300 percent just to get back to $100.) That could take 20 years.

During the bull run of the late 1990s, it seemed you could make a great return no matter what you did. That caused a large contingent to come to believe successful investing is easy—you could just as well do it yourself. New Internet sites popped up daily to assist do-it-yourselfers. All you needed to do was monitor past performance. And, how did that work out as a way of predicting future winners? Well, *Money* magazine used to publish an annual "Seven Best Mutual Funds" series; but, for three years, 1996, 1997, and 1998, its prior "best funds" *underperformed* the market. *Money* did finally stop this exercise, perhaps because it feared that somewhere, somebody might actually hold it responsible for its recommendations.

No matter how many times a mutual fund beat the market in the past, it has only a 50 percent chance of beating the market in the future. These apparently random outcomes are consistent with the fact that markets work.

One very famous study[2] tracked what percentage of mutual fund managers performed better than average for the subsequent five years. Their re-

---

[2] Edgar Barksdale and William Green examined the performance persistency of 144 institutional equity managers from January 1975 to December 1989. They ranked the managers based on their results over a five-year period. *Pensions &Investments* (September 17, 1990), p. 16.

sults showed that regardless of where a manager places in the first five years, she or he is about equally likely to be above average as below average during the next five years. Again, it's a random pattern that is consistent with the laws of pure chance.

These researchers concluded that, given only past performance information, index funds did better for both equity and fixed-income investments. Studies of mutual fund performance now span more than 40 years' investigation. The message is always the same: While an occasional mutual fund may beat the market, there is no indication to support the idea that performance may repeat or continue. There is actually more evidence that it will *not.*

The January 1996 cover story of *Fortune* magazine, titled "Let Them Make You Rich," listed stocks that had the approval of the top all-star analysts. Their long list of recommendations highlighted the following companies: Oracle at $72 was a great buy; CNGI had significantly declined at $44 and was now a great value; Global Crossing at $26 was expected to triple. The outcome was that Oracle went from $72 down to $7; CNGI dropped to 75 cents; and Global Crossing filed Chapter 11.

We could go on and on with examples. The point is, we appear to have no memory of past predictions and continue to succumb to hope and the belief that someone must know the future. Becoming knowledgeable is the only antidote for the grip of our emotions.

Our goal is for you to become an *educated* investor, instead of a *noise-and-nonsense* investor, so that the errors of "accepted" investment strategies will become clear to you. We want to demystify the whole investment process so you can discover, expose, and consider all the facts—just the opposite of a noise investor.

An educated investor takes the time to understand how financial markets actually work and knows how to use this financial market knowledge to consistently make money. An educated investor focuses on the overall investment strategy and portfolio, rather than viewing a specific investment in isolation, since academic studies tell us that each investment should be evaluated for its contribution to a portfolio's total return.

The best part about being an informed investor is that the confusion disappears, and you are completely able to properly evaluate the investment advice you receive and will never again be deceived or hoodwinked by misguided recommendations or advice. Through a combination of the efforts of academicians and real-world practitioners, you'll soon discover that nobody on TV or on Wall Street is keeping any secrets from you.

SUMMARY

What most people want is not truth, but validation. They want reinforcement for what they think they know. They'll seek out people and information (factual or otherwise) that support conclusions they've already reached. They only want to hear things that make them feel good and give them comfort about where they are right now. Some people prefer the passenger role because it imposes no pressure to decide or stand accountable for their decisions. If you're one of those people, you need either to wake up and take control or prepare to become one of life's crash test dummies.

Most people tend to consider news reports as accurate predictions. When a jump in a stock's price is accompanied by news that seems to support the price movement, we take that as a sign that the trend will continue. Conversely, when news reports justify a price decline, we tend to take that as an indication that the negative trajectory will prevail. As a result, we're likely to buy, buy, buy when the news is good and sell, sell, sell when the news is pessimistic.

Become an *educated* investor. Our goal is for you to become an educated investor, instead of a *noise-and-nonsense* investor. Nobody knows what stock is going up, or that a stock is worth more or less than the price shows. We want to demystify the whole investment process, so you can discover, expose, and unmask opportunities—not be restricted by them.

CHAPTER 4

THE REAL STORY

If we accomplish nothing else with this book, we must get this one point unequivocally straight: *There's no predictability to the market; it's random.* This fact cannot be mitigated by education or intelligence. Then, you might ask, why bother reading another word?

Because once you embrace this truth, you will finally have a chance at becoming a successful investor. You will no longer be drawn in by shrewd marketing techniques, sensational media headlines, or the emotional desire to "run for safety" or "make a killing." Free from the distractions of market volatility, you can employ proven academic investing strategies and tactics to reach specific goals in a way that reflects your unique circumstances. This book is called *The First Time Investor* because, for most people reading it, it will be the first time they invest knowing why and what they are doing.

The principles of investing are constant, but how to invest varies with individual circumstances. Our role here is simply to help you make informed decisions—not provide some type of investing magic. Education does make a difference in the decision-making process. If we can lay out the basics of investing, give you an understanding of how markets work, and show you how to keep your emotions out of your investment decisions, we believe you will then have an excellent chance of becoming a successful investor.

By the time you finish this chapter of the book, you'll know more than 90 percent of the people who work on Wall Street know. We believe the "state of the art" investment advice has been built over a basic flaw—a shortcoming that causes investors to fail over and over again. That flaw is the belief that superior stock selection can beat the market rate of return.

In fact, the entire industry thrives on this erroneous concept by focusing on past performance.

This belief system supports the sale of individual investment products and the competition for investable assets by funds. The people who work on Wall Street put together a good rationale for their stock picks; but the stock market is like the game of golf—it will humble anyone. The marketing departments at large firms study the prospect's every buying move. They learn everything about you and then they devise a product that's highly profitable for their company. They then sell it by using what they know about you. You need to remember that a broker doesn't work for you—he or she earns a living by selling investment products, just like the person who sells cars or appliances.

THE ORGANIC ECONOMIC MARKET

In 1776, Adam Smith, a moral philosopher in Edinborough, Scotland, wrote a book called *The Wealth of Nations,* which put forth the doctrine of economic freedom. Adam Smith is considered the father of economics (even though the word *economics* didn't exist then). Smith was intrigued with or concerned about a number of issues. One of them was the question: Why are we (England in the late 1700s) prospering today? Why are we doing so well while other countries are not?

In his book, he argued for economic liberalism; that is, free enterprise within a country and free trade among countries. He believed that governments should interfere less in the marketplace; that they should leave people alone to pursue their own self-interests. At the time, it was the policy of governments to engage in practices, rules, and regulations that they believed would help the home industries. That policy is still very much with us, but now we call it *protection.*

Adam Smith decided that countries ought just to get rid of all barriers to trade; that social welfare would be enhanced if the number of transactions occurring were simply increased. In an exchange economy, the more transactions we can foster, the better for everyone. That, by the way, is the definition of fair trade. Smith believed that there was an "invisible hand" that caused the producer to promote the interests of society. He stated that pursuing one's own interests frequently promotes the interests of society more effectively than really attempting to promote society's interests.

He also recognized that government intervention was allowable in some circumstances—for example, when the nation's defense was at stake. Smith was interested in the things that are necessary for civilizations to survive and perhaps prosper. He wrote that there must be a rule of law to protect private property, enforce contracts, and so on, and the rules of the game basically have to be fair. There must be freely floating prices; in other words, no impediment to the pricing of goods and services.

He built a very simple model, no mathematics involved, with three factors of production: land, labor, and capital. Then he gave examples of how the providers of goods and services will seek to input the best combination of those factors to provide for the production of outputs. And if prices are not interfered with, people will always know what is the most expensive material or service and what is the cheapest.

By relying on prices, people will generally produce output that exceeds the value of their input. The difference between the two, from an economic point of view, is what we call *profit*. So long as that's occurring on a fairly regular basis, that particular country or society as a whole will grow wealthier. But, if prices are interfered with, and attention isn't paid to what is dearest and what is cheapest, then outputs may soon become less valuable than inputs.

Now, let's suppose that everyone is knowledgeable about his or her own sphere of activity and people all know how much they are going to consume or produce. When we make a decision, we affect the prices for all goods and services by expressing our knowledge in our preferences. To keep it simple, let's say there are 6 billion such entities in the world. We're going to have basically 6 billion entities impounding their information into the worldwide set of prices of all goods and services. (See Figure 4.1.)

Think of the market pricing system as a vast information-processing machine that registers the implications of all available information. You may not know the information directly, but you have the implications of it in the set of market prices. So, when you make decisions by looking at stock market prices, you're essentially saying: "That price contains all the information of investors everywhere all over the planet." You don't need to spend too much time questioning the validity of that price; you are using approximately 6 billion times the information that you, individually, possess.

This is an oversimplified example of "efficient markets," a phrase coined in 1965 by Eugene Fama, a professor at The University of Chicago. Eugene Fama's efficient market theory is probably the most misunderstood hypothesis in economics. This hypothesis asserts that prices are probably

Timing of Each Additional Billion
of World Population   Approximate Years

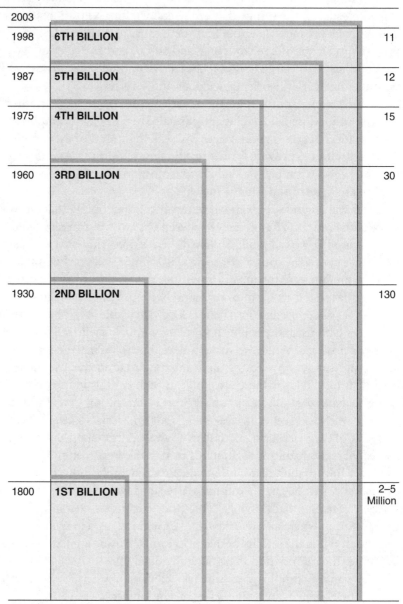

Year	Billion	Approximate Years
2003		
1998	6TH BILLION	11
1987	5TH BILLION	12
1975	4TH BILLION	15
1960	3RD BILLION	30
1930	2ND BILLION	130
1800	1ST BILLION	2–5 Million

FIGURE 4.1
Billions Added to Billions—A Projection of Population Growth
Source: U.S. News & World Report, *August 2, 1982, p. 48.*

wrong and that they're only right on average. In other words, the amount that a stock is over- or underpriced is randomly distributed.

Fama said that when markets are efficient, it's because information moves rapidly, and prices immediately reflect new information. Efficiency also means that the prices reflect the knowledge and expectations of all investors. That way no person can consistently know more about any individual security than does the market as a whole. The only condition necessary for market efficiency to occur is that nobody systematically profits more than expected by chance at the expense of other investors—so long as no one cheats.

Wall Street's Juxtaposition to an Efficient Market

After the stock market crash of 1929, a group of economists decided to find out whether traders really could predict how prices would move by looking at past patterns. They decided simply to pick stocks at random by throwing darts at the *Wall Street Journal* while blindfolded. At the end of the year, this random choice outperformed the predictions of top traders. The economists arrived at a devastating conclusion: It seemed just as plausible to attribute the success of top traders to sheer luck as to skill.

Once researchers were able to get their hands on the earliest computers in places like The University of Chicago, the IBM research labs, and the naval research labs, they confirmed that asset prices behaved in a purely random fashion. Soon there was a whole body of literature on the financial markets. By the early 1960s, there was no real controversy any more. Asset prices are random through time. Over the decades, we learned that the most anyone can say about a particular asset theory is what probability distributions it comes from. We can describe its mean, standard deviation, and variability, and we can describe how it correlates or moves with other asset classes. What we can't forecast is what's going to happen next.

It's ironic, then, that the most competitive sector of the economy, the financial service industry, is designed to give advice based on the belief that the very markets it trades in do not work. According to this view, prices react to information slowly enough to allow some investors, presumably professionals, to take advantage of market inefficiencies. But as good as Wall Street pundits are, given all the available information, they still do not know where or when the market is going to be inefficient.

There is no evidence of any large institution having anything like a consistent ability to get in when the market is low and get out when the market is high. Attempts to switch between stocks and bonds, or between stocks and cash, in anticipation of market moves, have been unsuccessful much more often than they have been successful.

There's a popular perception that investing is sort of a zero sum game where the winners take from the losers. In other words, if someone is to win, someone else must lose. In stock and bond investing, this simply is not the case. Not that people don't lose in the capital markets, because, obviously, they do. What people are saying is that being a speculator involves trying to guess the future in some manner. Another term for this would be *forecasting*.

All traditional Wall Street investment advice involves forecasting some future event, such as interest rates, the Federal Reserve's action, or whatever is on TV that day. Then, investments are made in anticipation of this action, and the portfolio is actively traded on an ongoing basis in an attempt to react to the accuracy of the forecast. The forecast is then regularly modified as new information enters the picture.

We call the people who believe they can do this *active managers*. Active managers believe that the market is not priced correctly and that they can exploit the mispricing, so that when other people find out, the price will go to what it should be and the active managers will have made money on the stock.

Traditional investment advisors try to guess which way interest rates will go, or which industry or sector of the market will "be in favor" over the next six months to a year. Each one is simply telling the investor that his or her "crystal ball" is better.

How does this misinformation get validated? Because every once in a while, someone like Warren Buffett or Peter Lynch gains fame for having done an extraordinary job of picking stocks that produce high returns. Of course, you don't hear about them until after the fact. In the same time frame, there were thousands of investment managers who didn't come close to beating the market. It's no different than if we were to have a coin-tossing contest, with "heads" as the winning toss, in which 1,000 people all tossed their coins at the same time. About half of them would toss "heads" and move to the next level. After about 10 sets of tosses, we'd end up with one or two players who had continually flipped "heads." The media would find their names, take their pictures, and then the top "heads" flippers would start writing books on how they flipped their coins to success.

But, investors are desperately seeking the next Peter Lynch to guide their decisions—someone else to take responsibility for the guesswork. We hear people say, "This manager has had a great track record for the past five years!" Here's the part most people don't understand: For that money manager to succeed, the markets must fail to efficiently price an individual issue of stock, and that manager must identify the mispricing and act on that information before it's corrected. That is why those who make predictions have one of the toughest jobs in the world—their best efforts at predicting are rendered ineffective by the invisible hand of free market competition.

Okay, what about when some mutual fund managers have produced a return greater than the S&P 500 index or the Dow Jones Averages? We can examine the top 10 funds for the last year, or five years, or ten years, or we can look at the top 20 funds—the winners don't repeat. It's simply probability that someone will be at the top of the list—but not because of any repeatable traits. There are some well-known academic studies from The University of Chicago that back up this statement. But you can show people the proof and they don't care; people want to believe that someone can predict the future.

The Investor's Paradox: Risk versus Return

The academic world has a different agenda. It is interested in finding a scientific method of creating portfolios using risk, not return, as the primary criteria in the design of the portfolio itself.

An investor should be asking how much her portfolio is moving relative to its asset class, relative to size, and relative to value. And if these three factors are independent, and are stated accurately, they're going to describe what that portfolio looks like simply by the amount of return in a given period.

Prior to 1952, major Wall Street gurus and investors essentially ignored the connection between risk and return, preferring to spend their efforts on varying views about diversification. In fact, a book by John Burr Williams, titled *The Theory of Investment Value,* published in 1932, was considered the authoritative work on how to value financial assets. The gist of this work seemed to imply it is better to concentrate your efforts on obtaining all available information on one company and then concentrating your portfolio in that company, rather than in a broad selection of companies of which you may not know as much.

Though shortsighted, this dominant view among investment professionals actually aided a young graduate student at The University of Chicago in 1952 to develop his view about the correlation between investing and the accompanying risk of the investment process. Harry Markowitz developed a keen insight that risk (which he defined as volatility) must be the central focus for the whole process of investing. What Markowitz found was an investment world blindly living in a paradox.

Although it was accepted that human beings, by their nature, are risk-averse, up to this point in history, investing had essentially ignored the interrelationship between risk and return. Through their in-depth analysis and research, Markowitz and others created a concept known as *Modern Portfolio Theory*, MPT for short. This revolutionary concept, which would earn Markowitz the Nobel Prize in Economics in 1990, involved a 180-degree change in viewpoint from what was (and largely still is today) considered the way to design and manage a stock and bond portfolio.

Until Markowitz's work was published and through the 1973–1974 bear market catastrophe, investment portfolio design centered on assembling a diversified portfolio of stocks and bonds that would achieve a desired target rate of return. These investments were evaluated on an individual basis. In other words, each stock or bond was required to stand or fall on its own merits.

Ironically, little has changed in regard to this methodology. Although it's been updated a bit, today's professional investors, stock brokerage firms, and money managers still follow this approach directly, believing they can somehow discover the one nugget of value and opportunity that no one else has seemed to be able to find and then repeat that process over and over again.

Markowitz, and the other financial academics who followed him in subsequent years, looked long and hard at the investor's paradox. Markowitz hit upon the concept of considering risk first, and returns second. In order to do this, the entire portfolio's risk or volatility should be the central issue, since the bottom line for the investor is what happens to the whole portfolio.

Markowitz stated that for every level of risk, there is some optimal combination of investments that will give you the highest rate of return. The range of portfolios exhibiting this optimal risk–reward trade-off forms what we call the *efficient frontier*, shown in Figure 4.2. The efficient frontier is determined by calculating the expected rate of return and standard deviation for each asset class.

By plotting each percentage combination of the various asset classes, we are able to view the efficient frontier curve. In this example, we see that a portfolio of 60 percent stocks and 40 percent bonds gives us a higher expected return than cash, without the volatility of 100 percent stocks.

Here's an example of how this works: Examine the period from 1982 to 1995 and track the best-performing asset class, then match it against the worst-performing asset class in each year. This is an interesting period of time because in 1982, foreign stocks filled the worst-performing sector, but in 1983, foreign stocks were the best sector. Government bonds were the worst-performing sector in 1983, but the top category in 1984.

If you'd been 100 percent invested in stocks over that time frame, you would have averaged an 11.2 percent return and you would have had seven down years. If you'd been 100 percent invested in bonds, you would have averaged an 8.7 percent return, and you would have had six down years. But, had you allocated your assets 60/40 percent in stocks and bonds respectively, you would have averaged a 10.5 percent return, with only three down years. If you'd been invested one-third each in stocks, bonds, and cash, you'd have averaged 9.6 percent and had two down years. This last simple asset allocation plan removed some of the bumps, or down years.

Markowitz created a concept of blending investments together in a manner that lowered the overall volatility of the total portfolio. Even though, if evaluated separately, the individual investments within the portfolio might

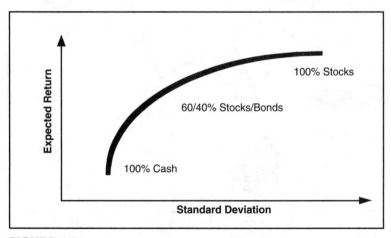

FIGURE 4.2
Efficient Frontier Curve

be considered too "risky" or volatile, Markowitz found that if you blend two investments, even so-called risky or volatile investments, together, the overall portfolio's risk or volatility may be reduced. This is possible if the two investments move up and down at opposite times to one another. The impact upon the total portfolio is a canceling out, or reduction, of the total portfolio's volatility. (See Figure 4.3.)

Out of this discovery, Markowitz created the concept of an *efficient portfolio*, which meant blending different investments together specifically for the purpose of controlling the volatility risk of the whole or total portfolio. The overall returns that the whole portfolio experienced could be enhanced, thereby adding value to the portfolio itself.

Modern portfolio theory was expanded and refined to further explain the relationship between a portfolio's risk measurements and the returns that resulted while exposed to that risk. It has evolved into the newest version, which Professors Fama and Ken French (professor of finance at the Tuck School of Business, Dartmouth) call the *three-factor model*. That model argues that 96 percent of returns in a portfolio can be explained by three factors.

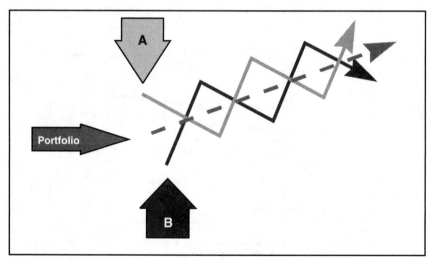

FIGURE 4.3
How Diverse Investments Reduce the Volatility of the Portfolio

The three factors are exposure to the overall market, exposure to size, and exposure to value. In concert, these factors drive all the variation in stock returns. The only way to get returns above the market is by increasing exposure to a risk that has been identified to deliver extra returns. Extra returns come from the small companies (size effect) and exposure to value companies (the value effect). The growth of these companies is riskier and, therefore, over long periods of time they have higher expected returns.

In a nutshell, the three factors explain returns; what isn't explained is what we call "residual risk," which is risk present by the concentration of a few securities, manager risk, stock picking risk, market timing risk, and foreign ownership risk.

But what do most investors do? They go into a bookstore and pick up *Fortune, Money,* and *Forbes,* where they read over and over again that companies that are profitable, healthy, well run, and have great management and great ideas have higher expected returns than companies that are poorly run and have stupid ideas, bad products, and low profitability. Everyone thinks that's correct. But it's wrong.

Do you remember Tom Peters' best-selling book, *In Search of Excellence?* It came out in the early 1980s. It was a fun book to read because it is like a bible for the armchair entrepreneur. Each of the book's 40 or so chapters is about a different company and what made that company so excellent. The book is not an academic text, but it was analyzed as such by an academic on the East Coast named Michelle Clayman.

Michelle wanted to put a study together to find out what really defined an *excellent company;* what was it about these companies in particular that was really excellent? She did what any decent academic would do—she made a value-weighted portfolio of the companies in the book. Her thinking was that these companies had fantastic profitability, great ideas, progressive management techniques, etc.

She decided to take the 40 lousiest companies she could find and use the same criteria. She wanted companies that had low profitability, really bad ideas, and used Dark Ages management techniques. She called these the *un-excellent companies.* Next, she measured different variables and found that on virtually every measure that had anything to do with earnings success and profitability, the excellent companies beat the un-excellent companies.

Think about it this way: When you're buying stock, what you're functionally doing is supplying capital to that company; that's your job as an investor. It's important that investors actually know this. Your function in a capital market is to provide capital for corporate operation (similar to the role a bank has) and for that function you get a return on your capital.

Suppose for the moment that you are the bank, and the owners of both Microsoft and Chia Pet Company come to you for a loan. Who's going to have to pay a higher interest rate? Chia Pet, obviously. It's the same when their companies issue stock. Which company has to promise investors a higher rate of return on its stock? Nobody thinks about how the Chia Pet Company is going to have to lower its price until the market in general buys Chia stock as readily as Microsoft stock.

If Chia's price isn't sufficiently low, investors are not going to buy it. But if the price is lower, it means that the buyer is getting a bigger chunk of Chia Pet's future earnings stream for his or her dollar of capital. Every share of stock Chia sells is return that the company is actually forgoing in the future. If Chia holds onto the stock, it keeps the return, so Chia's cost of capital is the investor's stock return.

Companies that are distressed and doing poorly must pay a higher cost for capital than companies that are healthy; otherwise, capital markets would be horrible at allocating resources. The reason capital markets work when all other systems fail is because prices are very good carriers of information and they allocate capital accurately based on the underlying risk of the venture across the marketplace. If Microsoft had to pay more for its capital than Chia Pet, the market would fall apart. We wouldn't have computers; instead we'd have a lot of little pots growing plants.

When the stock prices go up, expected returns go down. The problem is that this event is totally arbitrary. Here is what Michelle found in her studies: The un-excellent companies killed the excellent companies in terms of investment returns. (See Figure 4.4.)

Obviously, these un-excellent companies are the ones with the highest expected returns.

Here's the problem: No mutual fund is going to put together a 40-stock portfolio, call that the un-excellent company portfolio, and bring it to the market. That wouldn't work because of the residual risk. What you want is a 1,000- or 2,000-stock portfolio of un-excellent companies. Historically, in every long time period in every market around the world, the value stocks have outperformed the growth stocks and the small stocks have outperformed the large stocks. The small stocks do it with a higher standard deviation, but the value stocks beat the growth stocks without a higher

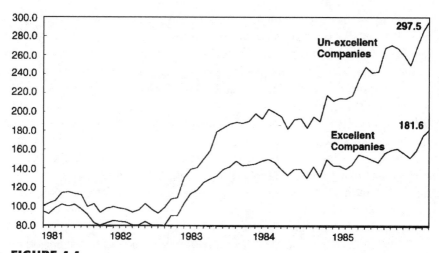

FIGURE 4.4
Un-excellent/Excellent Companies
Source: M. Clayman, "In Search of Excellence: The Investor's Viewpoint," Finan-
cial Analysts Journal, *May–June 1987, p. 63.*

standard deviation. Value stocks are companies that are distressed economically. Growth stocks are companies that have good sales and good
prospects for the future.

Standard deviation describes how far from the *mean* historic performance has been, either higher or lower. The mean is simply the middle
point between the two historic extremes of the performance of the investment you are examining. The standard deviation measurement helps explain what the distribution of returns likely will be. What this tells you is
that the greater the range of returns, the greater the risk. The lower the risk,
the lower the return expected.

The reason that, historically, value and growth stocks don't always pan
out is because we're in a multiple-factor world and don't realize it. We buy
mutual funds as if there were a single factor. What was needed was a way
to measure the relationship between a portfolio's risk measurements and
the returns that resulted while exposed to that risk. That is what Professors
Eugene Fama and Ken French did when they came up with their three-factor model.

The three-factor model basically takes a timed series of returns and runs
it through three filters to measure how much that timed series of returns

is varying relative to each filter. A metaphor is found in the printing process. The way the printing process works is by using the three primary colors: blue, yellow, and red. The printing industry has found specific shades of these three colors that are exactly right to capture the universe of colors that you see in the world. For example, if you have a photograph of a face printed in a magazine, photographic equipment examines the face and breaks it into its component three colors. It might make the face 50 percent blue, 30 percent red, and 20 percent yellow. The percentages change throughout the variations in the face. The camera assigns a percentage to each color throughout the face. Then it breaks the results into a pointillistic system with a filter that makes little dots in those proportions. When the dots are printed onto the paper, it makes a model of the face, because those three colors are perfectly specified.

The three-factor model does the same thing. It takes the time period of return and asks how much it's moving with these three factors. When the three factors are perfectly specified, they capture all the nuances of portfolio movement to such a degree that they can replay it the same way as that pointillistic map.

That's what the academics call an *expected return*. It's what the return should have been historically and ongoing based on assumptions about the price of each of the three risk factors. The Fama and French model argues that 96 percent of returns in a portfolio can be explained by these factors.

THE TRADITIONAL BROKERAGE MODEL IS DEAD

So how does the traditional brokerage model deal with this knowledge? It doesn't.

It used to be that advisors would do all this research trying to find good investments or smart managers to put your money with. Today, advisors are in a unique situation to help you decide on asset allocation and, more important, coach you through the times that the asset allocation does not work. Their job is to structure a plan that you can stick with and that also ensures that your return expectations are proportionate to the amount of risk you are taking. And those two tasks are virtually impossible in the face of fund managers who make asset allocation decisions in your stead. That model of how a manager is supposed to behave is worthless.

We used to feel betrayed by fund managers when, at the end of the quarter or the year, we would find the fund's investment style had been reversed and, therefore, *our selection* had been arbitrarily changed. You have got to understand what these people's agendas are. A mutual fund manager's job is to produce a yield that will attract new money, but if his or her style of investment starts doing poorly, the fund manager might *drift* to whatever group of stocks is currently doing well to prop up the returns. The result is that most fund managers drift toward the same asset class. Thus, we find our investments concentrated, rather than diversified.

There is an age-old investment rule that you must stay in the market. If you miss any number of days, your return could get killed. But if all your mutual funds are in the same asset class and that asset class gets killed, your mutual funds are all going to suffer. Don't set up a program that you can't stick with.

If you learn only one thing, it should be that you know what the sources of investment returns are and how they are delivered.

SUMMARY

Markets are, for all practical purposes, very efficient, which means: The prices at which securities are being traded reflect *all of the known* information, at all times. That information is available to anyone who wishes to know it. The ability to know something that no one else knows, and then act on that knowledge in a way that no one finds out about it, doesn't realistically exist today.

Most people believe investing is a zero sum game. In other words, if someone is to win, someone else must lose. In stock and bond investing, this simply is not the case.

For active management to work, the efficiency of market pricing must fail! By fail, we mean that there must be consistent areas of the free-market system that are "inefficient" and the free flow of goods and services is not occurring.

Efficiency means there is an unrestricted flow of goods and services between buyers and sellers. Stock and bond investing, in its simplest form, is the epitome of capitalism. People with capital (money) give it to people who want, or need, this capital. In exchange for this process, paper is exchanged in the form of company ownership, or stock, or as bonds with obligations of repayment from a company or the government. This exchange of capital comes with a price for the risk being born by the individual who is providing the money. We call that price a *return*. The level of return is influenced directly by the investor's perception of the amount of risk he or she is being asked to bear. As a result, one factor about capital market investing is absolute. Investors are risk averse, which means investors will only bear as much risk as they have to in order to receive a reward for that risk. And, if higher and higher levels of risk are involved, the bearer of that risk, the investor, demands higher and higher levels of reward.

Our social and economic system is characterized by open competition in a free market. And, with our system of capitalism, there is and has been a positive return on capital. That has to be or there would be no capitalism and no free markets.

In the next chapter, we will show you how to build academically tested portfolios. You will learn five lessons that will change your investment life.

PART TWO

HOW THE GAME IS PLAYED

A reporter once asked Michael Jordan, who was with the Chicago Bulls at the time, how one of the new players was doing. Jordan replied, "Fine, but every new player has to learn our system. The Bulls have a plan, and everyone who comes to the Bulls must learn the plan inside and out, forwards and backwards so it becomes part of him and he doesn't have to think about it. When the team is winning, they just play basketball. They don't worry about the plan or anything else. They just go. But when they're losing, when they get in trouble, they switch to the plan immediately. Everybody knows where to go and what to do. Everyone focuses on doing their job and when they get back on track, they just play basketball again."

Why relay this anecdote? Because that is exactly the way you should approach investing. What you're going to get in Part Two are the action steps that will lead to building your portfolio. It's your investment plan, a plan that you'll use for the rest of your investing life. It will not change because it's based on investment principles, and principles never change. When things are going well, when you're winning and the market is going up, just keep doing what you're doing. But when you perceive trouble—when the market drops and you don't understand why—then you can immediately go back and review the plan and know how to react.

It's following those principles that will get you to your destination. If these elements aren't in place or they're not set up and working properly, nothing else you do can make up for it. If you don't attend to them first, then you're going to waste an enormous amount of energy working on things that add little or no value. You will lose money, and no matter how hard you work or how many television news shows you watch, there will be nothing you can do to get it back.

So when bad events happen, do not let yourself get distracted by listening to the latest excuses. Look to your plan for direction and reassurance. If you have all these elements working for you, your investment program is going to be working. It's going to be moving in the right direction, and you won't have to be wondering what's wrong. I have never seen a failing investment plan that didn't have a problem in one of these principal elements.

CHAPTER 5

STRATEGIES THAT GIVE YOU THE EDGE

This chapter will show you how to build an academically tested portfolio in five easy-to-follow lessons.

LESSON 1 Know the Amount of Risk You're Willing to Take. Everybody is a long-term investor—until they get their quarterly statements. We want to ensure that your investment strategy is designed to reflect your personal risk tolerance. *Risk tolerance* is your capacity to tolerate unfavorable conditions during the time period you hold your investments without making changes. It has to do with your capacity to withstand negative returns without being tempted to abandon your investment program.

LESSON 2 Understand Asset Classes. *Asset class* is a term frequently used and often misunderstood in the investment world, but asset classes are really nothing more than categories of various types of investments. We're going to discuss what they are, one by one, and explain how they work together.

LESSON 3 Know the Six Principles of Successful Investing. There are six investment principles that will give you the highest possible probability for success. These principles work together to smooth out the roller-coaster ride associated with good and bad markets and produce steady results.

LESSON 4 Understand Your Investment Choices. When you build a portfolio, you want to combine funds for each asset class so that you can effectively build a diversified portfolio. You must understand your choices; frankly, as you will see, it's not that hard.

LESSON 5 *Know How to Design Your Own Investment Portfolio.* Having
   your own personal investment plan for accumulating capital will
   help you set reasonable goals and manage your expectations for
   reaching them. It will help you not to panic because you "heard
   something" on the news; and it will stop you from defaulting to
   short-term moves, thereby, potentially missing out on gains that
   long-term investors enjoy with much less effort.

LESSON 1 KNOW THE AMOUNT OF RISK YOU'RE WILLING TO TAKE

Everybody is a long-term investor—until they get their quarterly statement.

If you're like most investors, the important thing is to know that you're
not going to lose your principal. Unfortunately, there are only a few types
of investments that are guaranteed not to lose principal, and with those,
your earnings are only going to keep up with inflation. It's the oldest rule
in investing: No risk, no reward.

If you are absolutely terrified to be in the market, then you don't have
any business being in stocks or mutual funds in the first place. You'll have
to settle for money market instruments. There's no shame in that; the
stock market doesn't suit everyone's constitution.

Or you could be partially in the market—perhaps 20 percent, or 40 percent in the market and the rest in fixed income, such as money markets.
Don't hesitate to use fixed-income instruments at the same time; just realize that you're not going to make a lot of money.

We want to ensure that your investment strategy is designed to reflect
your personal risk tolerance. *Risk tolerance* is your capacity to tolerate
unfavorable conditions during the time period you hold your investments
without making changes. It has to do with how much you can lose and not
be tempted to abandon your investment program.

Determining risk tolerance is more than just filling out a questionnaire.
Reflecting on your past and looking at some of the major decisions you've
made over your lifetime can help in assessing your risk tolerance. What
motivated you to make those decisions?

Your risk tolerance is one of the most critical components for setting up
your portfolio mix. If you can't stand to lose more than 10 percent, then

you would be a candidate for a portfolio mix of 60 percent fixed income and 40 percent stocks.

If you can't stand to watch your portfolio drop more than 5 percent, you'd better be somewhere in the 30 percent stocks and 70 percent fixed income ratio. Or, if you can't bear to see it plummet more than 15 percent, you'd be well advised to have a truly diversified portfolio. If you're not diversified, all bets are off. Some equity portfolios lost 50 percent and more in the 2000–2002 years because they were not truly diversified. There's no limit to what you can lose if you're not diversified.

People don't like to lose money, and their anxiety about doing so can cause them to make unwise decisions. If that's the case, a more aggressive portfolio is not an appropriate choice.

MANAGING RISK

Start with less risk and gradually build up to a more aggressive portfolio. Before 2000, investors who were conservative by nature all of a sudden got very aggressive. That was because stock returns had been excellent for several years. Many people believed that the stock market "only goes up every year." *Wrong!*

You can increase risk little by little. Starting conservative will almost never be to your detriment. Say you start with a 60/40 ratio and later decide, "I can take more risk." Then add a little more risk to your portfolio.

What if you have only a few years left until retirement and you discover there is a huge gap between your assets and the amount of money you will need? Well, you are going to have to increase your investment risk to get higher expected returns. This may be the reverse of the advice you've been reading in other books. But, aside from greatly increasing the amount you're saving, how else can you make up for lost time?

You can start by identifying all the known variables, such as how much you currently have saved in all your asset pools, the size and frequency of your contributions, the amount of matches, investment allocations, and how much time you have before retirement.

Then, compare your long-term dollar needs with your portfolio performance and evaluate the probability of achieving those goals. In most cases, this evaluation will indicate a shortfall or a gap. At this point, your chances for success in achieving your financial goals are based solely on your current asset allocation and investment strategy.

Next, determine the maximum risk exposure you feel comfortable with. This will impact the probability of reaching your target retirement financial goals. If you are too conservative, that probability will decrease. You must make a decision to accept the downside of volatility and increased risk in order to realize the promise of a higher probability of success. Then, after you have determined the amount of risk you are willing to assume, you must attempt to solve for unknown variables, such as future capital market returns. The focus is on what is reliably predictable. Look at the stock market over different time periods, and then adjust your allocation to meet your future risk tolerances. This is where most people stop, because they don't know how much of an adjustment to make. You may need the help of an advisor.

If you have a long time horizon, you can do things more conservatively because time is on your side. But, if you discover that you still have a large gap, you may have to follow more aggressive strategies, such as concentrating more in equity investments, increasing your retirement plan contributions, or extending the age at which you wish to retire. Unfortunately, most people have lifestyle wants and needs that far exceed a reasonable growth rate of return on their retirement plans. Again, you have to think *not* in terms of how much you are willing to make, but how much you are willing to *lose*.

WHAT IS YOUR TOLERANCE FOR RISK?

The Lifeboat Drill

The most important thing about the lifeboat drill is that it's visual, and we are very visual beings. We react better to things we can see.

Assume for a moment that you have invested all of your money (we'll use $10,000 for simplicity). In the first quarter, your investment goes up 3 percent. You feel pretty good, right? In the next quarter, it goes up 2 percent more. You're feeling even better. But what if your money starts to decline? Your ship is taking on water—how low in the water will you let the boat sink before you abandon ship and get in the lifeboat?

Let's say your quarterly statement shows you that your $10,000 has become $9,700. Are you still on board? The next quarter, you're down to $9,400. Then you drop to $9,200. How are you feeling now? Are you still

TABLE 5.1   Decline Equation

Potential Quarterly Decline	Original Investment Is $10,000	Loss in Dollar Amounts
(3%)	$9,700	−$300
(7%)	$9,300	−$700
(10%)	$9,000	−$1,000
(15%)	$8,500	−$1,500
(23%)	$7,700	−$2,300

okay with doing nothing or are you getting your lifeboat ready? The following quarter, you drop to $9,000. Let's assume no action is taken and your assets go down further: to $8,500, $7,700, $6,500, and eventually to $5,000. At what point do you want to jump ship?

You might be willing to endure a 3 percent decline; you probably aren't very willing to sit still at 10 percent; and if you feel alone and emotional at a 15 percent drop, you'll want out. It's fear that gets someone out of the market.

What's interesting is that most investors are willing to accept a greater *percentage* amount of loss when it isn't related to a specific *dollar* amount. (See Table 5.1.)

Most surprising are people who have portfolios invested for maximum growth in very aggressive funds but indicate they are willing to take only a 12 to 13 percent decline in their principal. Clearly, something is out of whack. Either they must be able to accept more decline or they're invested completely inappropriately.

SUMMARY

The biggest mistake you can make is to go beyond your risk tolerance, your threshold of comfort. You may panic, jump ship, and get in the lifeboat, and then not make your destination because you're floating in the middle of the ocean waiting to be rescued. And you watch the ship, which is doing fine, as it picks up steam and leaves you afloat. If you bailed out of equity mutual funds at the end of March 2003, you missed an average 20 percent return for that next quarter. You just saw your ship sail away.

Now let's discuss asset classes, the subject of the next lesson.

LESSON 2 UNDERSTANDING ASSET CLASSES

Asset class is a term frequently used in the investment world to refer to a *category* of investment.

WHAT ARE ASSET CLASSES?

You're probably familiar with equity asset classes and fixed-income asset classes—the two main asset classes. For the purpose of our discussion, we are going to divide them into the following categories:

- Cash/money market
- Bonds
- Equities—Domestic
  U.S. large growth companies
  S&P 500
  U.S. large value companies
  U.S. small growth companies
  U.S. small value companies
- Equities—International
  Large companies
  Small companies

These asset classes are listed from the safest to the most risky, but as you will discover, there is no absolute ranking of risk in the equity market.

Cash

The first asset class, called *cash*, includes money market funds, which are made up of T-bills, certificates of deposit, and commercial paper. These are called cash because the NAV (net asset value) is always one dollar; in other words, the price doesn't fluctuate. Few people understand that when their holdings are in cash, they're still invested in an asset class.

Bonds

Also called *fixed income*, this asset class is divided into two main groups: stable bonds, such as U.S. government and AAA corporate bonds, and higher-yield bonds, such as bb corporate bonds and "junk bonds." We recommend only the first group. Within this category, we decide if we want long-term, intermediate, or shorter-duration bonds. We recommend short-term bonds, meaning five years or less to maturity, because a short-duration fund will give you 94 percent of the return without the long-term bond volatility. If you are in a long-term bond fund and interest rates move up, your fund can drop 25 percent in a day.

Never invest in junk bonds; it's not worth the risk. All you are doing is adding volatility without gaining the expected returns of a stock. We would never recommend junk bonds because they are actually unsecured loans to a company. Suppose a company goes bankrupt—that company's bondholders are secured and get paid before stockholders, but that is not the case with junk bond owners. These are usually general obligation instruments that are not backed up by any collateral, so you're last in line to get paid. When you think of bonds, think safety, not speculation.

Equities—Domestic

After cash and bonds, we subdivided asset classes into more specific categories distinguished by their unique characteristics. Equity, or stock, asset classes are often categorized according to the size of their market capitalization (number of outstanding shares multiplied by current stock price.)

How it's decided what stocks go into an asset class

The way academics built equity asset classes is quite involved. First, they took all the companies on the New York Stock Exchange, ranked them by size, and then divided them into 10 deciles.

They designated the largest one-tenth of the companies as Decile Number 1, including companies on the scale of General Electric or Chrysler. Decile Number 2 represented the next 10 percent graduating down in company size. Deciles 9 and 10 were the smallest companies, the bottom 20 percent in size. That's not an asset class yet, but it's part of an asset class.

Next, they looked at the Nasdaq (National Association of Securities Dealers Automated Quotation System) and Amex (the American Stock Exchange), and they filled in the same capitalization requirements that were in Deciles 1 through 10. Deciles 1 through 5 qualify as large-company stocks; small-company stocks are in the 6 through 10 deciles. Deciles 9 and 10 on the Nasdaq and Amex have over 2,000 small stocks.

The academic asset class of value stocks originally included every value stock across all those same markets. They discovered that was too cumbersome, so they divided it into asset classes called *large value* and *small value*. The same applies to *growth* and *international* equity asset classes.

Large growth

These are very large U.S. companies that are doing very well (they have an average capitalization of approximately $10 billion or greater). This type of company usually has good sales, good prospects for the future, and good earnings.

S&P 500 (Standard & Poor's Index of the 500 largest U.S. stocks)

It seems there is a lot of confusion between asset classes and indexes, but there is a distinction. Asset classes are academically defined, whereas an index is simply a numerical group of stocks. Indexes are commercial benchmarks. The S&P 500 is an index of 500 stocks. We also call it an equity asset class even though it contains both large-growth and large-value stocks. It's well known and it gives people something to compare to.

Asset classes for stocks are further refined into value and growth stock categories according to their potential total return over time.

Large value

These are large U.S. publicly traded companies that may be temporarily out of favor. They aren't doing well by any measurement. The companies are distressed economically.

Small growth

These are smaller publicly traded U.S. companies with an average capitalization of less than $2 billion. They have good sales and good prospects for the future.

Small value

These are smaller publicly traded U.S. companies (with an average capitalization of less than $2 billion) that aren't doing very well.

Equities—International

The last two equity asset classes are international. This group is generally composed of stocks of companies based outside the United States—from any part of the world with established free markets.

Large companies

These are large international companies that are doing very well, including growth to value stocks and everything in between.

Small companies

These are small international companies that aren't doing very well, also including both growth and value stocks.

It's important to be clear about definitions that get tossed around. For instance, contrary to what many people believe, technology is not an asset class; it's a sector. Anyone who invests strictly in high-tech and telecommunications (sector funds) is forgoing investment strategies in order to speculate in concentrated, high-risk sectors. Some would say anyone who does this is not only a speculator, but an outright gambler.

Table 5.2 shows how these seven equity asset classes have done individually compared to an entire diversified portfolio over the last 30 years. The first five asset classes across the top are domestic; the next two are international. And the last is a combination of all. Each column represents every stock in its respective categories. The columns are more precisely defined as follows.

TABLE 5.2   Rates of Returns by Asset Class

Year	Small Value	Small Growth	Large Value	S&P 500	Large Growth	Int'l. Small	Int'l. Large	Diversified Portfolio*
1970	0.31	(18.61)	11.90	4.03	(5.23)	0.90	(9.65)	(2.09)
1971	14.40	23.49	9.44	14.32	23.60	68.25	59.87	26.45
1972	6.96	3.75	15.97	18.98	21.65	64.22	53.25	22.52
1973	(26.01)	(39.10)	(2.75)	(14.67)	(20.34)	(13.68)	(22.34)	(20.06)
1974	(18.11)	(33.40)	(22.38)	(26.46)	(29.96)	(28.61)	(33.68)	(27.08)
1975	54.45	63.17	51.92	37.21	35.66	49.86	65.26	50.30
1976	53.55	43.51	44.98	23.85	18.38	11.46	5.55	31.18
1977	21.81	20.32	.75	(7.18)	(9.13)	74.08	40.61	15.72
1978	21.82	18.63	6.63	6.57	7.01	65.53	33.22	19.58
1979	37.95	47.26	23.78	18.42	20.69	(0.78)	2.11	23.83
1980	29.09	46.07	16.54	32.41	33.87	35.46	38.48	32.67
1981	10.54	(4.09)	11.23	(4.91)	(7.90)	(4.65)	0.86	0.40
1982	37.66	25.99	27.35	21.41	17.60	0.82	5.22	21.41
1983	44.22	26.92	26.77	22.51	16.23	32.40	22.23	27.33
1984	5.08	(8.87)	14.07	6.27	(1.07)	10.08	11.39	4.62
1985	34.73	28.51	29.46	32.17	31.45	60.11	48.28	35.85
1986	16.86	5.82	20.36	18.47	13.70	50.10	59.95	23.04
1987	(6.30)	(10.00)	2.32	5.23	6.40	70.55	41.43	10.82
1988	28.84	20.46	24.64	16.81	12.82	26.01	24.81	21.65
1989	19.69	19.09	28.35	31.49	31.52	29.34	14.67	25.22
1990	(20.81)	(18.13)	(13.94)	(3.17)	1.43	(16.77)	(18.38)	(12.25)
1991	39.37	52.11	29.82	30.55	41.14	7.05	13.95	32.98
1992	29.86	11.23	21.16	7.67	7.14	(18.37)	(9.44)	9.55
1993	22.56	14.04	21.16	9.99	2.01	33.49	36.44	18.15
1994	(0.95)	(2.88)	(4.57)	1.31	1.47	12.42	7.63	1.11
1995	29.24	31.28	37.19	37.43	37.92	0.48	13.72	29.11
1996	21.36	12.92	15.69	23.07	21.20	2.26	7.49	16.05

TABLE 5.2 *(Continued)*

Year	Small Value	Small Growth	Large Value	S&P 500	Large Growth	Int'l. Small	Int'l. Large	Diversified Portfolio*
1997	34.40	16.27	31.70	33.37	30.28	(25.11)	(4.37)	20.41
1998	(7.03)	0.38	14.93	28.58	33.61	8.04	15.46	13.63
1999	10.76	47.73	1.89	21.03	28.16	20.15	32.87	22.83
2000	1.03	(18.42)	8.20	(9.10)	(13.53)	(5.69)	(16.08)	(7.27)
2001	35.43	6.00	(0.47)	(11.88)	(15.17)	(10.69)	(22.03)	(1.05)
2002	(10.20)	(28.07)	(27.71)	(22.11)	(21.95)	1.78	(13.76)	(18.80)
Annualized Returns in Percentages	15.42	9.19	13.04	10.81	9.50	14.88	12.28	12.72
Standard Deviation	20.96	25.67	17.59	17.52	19.29	30.19	26.57	17.72
Years Best	8	4	5	1	4	8	3	0
Years Worst	2	9	4	1	6	7	4	0

*Diversified portfolio = 16 percent in each U.S. asset class, 10 percent in each international asset class.
Note: Past performance is not an indicator of future expected returns.
Source: Returns Program, Dimensional Fund Advisors (Rogers Capital Management, Inc.)

- *First column: small value stocks.* The smallest 8 percent of the market universe[1] *based on total capitalization.* From that range, a value screen is given in which the BtM (book-to-market value) of every issue is calculated. In other words, small value companies are very small in size, temporarily distressed, and there are a huge number of them, over 2,000.

  Book-to-market value is a ratio comparing the book value of a share of common stock with its market price. High BtM companies are companies in distress (and investors demand to be compensated for the perceived higher risk). Low book-to-market companies (like Microsoft and Wal-Mart) on average will do well, and because they

[1] *Market universe* is defined as all stocks in the NYSE, Amex, and Nasdaq. Source: Dimensional Fund Advisors Firm Profile & Returns Program.

are so popular, investors are not compensated so well. Their cost of acquiring capital is less than for other companies not in this group.

- **Second column:** *small growth stocks.* The smallest 8 percent of the market universe[2] *using the lowest book-to-market ratio.* These are small companies, but they are doing very well compared to small value companies. Their sales are good, price to earnings is good—everything is going great—they are just small. Because they are doing so well, they don't have to pay as much for capital as other companies.

- **Third column:** *large value stocks.* From the largest 90 percent of the market universe,[3] these *have the highest BtM ratios.* They are large companies that are distressed because they are not doing so well.

- **Fourth column:** *S&P 500 (Standard & Poor's 500).* An index of stocks composed of the 500 largest companies in the United States. The index is market weighted, which means the larger the company, the larger the weight in the index. The index is widely used as a stock benchmark for account performance measurement. This index includes 400 industrial stocks, 20 transportation stocks, 40 financial stocks, and 40 public utilities—whether growth, value, or those stocks in between.

- **Fifth column:** *large growth stocks.* The largest 90 percent of the market universe[4] with the lowest BtMs in the top tenth percentile are chosen. These companies are doing very well, and they just happen to be very big as well.

- **Sixth column:** *international large stocks.* The largest 60–75 percent by market cap ranking in Australia, Austria, Belgium, Denmark, Sweden, Finland, France, Germany, Greece, Hong Kong, Ireland, Italy, Japan, the Netherlands, New Zealand, Norway, Portugal, Singapore, Spain, Switzerland, and the UK.

- **Seventh column:** *international small stocks.* The smallest 8 percent of companies in the following regions: Japan, UK, Austria, Belgium, Denmark, Finland, France, Germany, Greece, Ireland, Italy, the Netherlands, Norway, Spain, Sweden, Switzerland, Australia, Hong Kong, New Zealand, and Singapore.

---

[2] Ibid.
[3] Ibid.
[4] Ibid.

■ *Eighth column: a diversified portfolio.* Made up of all asset classes. We wanted this diversified portfolio to be structured without bias, so it is a ratio of 80 percent U.S. stocks and 20 percent international. We divided 80 by 5, which gave us 16 percent in each of the five U.S. asset classes; and put 10 percent in each of the international asset classes. This portfolio is for the person who says, "Since I don't know what to do, I'll just divide my money equally among the asset classes."

The sun does not shine on the same dog's tail every day.

The light gray boxes depict the worst-performing asset class for that year. The dark gray boxes depict the best-performing asset class for that year. The black boxes represent years when the diversified portfolio out-performed the S&P 500.

Do you see any pattern in Table 5.2? Does it appear that one asset class is superior? No. If you look closely, it's totally random. The people who are trying to time the dark- and light-gray boxes will always fail miserably. (Dalbar studies support this claim.)

The down years of 1973 and 1974 are intentionally included in Table 5.2. Look at the best asset classes during those years. If we'd started the table in 1975, overall returns would have been a lot higher.

Now cover up the top row containing the names of the asset classes. Look at the data near the bottom of the table that shows the annualized return, standard deviation, and the number of years that the asset class was best or worst. If you had only this information and you could invest in just one asset class, which would you pick? You would most likely choose small value because of its annualized return of 15.42 percent.

Next, look at the year 1998. You'll see that small value returned a negative 7.03 percent, while large growth for that year was up 33.61 percent. That's a 40 percent difference. If someone had advised you in 1998 to invest in the "best" asset class of small value, you would have underperformed by 40 percent. And you probably would have sold out after it did so poorly, especially because the financial media was telling people that value would never be good again.

What this tells you is not to invest all of your money in any one asset class. The sea of light and dark areas in Table 5.2 shows that every asset class behaves differently and without predictability at any given time. This is why all of them are necessary to build a successful portfolio.

But in 2001, the table shows that small value was up 35.43 and large growth did a negative 15.17 percent, a 50 percent difference.

Let's compare small growth and small value over the 33-year period from 1970 through 2002. Small value outperforms small growth. During that same period, large value outperforms large growth. Why did value outperform growth? Value companies are the poorest companies and are therefore riskier. Their cost of capital is greater. It's the same principle that causes the person who can least afford the loan to pay the highest interest rates. During the years 1995 to 1998, there were hundreds of media articles proclaiming that value was dead. But look at 1995 on the table—large value was up 37 percent.

On the other hand, large growth companies, such as GE or Microsoft, are highly successful companies, but look at their returns. If asset classes all paid the same rate of return, we would all buy large growth because it's the safest. Small outperforms large because large is safer.

Academic studies have shown that international investing is no different when it comes to the risk factors—international value beats international growth; international small value beats international small growth. In other words, small has always beaten large over long periods of time. This is exactly the same for value versus growth.

Over 2,057 stocks make up the small value asset class. You could buy any one of the small value stocks and it might or might not perform like the asset class, but if you bought them all, you would get the return indicated. There is safety in numbers.

So, how do you find out the asset class of the mutual funds you're invested in? You can look up your fund on Morningstar.com or work with a knowledgeable investment advisor. They break everything down into asset classes for you.

Refer to the row near the end of Table 5.2 labeled "Standard Deviation." The number in the row under each asset class represents the volatility of the asset class. The higher the number, the greater the volatility or (risk). While it was generally accepted that the large growth asset class is safest, notice that the standard deviation for large growth is somewhat higher than for the large value or the S&P 500 asset class. However, it is lower than for either of the international asset classes and either of the U.S. small asset classes.

Why is this significant? Because it demonstrates the overlooked power of diversification. Notice that the diversified portfolio provides a 3 percent higher annualized compound return than large growth over the 33-year period; yet it had 1.5 percent less volatility. By combining asset classes that have individually high standard deviations (volatility/risk), you are able to diversify away the higher risk inherent to any one asset class and achieve a superior return when compared to the "safest" asset class.

You may be investing in your 401(k) plan and find you have no small funds and no international funds available to you. If you don't have all the asset classes in your 401(k) plan, then you need to insist that you have at least a representative fund in every asset class. That's one of your rights.

Let's say your 401(k) plan includes Vanguard Growth Index and Oakmark I. You should also have an S&P 500 index fund. But you would want to use all three of these funds to fill up the rows across the top of the table. The S&P 500 is a blend of value and growth. You may want to add Vanguard Growth Index for large growth and Oakmark I for large value. You have to have at least large growth and value and small growth and value funds. Forget the mid-caps if you have to, but you have to have international exposure to some degree. You need a pure international fund, not a worldwide fund such as Janus Worldwide (80 percent of Janus Worldwide was in U.S. stocks to attempt to boost its return). If you don't have international growth and international value, it's going to be hard to build a truly diversified portfolio.

SUMMARY

- Asset class refers to a *category* of investments.
- There are nine asset class categories.
- Asset class performance is totally random.
- You can combine asset classes in a portfolio to lower risk.

Diversification is just one of the six investment principles that will give you the highest possible probability for success. Learn what the principles are and how to put them to work for you in Lesson 3.

LESSON 3 THE SIX PRINCIPLES OF SUCCESSFUL INVESTING

Investing is a marathon, not a sprint!

Twenty-five years ago, before the "technology boom," the greatest technology company in the world was IBM. IBM dominated the market; no other company was even close. Logically, that should have been the best investment, but others were better. For example, Clorox Corporation, a bleach company, outperformed IBM.

Why can't people who are highly educated in the world of finance pick a superior stock or a mutual fund? Because they don't have a crystal ball, and no one knows what will happen in the future. But the good news is that it isn't necessary.

We know how to *blend* the markets to mitigate risk. There are six principles you can employ to put together the hand you've been dealt in a way that gives you a chance to smooth out market volatility and provides you with the highest possible probability for success. These principles work together to level out the roller-coaster ride associated with good and bad markets and produce steady results.

1. Dollar cost averaging
2. Diversification
3. Asset allocation
4. Asset class investing
5. Time
6. Rebalancing

The best reason we can give you for learning how to use these basic principles of successful investing is to lessen your *fear factor*. You will no longer have to play the role of the blind sheep, just following someone else's lead because you're unable to make informed decisions. Nor do you have to get a Ph.D. in finance; simple knowledge is your best protection. Once you have a grasp of how these concepts work, you can take an active role in putting them to work in your favor.

PRINCIPLE 1 DOLLAR COST AVERAGING

Dollar cost averaging is a systematic purchasing of shares with fixed dollar amounts at regular intervals, without regard to the share price. It has many advantages and very few drawbacks, if any.

It works like this. Say you decide to defer $100 of your paycheck every pay period into your retirement plan. Your paychecks are semimonthly. So, twice each month your plan automatically buys $100 worth of shares, purchasing more shares when the price is down, and fewer when the price is up. It has been academically proven that this method will lower your average cost per share over time.

Example: You decide to invest $100 per month to buy an index mutual fund. In **January**, the price of the fund is $10 per share, so a hundred dollars buys 10 shares. (See Figure 5.1.)

In **February**, the price of your fund's shares drops 50 percent to $5 per share. That means the original investment is worth only half as much. It also means $100 now buys 20 shares of the same mutual fund.

In **March**, the following month, the price has dropped again and your original investment is down 75 percent, but now you can buy 40 shares with your $100. The price starts to rebound in **April** to $5 a share, so you buy another 20 shares. Finally, in **May**, the price of the fund is back to the original purchase price at $10 per share and you buy 10 shares. At this point, you decide to check your accounting. So far, you have spent $500 and bought 100 shares of an index mutual fund. At the end of May, the fund shares are selling for your original purchase price of $10 per share, so your 100 shares are worth $1,000 gross. After deducting the $500 you invested, you actually made $500 on an asset that never appreciated above the original purchase price!

Monthly Commitment ... $100.00 to shares of a mutual fund			
January	$100.00 / $10.00	equals	10 shares
February	$100.00 / $ 5.00	equals	20 shares
March	$100.00 / $ 2.50	equals	40 shares
April	$100.00 / $ 5.00	equals	20 shares
May	$100.00 / $10.00	equals	10 shares
Total of:	$500.00 spent to purchase:		100 shares
	$1,000.00 Sales proceeds yield profit of		
	$500.00 on a nonappreciating asset		

FIGURE 5.1
Dollar Cost Averaging

Dollar cost averaging keeps investors from making some critical mistakes, such as market timing, and trading themselves into oblivion. Here are examples of the two most common investing errors.

Investor A has a diversified portfolio, but can't control his emotional reactions. He receives a quarterly statement in which three of his funds show a modest gain and two funds show a 15 percent loss each, resulting in a portfolio total that is down for that period. At this point, most "long-term" investors become quarterly investors, meaning they are overwhelmed with an urge to "fix" their portfolios by putting new money only toward the funds that made money and dumping the two that lost money.

Does this make sense? Of course not, because it means the investor is "buying high and selling low." Everyone, regardless of his or her investment experience, knows how important it is to do the opposite: "buy low and sell high." Yet, it's the hardest of all principles for investors without guidance to follow! It's not in our nature to buy funds that are struggling, and it is in our nature to join the bandwagon of the latest winner.

Almost without fail, Investor A will dump his mutual funds that have lost money and take the 15 percent loss (which, before selling, was only an UNrealized loss). Then, to make matters worse, Investor A buys more of the "best" fund, which happens to be the highest priced. Now the funds switch and the two that have lost money begin to rebound and the recent winners start to lag. And the losing cycle is born.

Investor B suffers from market timing. Although she also has a diversified portfolio and is able to overcome her urge to sell her securities when they are down, Investor B instead decides to sit on the sidelines during bad markets. In other words, she thinks it is wiser to stop contributing altogether during bear markets and will come back when the market is "good" again. Essentially, this investor has acknowledged that the market will turn around again.

So why not buy shares at cheap prices when the market is down if you think it will eventually go back up? In fact, it's the best time to buy, and definitely not the time to stop your contributions to your 401(k) plan. Additionally, if the employer provides a match, then free money is being left on the table. That's like walking past a $100 bill and being too lazy to bend over and pick it up.

In both of the above cases, the discipline of dollar cost averaging takes the worry and guesswork out of investing and is a more methodical and sensible way to invest. By setting up dollar cost averaging contributions in a diversified portfolio, you'll always own some things that perform better than others. However, by making regular deposits and purchasing more shares on a consistent basis, you're not as worried about which ones are up or down. In fact, you can take comfort in knowing that you are purchasing more shares with your contribution when certain funds may be down; and when the funds turn around, the investor with the most shares will be in the best shape!

If you decide to sit on the sidelines and not continue to invest, the rest of these principles won't matter.

PRINCIPLE 2 DIVERSIFICATION

The biggest mistake most investors make is attempting to diversify within the same asset class.

Diversification may well be the most misused word in the English language. People frequently tell us, "I'm well diversified; I have four funds." But, they're not really diversified because their four funds are all in the same asset class—large growth funds for instance. Suppose you are invested in a 401(k) plan that has many choices, but they're all in the same asset class. How could this happen? Your 401(k) provider probably picked them based on best performance, which would have come from the same asset class. So it ended up with three large-cap funds, thinking it was making the plan diversified. This is why you have to know what you're doing, or at least have an advisor who does.

Harry Markowitz, a Nobel Prize winner in economics, said that while almost all diversification is good, there is *effective* diversification and *ineffective* diversification. Simply put, if your investments move up and down together, that is ineffective diversification and has the same effect as being invested in just one fund. Chances are, there is also a tremendous stock overlap in these funds.

A diversified portfolio provides stability and, hence, a larger long-term return, but only if you spread your money among the various asset classes that don't always have the same price movements—for example, between value and growth, small and large, and international growth and value. A truly diversified portfolio comprises many asset classes, some of which are doing well, and some of which are not doing so well. Thus, the total return of a diversified portfolio will never be as good as the current best asset class; nor will it ever be as poor as the worst. But the ride will be smoother and the end result will be a superior return.

PRINCIPLE 3 ASSET ALLOCATION

Asset allocation simply means determining what proportion of your money is going to be invested in which asset classes—stocks, bonds, and cash investments—in order to maximize the growth of your portfolio for each unit of risk that you take. This may be the single most important determinant of the long-term performance of any investment portfolio. The confusion occurs when the terms *asset allocation* and *diversification* are used interchangeably. Even if you are 100 percent invested in money market funds, that is still a form of asset allocation.

The first step is to identify what asset classes are represented by the mutual funds in your plan and then spread, or allocate, your contributions among them to minimize risk.

You should insist on a mutual fund that represents every asset class we just discussed. You may discover that your employer has given you only cash, a bond fund, and four large growth funds. That's not asset allocation.

Now, how do you determine what percentage of each asset class you should own? Selecting asset classes with a low correlation to one another is the Nobel Prize–winning secret for achieving more consistent portfolio performance. Academics have actually calculated methods to measure correlation in a portfolio, thereby enabling one to measure the volatility or risk of a portfolio. By using these tools, portfolios can be more systematically created with greater degrees of predictability in terms of risk and return.

Because of these measurement tools, it is possible to combine, in one portfolio, assets that have the potential to generate higher returns due to their volatile nature, but whose market performances have a low correlation to one another. This achieves the result that the portfolio as a whole will actually be less risky than any one of the individual investments, yet generate a higher overall return than a portfolio made up solely of low-risk investments.

Table 5.3 illustrates the correlation coefficients for each of our asset classes for the years 1973 through 2002.

As you can see, their prices move in different directions. A perfect correlation is +1, and an opposite correlation would be −1. You would want the −1 correlation in your portfolio because it provides you with dissimilar price movements.

In the real world, however, there is no −1 correlation, but you try to get the lowest correlation you can in your assets. To determine the suitability of an asset, you look at the correlations among the assets, and if they come out low, then the given asset will provide you with further diversification. The correlation measures are very good at telling us what asset classes or investments should go into our portfolio, but not necessarily how much we should put into each. To determine how much to put in each depends on time horizon, risk tolerance, and long-term rates of returns for the individual asset classes. See Appendix B for the formulas.

PRINCIPLE 4 ASSET CLASS INVESTING

Asset class investing is easy to understand. First, determine what proportion of your money is going to be invested in which asset classes. Select your allocation. And then leave it alone!

Asset class funds are *passively* managed, which means there is *no* "active" decision making occurring about buying and selling the issues that are contained within the mutual fund. Their sole purpose is to mimic the markets while experiencing very low turnover and significantly below average costs.

The best way to do asset class investing is by owning academically defined asset class mutual funds because they are more reliable in concentrating on a specific asset class. These funds are a relatively new hybrid created by Dimensional Fund Advisors, an institutional money manager. Although not available to the general public, institutional asset class mutual funds can be purchased by individuals through selected groups of investment advisors who are required to educate their clients on the benefits of passive asset class investing.

Some of the more progressive 401(k) plans have predefined asset class *portfolios* representing various levels of risk; these portfolios vary only by

TABLE 5.3 Asset Class Correlation Coefficients

	Fixed			Domestic		International	
	MMF T-bills	1-Year Fixed	5-Year Notes	U.S. Large Co. Stocks	U.S. Small Co. Stocks	Large Co. Stocks	Small Co. Stocks
Money Market Fund	1.000						
1-Year Fixed	0.852	1.000					
5-Year Treasury Notes	0.198	0.622	1.000				
U.S. Large Company Stocks	−0.106	0.153	0.253	1.000			
U.S. Small Company Stocks	−0.010	−0.043	0.096	0.666	1.000		
Int'l Large Company Stocks	−0.005	−0.053	−0.009	0.575	0.456	1.000	
Int'l Small Company Stocks	−0.027	−0.114	−0.096	0.278	0.263	0.883	1.000

the percentage allotted to bonds. For example, a conservative portfolio may have 40 percent stock mutual funds and 60 percent bond mutual funds, while an aggressive one may have 80 percent stock and 20 percent bond funds.

Actively managed mutual funds (especially the advertised ones that appeal to the retail market) tend to do what we call *style drift*. Active managers are under tremendous pressure to deliver returns, even though that may not be the function of a particular fund. They will drift out of their asset class into another asset class in an effort to, hopefully, boost their returns.

It is very difficult to maintain a balanced portfolio with actively managed funds because of style drift. Let's say you wanted a portfolio that is a 50–50 mix of large growth companies and small value companies. If the manager of the fund of large growth companies starts buying small value companies because the large growth asset class isn't doing well, or vice versa, that messes up your 50–50 allocation.

And, if every fund went to large growth when growth is doing well, then when growth plummeted, your whole portfolio would plummet. That's why many investors today are down 70 percent. They may have tried to remain diversified, but the managers of those funds drifted. If each one "fudged" just a little in the direction of whatever was up at the time, it would be enough to cause big trouble to a portfolio.

Your advisor should search for managers who have been consistent and will not chase returns in a neighboring asset class to prop up returns. Advisors should monitor the managers, and if they start drifting, they should be replaced.

Investors without any knowledge or advice naturally pick the funds with the best returns for the last period, and that's how they end up with everything in one asset class.

Then if the fund doesn't deliver performance, investors take their money out of that mutual fund and go elsewhere. And the fund manager gets fired. The average tenure of an active manager is around three years. Robert Sanborn was fired as the manager of Oakmark, a top value fund, for *sticking* with value companies when growth was in vogue. He was later exonerated because, after a few years, value was again back in vogue.

Asset class funds and index funds are not under pressure to perform like actively managed funds. If asset class funds are not available, the next best alternative is to build a portfolio of index funds. Even though they are only numerical commercial benchmarks and not academically defined as asset class funds are, it is still possible to build a superior portfolio with index funds. For example, the S&P 500 is a good one to utilize, and frankly, the large growth managers have trouble beating it. Each year, the S&P 500 index outperforms 82 to 95 percent of the actively managed funds whose stated goal is to beat the S&P 500.

PRINCIPLE 5 TIME

The longer the time period you hold your investments, the closer you will come to the expected average. This means short-term market fluctuations get smoothed out over time.

No serious investor would knowingly hold a stock for only one day, one month, or even one year. Such brief time periods are clearly too short for investment in stocks, because the expected variation in returns is too large in comparison with the average expected return. Such short-term holdings in stocks are not investments; they are *speculations.*

Equities become much less volatile the longer they're held. Bonds and money market funds are lower risk, lower return, and can be held a shorter time.

If you study Figure 5.2, you will see that the common stock investments made in any one-year period could have gone up 53.99 percent or dropped 43.34 percent. But, when you look at any 20-year period, you will see that there are no down periods—only gains.

If we measure an investment every three years, rather than every quarter, we can see satisfying progress that wouldn't be apparent in a quarterly measurement. In most cases, the time horizon that investors use as the standard to measure results is far too short, causing dissatisfaction with investment performance.

The Power of Compounding Is Just a Function of Time

Compounding is the process of earning a rate of return on your money that is invested, and then reinvesting those earnings at the same rate. This can be done with dividends, interest, or new contributions. For example, a $100 investment earning compound interest at 10 percent a year would

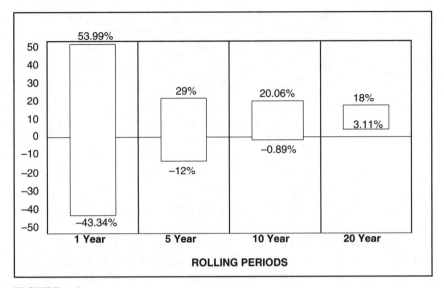

FIGURE 5.2
Risk over Time
Source: Ibbotson Associates.

increase to $110 at the end of the first year, and $121 at the end of the second year, and so on. The actual formula is:

Compound sum = (principal) (1 + interest rate), to the Nth power

where *N* is the number of years

The essence of the formula is that at the end of each year, interest is earned not only on the original amount, but also on all the previously accumulated interest amounts—you are earning interest on interest!

The typical compounding table (Table 5.4) shows you how a single investment of $10,000 will grow at various rates of return. Five percent is what you might get from a certificate of deposit (CD) or with a government bond; 10 percent is about the historical average stock market return; and 16 percent would have been possible over the last 20 years. But historically, you should average around 11 percent.

A simple way to figure out how long it takes your money to double is the *Rule of 72*. Divide the number 72 by the interest rate or rate of return you are earning and the result is the number of years it takes your money to double. For example, if you are earning 10 percent, your money will

TABLE 5.4   Compounding

	Growing at		
Year	5%	10%	15%
0	$10,000	$ 10,000	$ 10,000
5	12,800	16,100	20,100
10	16,300	25,900	40,500
15	20,800	41,800	81,400
25	33,900	108,300	329,200

double in 7.2 years. If you are earning 12 percent, it only takes 6 years for your money to double.

Your goal is to maximize the rate of return you are earning, while also minimizing the risk you are taking. If you can earn just 10 percent, in 20 years, because of compounding, your money will have grown by almost 800 percent.

PRINCIPLE 6 REBALANCING

More frequent rebalancing improves results, which would indicate that a style that is outperforming the broad market does not stay in favor for long periods of time. The same holds true for a style that is underperforming the broad market: Its out-of-favor status is not sustained for long periods of time.

Rebalancing an investment portfolio seems simple on the surface, but as you start to think through the method, frequency, tolerance limits, fees, and commissions, the subject reveals itself to be quite complex and without easy answers. This is probably not an exercise that an average first time investor would pursue on his or her own. Here's where a qualified advisor can help.[In a progressive 401(k) plan, you can go to your computer, push a button, and it will automatically rebalance your portfolio.]

The principle of rebalancing is to maintain the same percentages in the various asset classes you have chosen to maintain proper diversification in all market environments. By rebalancing, you may give up some short-term gains if you reduce your holdings of winning stocks prematurely, but you'll also miss the big losses when and if they collapse.

Although the mechanics of rebalancing are fairly straightforward, there are a variety of methods that could be used to reach that optimal portfolio goal of maximizing returns while minimizing risk.

Many investment advisors rebalanced their equity positions down to their allocation targets as the bull market pushed equity values upward. Then, after 2002, they increased equity positions as the declining markets dropped those positions below targets. As a result, they have been selling high, then buying low. See the logic?

When the price is down, you are able to buy more shares. Plus, you're reinvesting the money you've made along with your principal and *compounding* your growth.

An investment advisor or consultant should be knowledgeable about the various issues surrounding rebalancing and, ideally, should be able to explain them to you in a way that makes the desired method acceptable and practical to apply.

SUMMARY

- Dollar cost averaging
- Diversification
- Asset allocation
- Asset class investing
- Time
- Rebalancing

These principles work together to level out the roller-coaster ride associated with good and bad markets and produce steady results, but you still need to understand your investment choices. This is the subject of the next lesson.

LESSON 4 UNDERSTANDING INVESTMENT FUNDS

With the addition of hundreds of new funds annually, it's safe to say they represent the number one investment choice—and for many good reasons. But, not all mutual funds are created equal. Although a fund is sold as representing a specific asset class, the management is crucial to maintaining that focus. Your portfolio can contain a variety of funds to achieve the diversification required to meet your risk tolerance. Following are descriptions of the types of funds you will want to look for in assembling your portfolio.

MUTUAL FUNDS

Think of a mutual fund as a financial intermediary that pools all its investors' funds together and buys stocks, bonds, and/or other assets on behalf of the group as a whole.

Mutual funds continually issue new shares of the fund for sale to the public, and every new purchase results in new shares being issued. The number of shares and the price are directly related to the value of the securities the mutual fund holds.

A fund's share price can change from day to day, depending on the daily value of its underlying securities. Each share's value is computed by dividing the total value of all the assets held by the fund by the number of shares issued and outstanding.

The NAV (net asset value) reflects the daily change in the price of the securities within the fund's portfolio and is computed at the end of every day the markets are open for trading. In a regular mutual fund, which includes thousands and often millions of shares, the NAV is calculated on a daily basis without commissions, in full and fractional units, with values moving up or down along with the stock and bond markets.

FIXED-INCOME FUNDS

Most fixed-income funds will be called bond funds because the primary investment is in bonds, the most common form of debt instrument. Other debt instruments include government and corporate issues. The purpose of fixed income is to provide safety of your principal as well as to produce income on your investment. Another benefit is that fixed income of the right type can dampen (reduce) the volatility of your investment portfolio.

The main risks associated with bond funds are market, or price, risk if interest rates rise; and credit risk if the ability of the borrowers to repay the debt declines. The longer the maturity of the bonds in the fund, the more susceptible the fund is to price risk if interest rates rise. For example, a fund with two-year average maturities on its bonds will not suffer a decline in value nearly as much as a fund in which the bonds average eight- to ten-year maturities.

For safety, look for U.S. government bond funds or, at least, corporate bond funds that invest in bonds that are AA to AAA quality.

Classes of Fixed-Income Funds

Money market funds

Money market funds are the safest type of mutual funds if you are worried about the risk of losing your principal. Money market funds are like bank savings accounts in that the value of your investment does not fluctuate. Money market funds, however, are not insured like bank certificates of deposit. The interest rates are generally lower than for other forms of fixed-income funds.

Government bond funds

These funds invest in debt from the U.S. government. They are by their nature quite conservative, depending upon the maturity of the underlying bonds. They generally invest in all types of government bonds, including those backed by the government but not directly issued by the government. Look for bond maturities of five years or less.

U.S. fixed-income funds

These are funds that invest in all types of U.S. bonds, including government and corporate bonds. They will typically invest in higher-quality investments with little risk of default across a broad range of maturities. Check to see that the credit quality of the bonds is primarily AAA or AA and the average maturities are no longer than five years.

High-yield funds (junk bonds)

These funds typically invest in low-quality corporate debt and are subject to high risk of default. They, therefore, tend to offer a higher yield. If safety and stability are important to you, avoid this choice. For similar risk, you could have higher potential returns in equity mutual funds.

Global bond funds

These funds invest in foreign and U.S. bonds. Historically, global bond funds have outperformed domestic bond funds, but you do assume some additional risk.

International bond funds

These funds specialize in investing in bonds of foreign governments and companies and are usually riskier than U.S. investments. However, you may realize additional income as compared to U.S. fixed income.

EQUITY FUNDS

A stock mutual fund is called an *equity fund*, which is usually a higher-growth vehicle than a bond fund. Over the last 15 years, the average stock mutual fund has returned about 11.3 percent on an annual basis. But remember the rule: the greater the return, the greater the risk and volatility. Obviously, an equity mutual fund, because of its investment risk, is not an appropriate investment for your short-term money or for your intermediate money. But, if the time frame for your long-term money is eight to ten years or more, an equity mutual fund is a good choice.

Classes of Equity Funds

Growth mutual funds

A growth company is one that is doing very well, by any measurement. A growth mutual fund is typically defined as one that invests in companies that are exceeding the growth of the economy. Investors look for companies and industries with a strong growth trend in sales and earnings. Growth companies typically sell at high price/earnings (P/E) ratios, reflecting the expectation that their growth will continue and that the earnings will eventually "catch up" with the high valuations awarded the companies. Growth companies and growth mutual funds can cover all capitalization ranges.

Large-Cap Growth.   An investment strategy that invests in stocks of large high-growth companies with an average capitalization of approximately $10 billion or greater.

Mid-Cap Growth.   An investment strategy that invests in stocks of mid-sized companies with an average capitalization of between $2 billion and $10 billion.

Small-Cap Growth.   An investment strategy that invests in stocks of smaller companies with an average capitalization of less than $2 billion.

Value mutual funds

Value mutual funds invest in companies that are temporarily distressed. Value stocks have high book-to-market ratios, which means the stock is trading at a low price compared with its book value. (*Book value* is defined as the company's assets on a balance sheet, less its liabilities, and is often figured on a per share basis.) In addition, the price/earnings ratio is lower for value stocks, and for this reason, they are generally considered to be less volatile. As with growth stocks, value stocks can cover all capitalization ranges.

Large-Cap Value.   This type of fund utilizes an investment strategy that invests in stocks of large companies with an average capitalization of approximately $10 billion or greater.

Mid-Cap Value.   This type of fund utilizes an investment strategy that invests in stocks of mid-sized companies with an average capitalization of between $2 billion and $10 billion.

Small-Cap Value.   This type of fund utilizes an investment strategy that invests in stocks of smaller companies with an average capitalization of less than $2 billion.

Value and growth stocks tend to behave differently. There are market cycles when value stocks outperform growth stocks, and other periods when growth stocks outperform value stocks. In general, a growth investor's returns are somewhat more volatile than a value investor's returns. Both styles in a portfolio can even out performance over time. When one group is underperforming the market, the other is outperforming it. While value stocks have outperformed growth stocks over long periods of time, it is important to have both in your portfolio to stabilize returns.

International equity funds

The principles of international growth and value are the same as those of domestic growth and value. Growth companies are those that are doing very well. Value companies are those that are distressed and doing poorly by almost any measurement.

International Growth. This type of mutual fund utilizes an investment strategy that focuses the portfolio on stocks of high-growth international companies.

International Value. This type of mutual fund utilizes an investment strategy that focuses the portfolio on stocks of distressed companies worldwide.

Just as important as selecting the right investment vehicle is building an appropriate core investment *strategy* that the investor can adhere to and that delivers a consistent and specific result. Lesson 5 will show you how.

LESSON 5 HOW TO DESIGN YOUR OWN INVESTMENT PORTFOLIO

Most first time investors have no investing experience. Fewer have ever read the academic research on investing, some of which has won the Nobel Prize. What little information they do have comes from television, newspapers and magazines, or coworker conversations—most of this "noise" is misguided, sensationalized, and lacks any foundation. Many false ideas are so widespread that the public, for the most part, simply accepts them as fact. Often, intimidating legal jargon and overriding priorities of the moment may force a selection of anything familiar, usually whatever low-risk, fixed-income vehicle is available. After all, this is retirement money we're talking about here! But, in truth, that's exactly why you want to take an active role in directing the investments that will become a contributing factor in the comfort level you will enjoy later in life.

Here are some popular *false ideas* that people insist on believing:

1. It's possible to beat the market by picking mispriced stocks, timing the market, or doing both. Under the law of probability, many investors, advisors, mutual fund and money managers will beat the market in any one year; a few of them two years in a row; and an occasional person will be able to consistently beat the market over a five- or ten-year period. An academic study shows that the number of people who beat the market over long periods is exactly the number you would expect to find due to pure mathematical chance.

2. A broker, since he or she does it for a living, must be better at picking stocks than you are.

3. Big brokerage firms, because of their resources, have valuable advice to convey about buying stocks and timing the market.

4. Because brokerage firms are members of NASD and NYSE, they must have significant financial resources that are used to help me.

5. If I invest in bonds, my portfolio is safe.

INFORMED CHOICES

Arm yourself with the basic investment terminology and strategies in this book before you make any investment decisions. If you're going to direct your investments, you will need to know how you can receive periodic performance (gain and loss) results—and what to do with that information.

Protecting Your Investment

The only way to protect against investment losses and still achieve a reasonable growth rate of return is by creating a portfolio with an optimal combination of investments for a specific level of risk. Risk is the uncertainty of future rates of return. We can't tell you this often enough: The higher the expected growth of the investments, the higher the risk. The lower the risk, the lower the expected return. The *real* risk is not the volatility of periodic returns; rather, it is the probability of not having enough money to meet a financial goal, such as retirement.

How Aggressive Do You *Need* to Be?

There are three factors that determine how aggressive you should be.

1. The amount of *gap* between the current rate of accumulation of your investments and your financial goals.
2. The amount of *time* you have before retirement. The more time you have to accumulate assets and recover from potential losses, the more aggressive your portfolio can be. Or, you can be more conservative if you will have more time to compound the earnings in lower-return investments.
3. Your fear factor. When do you jump ship and not follow your plan? Determine your risk tolerance percentage.

If we ask 401(k) plan participants how much they want to make, "As much as I can," they all say. Everybody thinks they'd love to be ultra-aggressive. Who wants to make 3 percent per year? Everyone wants to make 15 percent, but most don't understand the amount of risk they may have to take to get it. This is where participants get into trouble. You have to think not in terms of how much you are willing to make, but how much you are *willing to lose*. That's the more important part of the equation. Determine a percentage of your assets that you can lose and still stick with the program. Then convert that to a dollar amount, so that it becomes tangible.

What Is a Reasonable Growth Rate of Return?

An informed investor needs to establish his or her personal expected *reasonable* growth rate of return. The general rule of thumb is that if you take the percentage of decline tolerance (how much money you could stand to lose) in a given quarter that you are comfortable with, divide that percentage in half, and add a money market rate (typically 3 to 4 percent), the result is a reasonable rate of growth over a 10-year period.

In calculating the expected rates of return for each asset class, you must recognize that these are theoretical returns. The expected rate of return is the forecasted return based on the historical arithmetic average returns for each asset class.

Again, how little or how much risk you take directly affects how much growth you can expect. For instance, if you are willing to take a 10 percent decline quarterly, divide that number in half (5 percent), and add 3 to 4 percent. A reasonable rate of growth that you can expect to capture is 8 to 9 percent annually over a three- to five-year period.

It is important to know, *and remember,* that there will be some times when you will experience declines in excess of this amount and your returns might be superior at other times.

How Do You Measure the Risk of an Investment?

Securities within the asset class are priced to reflect their perceived risk by the market. You may have seen one of the old investment risk "pyramid" charts. They're in almost every basic investment book and are used to explain risk and reward. A broad base of safe investments such as cash is at the bottom; bonds, stocks, and real estate are in the middle; and more speculative investments are at the top. Most investors understand this hierarchy, but it's overly simplistic and not useful in designing portfolios.

In the financial industry, we use academic terms like *beta, volatility,* and *standard deviation.*

> *Beta* is a measure of the risk of an investment compared with that of the market. This is a good way for institutions to measure risk; however, it is often not very useful for you, the individual, since you don't look at risk in relative terms (meaning in relation to something else). The market is said to have a beta of 1.0. If a mutual fund has a beta of 0.8, it is said to be 80 percent as risky as the market.

> *Volatility* is simply investment jargon for frequency and amount of change. Volatility is a measure of *total risk,* instead of *relative* risk like beta. It can be statistically measured using standard deviation.

> *Standard deviation* describes how far from the average performance the actual performance has been, either higher or lower, and helps explain what the distribution of returns will likely be. The greater the range of returns, the greater the risk. You can calculate standard deviations for yourself using a spreadsheet program if you have the

historical return data for the asset classes you are considering. (See Figure 5.3.)

If you invest for a short-term goal, you will probably want lower volatility and be willing to accept lower returns. If you invest for the long term, you can probably tolerate greater volatility in order to anticipate the potential for greater returns.

People are willing to accept risk when buying real estate because they don't purchase a house thinking that they might sell it tomorrow. They know that, despite occasional drops in the real estate market, their house is probably going to increase in value by the time they've paid off the mortgage in 15 years or more. When you bought your house, you weren't thinking, "What are housing prices going to do tomorrow?" You were

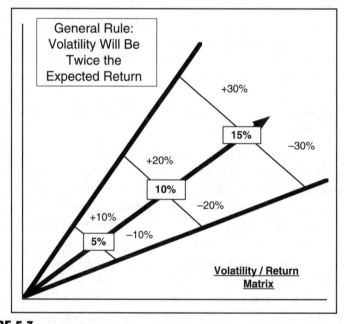

FIGURE 5.3

Risk Increases as Reward Increases

Note: Investors should never rely solely on this or any chart to make investment decisions.

Source: Data by Ibbotson 1926–1994.

investing over a 10- to 20-year time period, so you bought a home that met your needs and that you believed would increase in worth over the long term. Consider how you would feel about the risk of owning a home if you looked at the market prices every day: "The water main on Sixth Street broke; my house just dropped in value 10 percent." Odds are you wouldn't be a happy homeowner if you monitored your home's market value daily.

The same is true for stocks held over long periods. But, for some reason, people don't think about stocks the way they think about real estate. "Long term" is next quarter for most investors.

Different investments behave differently during different times. As an example, when the real estate market was booming in the 1970s, the stock market had some of its worst years. Large-cap stocks were the top-performing asset class in the late 1990s, but did poorly in the 2000, 2001, and 2002 years. Through 2003, large-cap stocks (growth and value) were up substantially.

Learn to expect the unexpected. What we want you to do is try to mentally prepare for market "corrections," commonly referred to as a bear market, when the stock market experiences a decline of more than 20 percent. At times, the market has gone down and stayed down for a long time. At other times, it just dipped and flipped back up again.

The 1990s were a time of sharp, quick drops and dramatic movements upward. This might have been because the inflow of information was much faster or it may just have been due to the economy. Our inflation rate was down, our political system was stable, and corporations were generating steady profits. All of these factors combined to create a bull market.

Since World War II, there have been 42 years with positive market returns and only 11 years with negative returns.

The best return was +45 percent in 1954.

The worst return was −29.7 percent in 1974.

The median was +16.5 percent.

The market has gone down two or more years in a row only twice, in 1973 and 1974 and again in 2000, 2001, and 2002.

The good times in the market have far outpaced the down periods, as you can see. When the economy is healthy and the market is on a roll, stock prices can rise for years. During the last 50 years, the stock market has seen four major bull markets, with moves over 100 percent; however, there were meaningful declines in between, even in those positive environments.

The main problems are that you don't have time to be checking on stocks or funds every day, all day, and you don't have the expertise to trade in and out of the market during the up and down periods. (Don't feel badly—no one does.) Protecting your plan also saves you time. Your time is better spent concentrating on your work.

If you have access to an advisor, work with him or her to develop a personal strategy in the form of a statement of investment objectives, then commit to it in writing and stick with it. Having your own personal investment plan for accumulating capital will help you set reasonable goals and manage your expectations for reaching them. Plus, it will help you avoid investor panic because you "heard something" on the news, and stop you from defaulting to short-term moves and potentially missing out on gains that long-term investors enjoy with much less effort.

Academic research has found that 96 percent of returns are generated from making the right asset allocation decisions. A portfolio containing only one type of investment is unbalanced, having no dissimilar investments that could help carry the portfolio through tough times. Likewise, a portfolio of six or seven mutual funds in the same asset class is also unbalanced. (See Figure 5.4.)

In the practical application, consider an employee who at age 39 has over $100,000 in her 401(k) plan. She's been funneling 8 percent of her $90,000 yearly salary into her 401(k) plan, plus she receives a 50 percent match from her employer. She is an informed investor, so she shifted her plan to a 75 percent stock and 25 percent fixed-income mix.

As long as her stocks and bonds maintain their historic norms (11.35 percent for stocks and 5 percent for bonds), she has the potential of retiring at age 65 with over $2,770,000.

Another employee of the same age, saving the same dollar amount with the same employer match, doesn't understand risk and is intimidated by it, so he is investing mostly in fixed-income bonds. When he reaches 65, he'll have just under $1.5 million in his account. Not bad, but with a little investment knowledge, he could have had over $1 million more at retirement.

Since we can only guess about the future, we put emphasis on the things we can control—factors such as contribution amounts, retirement age, and investment mix.

When you follow an asset class investment strategy, you have to know which mix of asset classes stands the best chance of meeting your objec-

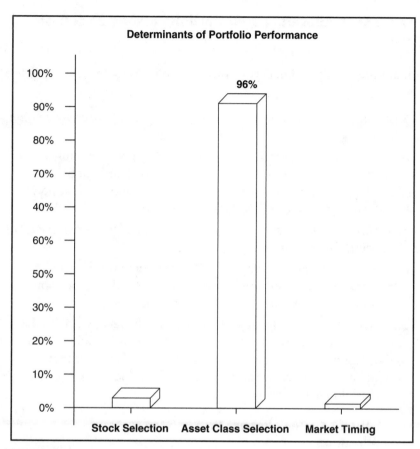

FIGURE 5.4
Making the Right Asset Allocation Decision

tives. Since risk is mitigated by blending asset classes and expected future returns in an optimal manner, by using a core strategy, you never shoot the lights out, but you never go bust either.

While speculators might claim that this is nothing but a guarantee of mediocrity, academic research belies their position. There's nothing mediocre about being able to sleep at night while achieving a superior return, enabling progress toward your financial goal.

Five Steps in Allocating Your Portfolio among Each Asset Class

You are now ready to build your own portfolio using the following five steps.

Step One: *Determine how much money you have available in your plan and what percentage you are going to invest.*

Step Two: *Match your risk tolerance to an asset mix.* Remember your "risk tolerance" has to do with staying invested and not being tempted to get out of your program or jump ship. At what point did you run for the lifeboat? (See Table 5.5.)

Step Three: *Select asset class mutual funds that will fit the parameters of the portfolio you selected.*

Step Four: *Add time to your plan.* The more time you have before needing to access your funds, the longer the funds will be compounding, earning, and recovering any losses.

Step Five: *Rebalance annually.* By systematically rebalancing to the original model portfolio at least annually, you will gradually sell those asset classes that have gone up while buying those that currently have lower returns. This approach eliminates the negative results of being driven by emotions.

TABLE 5.5   The Lifeboat Drill Related to Asset Allocation

Potential Quarterly Decline	Appropriate Original Investment of $10,000	Asset Allocation Based on Your Risk Tolerance
(3%)	$9,700	Portfolio 1—Defensive
(7%)	$9,300	Portfolio 2—Conservative
(10%)	$9,000	Portfolio 3—Normal
(15%)	$8,500	Portfolio 4—Aggressive
(23%)	$7,700	Portfolio 5—Ultra-Aggressive

Match the model portfolio that most closely aligns with the potential quarterly decline (your risk tolerance).

Doing the math

The mathematical calculations necessary to determine the range of efficient portfolios are included in Appendix B. Mathematical formulas can sidetrack many investors and can sometimes seem overwhelming and complicated.

We've calculated the expected rates of return, standard deviations, and correlation coefficients for each of our asset classes to determine the optimal combination of asset classes in a portfolio that results in the highest rate of return for each level of risk.

We have constructed several portfolios ranging from defensive to ultra-aggressive. These model portfolios use very basic allocations that we wanted to give you as guideposts—a professional advisor might certainly do something more sophisticated.

> *Portfolio Objective:* To design a portfolio that will outperform a "traditional" market-based portfolio with the same or less degree of volatility risk.
>
> *Reward Objective:* Our goal here is to add 2–3 percent of additional return annually to the "traditional" portfolio.
>
> *Investments Used:* We will use asset class funds that are institutional, no-load (no commission) mutual funds that buy and hold a representation of a very specific segment of the market (e.g., U. S.-based large company value stocks).

Figures 5.5 through 5.9 are based on a buy-and-hold strategy from January 1973 to December 2002. (They do not include the impact of taxes or expenses.) Typically, if you buy index funds, you will reduce these numbers by about 50 to 100 basis points.

Let's look at Figure 5.10 to see how these model portfolios and the S&P 500 did for 2003.

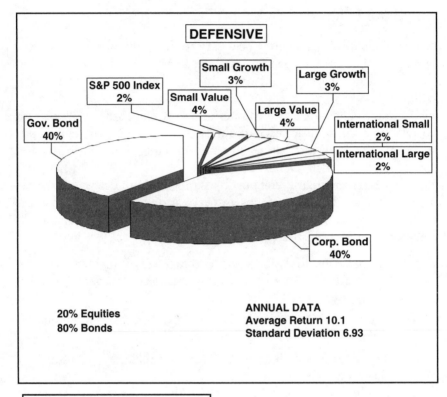

Corp. Bond	40%
Gov. Bond	40%
S&P 500 Index	2%
Small Value	4%
Small Growth	3%
Large Value	4%
Large Growth	3%
International Small Co.	2%
International Large Co.	2%

FIGURE 5.5
Portfolio 1–Defensive (20% equities/80% bonds)

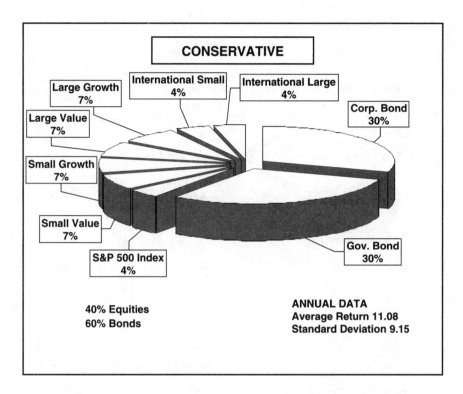

CONSERVATIVE

Large Growth 7%
International Small 4%
International Large 4%
Corp. Bond 30%
Large Value 7%
Small Growth 7%
Small Value 7%
S&P 500 Index 4%
Gov. Bond 30%

40% Equities
60% Bonds

ANNUAL DATA
Average Return 11.08
Standard Deviation 9.15

Corp. Bond	30%
Gov. Bond	30%
S&P 500 Index	4%
Small Value	7%
Small Growth	7%
Large Value	7%
Large Growth	7%
International Small Co.	4%
International Large Co.	4%

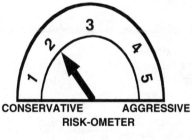

CONSERVATIVE   AGGRESSIVE
RISK-OMETER

FIGURE 5.6
Portfolio 2–Conservative (40% equities/60% bonds)

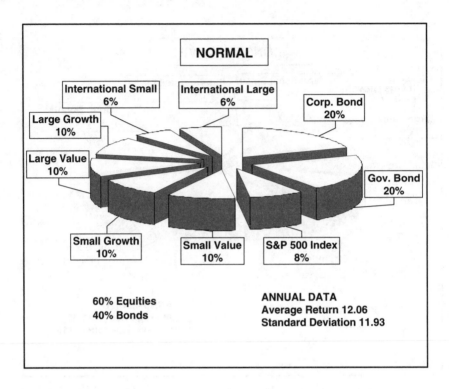

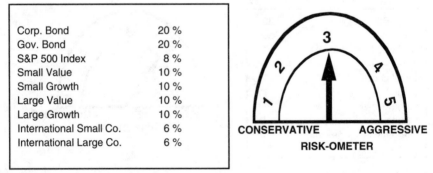

FIGURE 5.7
Portfolio 3—Normal (60% equities/40% bonds)

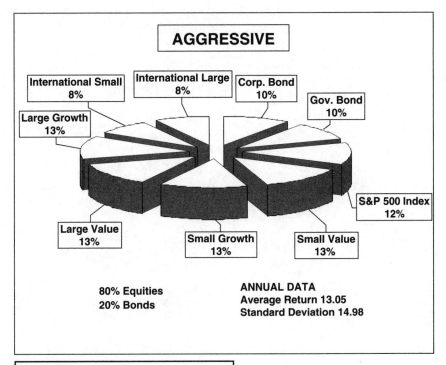

AGGRESSIVE

International Small 8%
International Large 8%
Corp. Bond 10%
Gov. Bond 10%
Large Growth 13%
S&P 500 Index 12%
Large Value 13%
Small Growth 13%
Small Value 13%

80% Equities
20% Bonds

ANNUAL DATA
Average Return 13.05
Standard Deviation 14.98

Corp. Bond	10 %
Gov. Bond	10 %
S&P 500 Index	12 %
Small Value	13 %
Small Growth	13 %
Large Value	13 %
Large Growth	13 %
International Small Co.	8 %
International Large Co.	8 %

3
2 4
1 5
CONSERVATIVE   AGGRESSIVE
RISK-OMETER

FIGURE 5.8
Portfolio 4–Aggressive (80% equities/20% bonds)

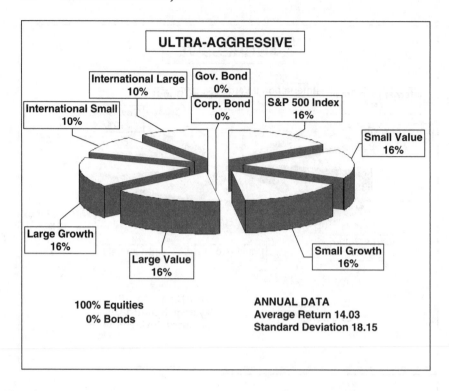

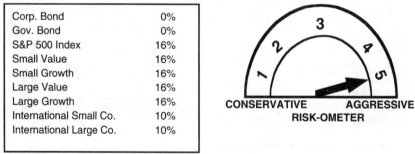

FIGURE 5.9
Portfolio 5—Ultra-Aggressive (100% equities/0% bonds)

Defensive 2003—9.77% Annualized 5 yr.: 6.01% Annualized 3 yr.: 6.21%	Aggressive 2003—32.64% Annualized 5 yr.: 6.06% Annualized 3 yr.: 5.68%
Conservative 2003—17.53% Annualized 5 yr.: 6.28% Annualized 3 yr.: 6.41%	Ultra-Aggressive 2003—40.07% Annualized 5 yr.: 5.67% Annualized 3 yr.: 4.90%
Normal 2003—24.95% Annualized 5 yr.: 6.19% Annualized 3 yr.: 6.08%	S&P 500 2003—28.67% Annualized 5 yr.: −0.57% Annualized 3 yr.: −4.05%

FIGURE 5.10
Comparative Portfolio Returns for 2003

SUMMARY

It is your responsibility to understand the investment choices. There are three factors that determine how aggressive you should be:

1. What is the amount of *gap* between the current rate of accumulation of your investments and your financial goals?
2. How much *time* do you have before retirement?
3. What is your fear factor?

Now, act on the information in this chapter to measure the risk of your investment choices so you don't exceed your risk tolerance and build your own portfolio according to the five steps. You can use the five model portfolios provided as Figures 5.5 through 5.9 to get you started.

PART THREE
TACTICAL TO PRACTICAL

If you knew just how much money you'll need at retirement, you could figure out how much risk you'll have to take to get there. And if you knew you ultimately couldn't lose, that there were no secrets, that it could all be explained, wouldn't investing take on a whole new appearance?

You could stop focusing on trying to find the hot mutual fund and set about building your overall net worth. You'd have a plan. You could begin to manage your existing assets and future resources to meet your future needs. You wouldn't run out of patience, or feel overwhelmed and just give up and do nothing. You'd settle in and confidently wait for the inevitable gain to occur. The ability to be patient during difficult times requires an understanding of not only the stock markets but also your own reactions to uncertainty (risk).

CHAPTER 6

HOW MUCH MONEY IS ENOUGH?

In the past, planning for retirement was somewhat irrelevant because most people died before reaching retirement age. The average life expectancy throughout most of the history of humankind was less than 18 years. But in the last thousand years, life expectancy skyrocketed to an average age of 47 at the turn of the twentieth century to 76 years today. And now, because of increased health and vitality, tomorrow's elderly will, in likelihood, live even longer. Around 1965, sociologists and the futurists were predicting a population boom. They thought it would come from having too many kids—they didn't realize it would come from living longer.

According to the U.S. Census Bureau, by the year 2035, some 70 million people will be 65 years of age or older. The United Nations expects that by the year 2050, there will be nearly 2 billion people in their sixties, a number equal to the current populations of Europe, North America, and India combined. At the same time, while the population is living longer, the work population is declining.

In the next 30 years, the total net growth of the American population will be 44 million. But 40 million of that number will consist of people over the age of 50. The downside is grim: Millions could spend their final decades struggling. Can we avert a possible troubled future? Yes, but it's going to take education, personal sacrifice, and intentional planning. What that means to the average person is that in order to achieve financial freedom, you are going to have to take some degree of risk.

Where do you start?

Begin by looking at how long you have before you retire and how much money you're going to need when you get there. If you first determine your projected monthly retirement expenses and income, then you can easily see any shortfall. A *shortfall* is the difference between what you will realistically need to have and what you will actually have. It's what happens when your anticipated income and other earnings do not cover all your expenses.

Let's assume you've started investing because you plan on retiring and will need your money in 10 years. You can determine, based upon your age, your lifestyle, and by making adjustments for future inflation estimates, how much capital you will need in 10 years to meet your objectives. This is assuming you know how much capital you're starting out with today, and you know roughly how much you can contribute to your plan over the next 10 years. With that information, we can determine the average rate of return you need over the 10-year period to achieve your objective. Let's assume the average rate of return is 7 percent per year. You know with certainty that if you achieve a rate of return less than 7 percent, you *will not* meet your objective.

You can make these calculations on the back of a napkin or fill out a comprehensive financial planning form. We've included some Internet sites where you can find calculators that will help you determine the amounts needed to make up for any shortfall, the rate of return you will need to achieve, and the number of dollars you will need to add annually to close the gap. Just knowing that should take some of the pressure off and should make the unknown less mysterious.

Let's say you figure out that your shortfall is about $300,000 and you have 20 years or so left before retirement. You have $50,000 from the sale of property to invest. What would most people do? They would jump at one of the advertisements in a money magazine, or they would seek out help from a traditional financial planner, stockbroker, or financial advisor. But if you take one of these approaches, you may still have a problem. Most investment sales organizations operate within the framework of pretax returns and relative performance.

Total return based on historical performance has become the only financial gauge for most investors. But total return is nothing more than a visual display of the past, and only certain aspects of the past at that. It's not an indicator of the future. Historical performance tells only a fraction of what you need to know and can be very misleading.

You may be shown a dollar goal projection, illustrating the magic of compounding using the historical rate of return of 10 percent. That 10 percent figure sounds conservative. If the potential for the investment program will cover your shortfall at this 10 percent figure, you're impressed. At 10 percent, your $50,000 grows to $336,000 in 20 years and $872,000 in

30 years. You think, *I'm there!* And you invest in that fund. But here's just one of the *dangers:* Total return drastically overstates the purchasing power that you will have because it ignores taxes, fees, and inflation.

Together, these three asset eroders can bring your expected return down to as little as zero. Studies by Ibbotson and Associates show that historical after-tax, after-fee, after-inflation rates of returns on corporate bonds are about zero, and the return on stocks, while higher, can be as low as 2 percent after all expenses are subtracted, including the advisor's fee. Sometimes experienced practitioners deduct for taxes and factor for inflation, but do not figure in the fees.

What a difference these oversights can make! With typical taxes of 2.5 percent plus fees, including the broker's fee of 2.5 percent, your 10 percent return assumption is reduced to 5 percent. So after taxes and fees, your $50,000 in 20 years is worth not $336,000, but only $132,000. Subtract 3 percent for inflation, and real dollar projections drop to $74,000. *Whoops!* You will not hit your target!

You could be off by hundreds of thousands of dollars and not have the time needed to make it up. This creates frustrated investors who become, in effect, market timers—often selling an existing fund and buying a new one in hopes of gaining back lost ground. The classic buy-high, sell-low syndrome results. Investors who do this a few times become disillusioned with the never-ending process of picking new actively managed investments, and many quit investing altogether.

Your goal should be to focus on the dollar amount you will need and on the total after-tax return. Total *after*-tax return is after fees, after expenses, after anything and everything that stands in the way of achieving your goal.

Unfortunately, selling past performance has become so hardwired into the investment profession's delivery system that most of us don't think twice about it. The tools that brokers and financial consultants have at their disposal, such as risk/return graphs, style analyses, and Morningstar data, are all based on historical performance. Why is this? Because Wall Street has been selling to huge pension plans for the last 50 years. The managers of pension plans need to sell past performance to defend their investment decisions. But a pension manager is subject to different motivations than you are.

The solution to this problem is to control what you can control: Understand what combinations of investments will give you the highest probability of making up any shortfalls, will lower your costs, and will operate your investment program with full awareness of the tax consequences.

STEPS TO FOLLOW

If you've never even tried to figure out how much you'll need to save for a comfortable retirement, rest assured that you're not alone. Two-thirds of all American workers fall into that category, according to a recent national survey. There are, though, some steps you can take to get you closer to a comfortable retirement.

1.   Calculate your monthly retirement expenses. Figure out how many dollars will be required to satisfactorily meet your monthly retirement expenses. First, estimate your current costs and those you expect to decrease when you retire. Then, record your current costs and the projected costs that might increase when you retire. The total represents your estimated annual retirement expenses.

2.   Calculate your retirement income. Primary sources of retirement income typically include employee-sponsored retirement plans, individual retirement accounts (IRAs), Keogh plans, SEP IRAs, Social Security, and personal savings. Identify all the known variables that are under your control, such as time periods, tax rates, required cash flows, and fees. The focus should be on what's reliably predictable.

3.   Calculate the amount of money you'll need to save for retirement. Keep adjusting the known variables. View financial goals as future liabilities that need to be met. This will help you to take the amount of risk needed—not too much or too little. You may think of yourself as a conservative investor, but if your shortfall is too large, you may have to become a more aggressive investor and take greater risks. Your investment program should be designed to overcome any shortfalls, not to beat the stock market.

INTERNET RETIREMENT CALCULATORS

People who are reluctant to share details of their financial affairs with others may prefer the impersonal—and nonjudgmental—approach of a Web-based retirement calculator. Even simple retirement calculators can be useful because they perform sophisticated computations that most people cannot do on their own.

In theory, most retirement calculators are simple enough. You enter your age, salary, pension (if you will have one), and current assets and investments. Next you plug in how much of your salary you're saving, the age at which you'd like to retire, and the income you'd like to have in retirement. The retirement calculator typically supplies an estimate of your future Social Security benefits and then renders a verdict: Yes, you're on the right track, or no, you'll fall short.

The simplest retirement calculator of all—and a good place for novices to start—may be "Ballpark Estimate," a planning tool developed by the nonprofit American Savings Education Council (ASEC). It's designed to provide a first-cut rough estimate of what you'll need to save each year to fund a comfortable retirement.

> *American Savings Education Council.* ASEC's "Ballpark Estimate" worksheet is part of the free "Financial Facts Tool Kit" developed by the Securities and Exchange Commission; you can get a copy at www.sec.gov/investor/pubs/toolkit.htm or by calling (800) 732-0330. ASEC offers more than a dozen other retirement calculators at www.choosetosave.org/tools/fincalcs.htm.

> *AARP Retirement Calculator.* You can find it at www.aarp.org/bulletin (click on "Online retirement calculator").

> *Quicken.com Retirement Planner.* *USA Today* calls it the "Cadillac of retirement calculators," partly because it factors in your tax rate after retirement: www.quicken.com/retirement/planner.

> *Rogers Capital Management Inc.* A simple pension calculator is offered by Rogers Capital Management Inc. Enter their Web site at www.RogersCo.com and click on "401(k) services" to find the calculator.

SUMMARY

When the concept of retirement was initially conceived in the early part of the century, retirement was expected to cover a period of a year or two. Now the average length of retirement is 20 years. You must prepare for 20 years of nonproductivity, and that may require some sacrifice today for a better future.

With all the new twists and turns in our lifestyles, with kids returning home like boomerangs, with second marriages and/or recycled careers, and new ideas and dreams for our maturity, more than ever before, the average person needs to sit down with someone who can tell them not only about financial products, but can help them plan the next stage of the life they've yet to live.

CHAPTER 7

WHERE DO YOU GET HELP?

There is no investment decision that you will make that is more important than who you hire to help you build an investment portfolio. A wrong choice can set you back many years, and time is an important facet to your equation for financial success. Before you go looking for investment advice, spend some time redefining your personal investment profile: your investment attitude, objectives, and time frames. An advisor can then help you determine whether your investment philosophy is actually in line with the return expected from your portfolio mix.

Hiring an advisor doesn't mean you must give up all control of your portfolio. The precise role an advisor plays in your individual investment process is up to you. Any advisor should provide you with an agreement that outlines expectations for the relationship: the roles each party will fulfill and will be accountable for. You may opt for a broker who executes the trades you direct, or an advisor who analyzes your financial condition, strategizes with you on the best path to take in the future, and then sends you on your way—in other words, one who educates you and then empowers you to take action on your own. The more continuous hands-on help you want, the more it will cost, but an ongoing relationship may be worth it.

THE FINANCIAL ADVISOR COMMUNITY

Unfortunately, the public doesn't know the difference between stockbrokers, fee-only advisors, and fee-based advisors. While the joint mission of all these professionals is to help clients meet their financial goals, that is where the similarity ends. The following descriptions will help clarify the differences between these financial professionals.

Stockbrokers

Whether employed by a giant broker-dealer, a small local broker-dealer, or even a bank, stockbrokers have exactly the same function. A few years ago, banks decided to cross over the line and offer investments through subsidiaries or affiliates, since banks are prohibited from offering investments directly. These bank affiliate advisors have the same securities licenses as other brokers, and many have gone through traditional Wall Street training programs.

Brokers are compensated by commissions for executing trades of stocks, bonds, and many other financial products, such as mutual funds, variable annuities, and even life insurance.

The key is to understand that brokers work for their employers—not you. They are there to sell products that will make the company (and the broker) money. The company has no incentive to cut commissions on trades or products since that is the company's lifeblood. It is in their best interest to sell you the highest-loaded product possible.

When you go to the Ford dealership, do you expect the salesperson to say, "This year's model is okay, but Chevrolet has a vastly superior product this year"? No! Think of the broker in the same way and you won't be surprised that you were sold a high-commission variable annuity that was not necessary—and, you will be better prepared to get what you need when you do business with a commission-based broker.

This is not to say that most brokers are not trying to deliver the best for their clients—but the system and method of compensation make it impossible for them to avoid inevitable conflicts. Let the buyer beware!

Questions to ask commission-based brokers or mutual fund salespersons

These questions came from Dan Solin, author of *Does Your Broker Owe You Money* (Alpha Press, 2003):

1. Why do you think this stock/bond/fund/annuity is right for me? How does it fit in with my investment goals and risk tolerance?

2. What is your commission on this stock/bond/fund/annuity? Are you being given any other special incentives to sell this recommendation? (Yes, you have the right to know this.)

3. Does your firm or any subsidiary of your firm manage this fund or product?

4. If it is a stock: Are you buying this stock out of your firm's inventory? If your firm is rating this stock a buy, why is your firm selling the stock from its inventory?

5. Did your company underwrite the stock?

6. Why are you recommending this purchase now as opposed to some other time?

7. Will you show me your account so I can see that you own what you are selling to me? On any product or service, ask the brokers to print their personal accounts from the computer (and they all can) and show you what they own and especially if they own what they're selling to you.

8. What is the standard deviation of this investment and how does this affect the standard deviation of my portfolio? (Standard deviation is a measurement of risk. For more information about this term, see Chapter 5.) This is critical to maintaining the risk level of your portfolio. The principle is the same whether your portfolio is $1,000 or $10,000,000.

Fee-Only Advisors

Fee-only advisors (registered investment advisors—RIAs) are compensated for portfolio investment management on a fee for service basis only. The fees charged by RIAs vary from larger fees for small accounts to less for large accounts, but 1 percent is fairly typical.

Fee-only advisors cannot accept any commissions associated with recommendations they make. Thus, unlike with some commissionable products sold by brokers, you will not incur any surrender fees or back-end loads should you wish to leave the RIA. Fee-only advisors don't make any more money, no matter what you do. These advisors have 100 percent incentive to deliver an investment portfolio to you commensurate with your risk tolerance at the lowest possible cost. If they do a good job, you'll stick around and they'll make more fees.

The biggest difference between fee-for-service investment advisors and commission brokers is the advisors' commitment to the continuing study of Modern Portfolio Theory. If you talk to a fee advisor who is not an expert (or close to an expert) in Modern Portfolio Theory, academic research such as that conducted at The University of Chicago by Professor Eugene Fama or at Yale by Professor Ken French, and is not utilizing academically defined asset class investing, then you are at the wrong place. Leave!

The largest 25 percent of RIA firms are registered directly with the Securities and Exchange Commission (SEC). The smallest 75 percent register in the state in which the advisory firm is domiciled. (For example, Rogers Capital Management, Inc., is registered directly with the SEC). But size is no indication of competence—big only means big, not good or great. Most older RIAs or RIA agents were former brokers who left the commission world to offer fee-based services. Newer RIA agents take an exam through the National Association of Securities Dealers (NASD) called the Series 65—National Investment Advisor Law Exam.

RIA firms must file an informational return (ADV) annually with the SEC as well as pay associated ongoing fees. Any change in personnel or structure must be filed quickly, amending the ADV. By law, these advisors must give you Part II of the ADV, which covers fee structures, financial services, and investment strategy. But you should also ask to see Part I and the accompanying schedules, which detail any disciplinary actions, education, account custody arrangements, and the number of clients the advisor counsels.

If your assets are very small, you may not be able to afford the minimum fee the RIA must charge. However, ask for advice on how to invest until you meet the minimum. Most will be happy to direct you to a discount brokerage or fund company that offers no-load index funds and will tell you approximately how to allocate your funds among the various indexes to start. While index funds are not academically defined asset class funds, they are the next best alternative. Remember, they want you as a client later, so it is in their best interest to guide you properly.

Fee-Based Advisors

These advisors charge a fee for their service, but, unlike *fee-only* advisors, they also charge commissions on the sale of investment products. The concern is that they may favor products that have loads and commissions. You must be very careful to compare all facets of the commission and fee schedules.

Since fee-based advisors also have a sales connection with a broker-dealer, you should ask the same questions that are important to ask the brokers—*and* be certain they meet the same requirements listed for fee-only advisors.

It's still up to you to do your homework. You really need to establish a list of criteria for your specific needs. Ask the appropriate questions, and if any answer is unacceptable, go on to the next advisor. Take your time. Don't be pressured.

Questions to ask fee-only and fee-based advisors

1. What is your investment strategy?
2. Do you follow the principles of Modern Portfolio Theory?
3. Do you believe that free markets are efficient?
4. What is your primary source of research?
5. How are tax considerations factored into the investment process?
6. Do you object if I talk to current clients?
7. Do you manage portfolios using asset class or index funds?
8. Will you allow me to see your investment portfolio?

SUMMARY

- An advisor can help you determine whether your investment philosophy is actually in line with the return expected from your portfolio mix.
- Hiring an advisor doesn't mean you must give up all control of your portfolio.
- The investing public doesn't know the difference between brokers, fee-only advisors, and fee-based advisors.
- Brokers are compensated by commissions for executing trades of stocks, bonds, and many other financial products, such as mutual funds, variable annuities, and even life insurance.

- Fee-only advisors (registered investment advisors—RIAs) are compensated for portfolio investment management on a fee for service basis only. A fee-only advisor cannot accept any commissions associated with a recommendation he or she makes.

- A fee-based advisor has a sales connection with a broker-dealer. You should ask the same questions that are important to ask the brokers—and, be certain they meet the same requirements listed for fee-only advisors.

- It's still up to you to do your homework.

CHAPTER 8

SOCIAL IN-SECURITY

Many people believe that Social Security is in place to take care of them when they are no longer earning money. In fact, they depend on it. The problem is that Social Security was never set up to do that. It was meant to be a safety net and a last resort.

Social Security originated in 1936 during the Depression years. Working people would pay a small portion of their wages into the Social Security system with the idea that the current working population would support the retirees of that time. So money went in and right back out again. It worked because in 1937, the first full year of operation, there were 33 workers for every 1 retiree. The annual contribution of a working person was only $30, so the system was workable. The difficulty with the system is that in 1951, there were 29 workers for every retiree. Today, there are only 5 workers for every retiree. In the year 2015, there will be 2 workers for every retiree.

For Social Security to continue to exist, the funding will have to come from two places: astronomically increased taxes or savings from cutting benefits. There is no other place it can come from. Why debate whether Social Security will be there when you retire? In some form, it will be. However, the percentage of wages that is currently paid as Social Security when you retire will be drastically reduced.

For now, let's assume Congress will do something about saving the Social Security system. You can figure that into your calculation of how much income you'll have at retirement. Obtain an estimate of your future benefits based on what you have been credited for and project what you will be credited for by the time you reach retirement age.

Figure 8.1 is the Request for Earnings and Benefits Statement. It will take you about five minutes to complete this form. You can send it to your

1.   Name shown on your Social Security card:

First   Middle Initial   Last

2.   Your Social Security number as shown on your card:

3.   Your date of birth:
                                Month   Day   Year

4.   Other Social Security numbers you have used:

5.   Your sex: ☐ Male ☐ Female

6.   Other names you have used (including a maiden name):

First   Middle Initial   Last

7.   Show your actual earnings for last year and your estimated earnings for this year. Include only wages and/or net self-employment income covered by Social Security.

A. Last year's actual earnings:
$ ___ , ___ . ___
Dollars only

B. This year's estimated earnings:
$ ___ , ___ . ___
Dollars only

8.   Show the age at which you plan to retire:
(Show only one age)

9.   Below, show the average yearly amount that you think you will earn between now and when you plan to retire. Your estimate of future earnings will be added to those earnings already on our records to give you the best possible estimate.

Enter a yearly average, not your total future lifetime earnings. Only show earnings covered by Social Security. Do not add cost-of-living, performance, or scheduled pay increases or bonuses. The reason for this is that we estimate retirement benefits in today's dollars, but adjust them to account for average wage growth in the national economy.

However, if you expect to earn significantly more or less in the future due to promotions, job changes, part-time work, or an absence from the workforce, enter the amount in today's dollars that most closely reflects your future average yearly earnings.

Most people should enter the same amount that they are earning now (the amount shown in 7B).

Your future average yearly earnings:

$ ___ , ___ . ___
Dollars only

FIGURE 8.1
Request for Earnings and Benefit Estimate Statement

10. Address where you want us to send the statement:

Name

Street Address (Include Apt. No., P.O. Box, or Rural Route)

City   State   Zip Code

I am asking for information about my own Social Security record or the record of a person I am authorized to represent. I understand that if I deliberately request information under false pretenses I may be guilty of a federal crime and could be fined and/or imprisoned. I authorize you to send the statement of earnings and benefit estimates to the person named in item 10 through a contractor.

Please sign your name (Do not print)

Date   (Area Code) Daytime Telephone No.

ABOUT THE PRIVACY ACT
Social Security is allowed to collect the facts on this form under Section 205 of the Social Security Act. We need them to quickly identify our record and prepare the earnings statement you asked us for. Giving us these facts is voluntary. However, without them we may not be able to give you an earnings and benefit estimate statement. Neither the Social Security Administration nor its contractor will use the information for any other purpose.

FIGURE 8.1
(Continued)

TABLE 8.1   How Social Security Income Builds

These figures represent the approximate yearly income from Social Security
benefits for a single person and, on the following line, for a worker and a nonworking spouse of the same age, when they become eligible for full Social
Security benefits at age 65 to 67. All of the amounts in the table are Social
Security Administration projections, based on continuous employment throughout an adult lifetime.

Annual Social Security Benefit

Your Age in 2000		Your Earnings in 2000				
		$20,000	**$25,000**	**$30,000**	**$35,000**	**$45,000+**
25	Individual	11,796	13,548	14,568	15,600	17,652
	Couple	17,688	20,316	21,852	23,400	26,472
35	Individual	10,896	12,540	13,476	14,436	16,296
	Couple	16,344	18,804	20,208	21,648	24,444
45	Individual	9,972	11,496	12,360	13,104	14,412
	Couple	14,952	17,244	18,540	19,656	21,612
55	Individual	9,048	10,344	10,920	11,352	12,036
	Couple	13,572	15,516	16,380	17,028	18,048
65	Individual	8,100	9,216	9,564	9,792	10,056
	Couple	12,144	13,824	14,340	14,688	15,084

nearest Social Security office or to Social Security Administration, Wilkes-
Barre Data Operations Center, P.O. Box 20, Wilkes-Barre, PA 18711-2030.
Or go to Social Security at www.ssa.gov.

Table 8.1 shows how your benefits were calculated by the Social Security
Administration.

SUMMARY

- Social Security benefits will be drastically reduced by the time you
  retire.
- Complete the Request for Earnings and Benefits Estimate Statement
  and find out where you stand.

CHAPTER 9

HOW TO PAY FOR YOUR CHILDREN'S COLLEGE

You have a retirement plan going and investments are working, and you are right on target to continue your lifestyle when one day your kid tells you he or she wants to go to Harvard.

You think, "I could take a loan from the $200,000 in my 401(k) plan." But it could devastate your planning and you may never be able to recover. Taking an early withdrawal from your 401(k) plan could cost you dearly. Better ways to go if you haven't set aside a separate savings account for your children's education are to pay as you go or to pay with student loans and scholarships.

If you have a long time before your children are college age, start a 529 savings plan. When the relatives want to give the kids something, ask them to make a contribution to their college savings plans. The point is not to mix up your retirement money with their needs.

The best way to pay for college is to motivate your kids to achieve high grade-point averages for scholarship eligibility. Help them search the Internet for grants and scholarships in high school. Every kid thinking about college must read *How to Go to College Almost for Free* by Ben Kaplan (HarperCollins Publishers, 2002). Go to www.scholarship Coach.com and Kaplan will coach them how to do it. The author himself amassed nearly $90,000 in scholarship awards, and virtually the entire cost of his Harvard education was covered.

Find an advocate or counselor at your child's school who can alert and steer him or her toward scholarships. I found that many states have *college fee waiver programs* for children and dependents of veterans with service-connected or service-related disabilities. Most of these college fee waiver programs are not public knowledge, so it takes a little research that is well worth it. Check with your state Veterans Affairs office if you believe you may be eligible.

In addition to scholarships, grants, or waivers, you may still need extra money. And providing a college education today (and even more so tomorrow) can cost as much as buying a house. It's going to require some careful advance planning. [For more information, call the Federal Student Aid Information Center, (800) 333-4636.]

Tuition at public four-year colleges jumped in 2003 to the highest rate in 20 years, according to the College Board's annual survey of tuition and financial aid. At these institutions, tuition in 2003 was 9.6 percent higher than it was in 2002. At private four-year colleges, it rose by 5.8 percent, and at public two-year colleges, it rose by 7.9 percent.

The increases came as no surprise to many college leaders, reflecting the budget difficulties of colleges in an era of shrinking state coffers and diminishing endowments. The tuition increases for 2003 were far greater than the rate of inflation over the previous 12 months, as measured by the Consumer Price Index, which was 1.5 percent in the year ending September 30.

In fact, the news may not be all bad for the average student, because financial aid increased at a record rate as well, rising 11.5 percent, according to the College Board's survey. Not every student is able to take advantage of the increased aid, however, since the survey showed an increase in aid given based on factors other than need, such as merit-based scholarships, which tend to go to middle-income students.

Many students are not paying the published tuition prices. Why? Because of various grants, student waivers, and other in-school programs. It's up to you to find out about these discounted tuition prices.

Those published prices, according to the College Board's survey, were, on average:

- $18,273 at private four-year colleges, an increase of $1,001, or 5.8 percent. The increase in 2002 was 5.5 percent.
- $4,081 at public four-year institutions, an increase of $356, or 9.6 percent. The increase in 2002 was 7.7 percent.
- $9,890 at private two-year colleges, an increase of $690, or 7.5 percent. The increase in 2002 was 5.5 percent.
- $1,735 at public two-year colleges, an increase of $127, or 7.9 percent. The increase in 2002 was 5.8 percent.

Out-of-state students at public four-year colleges were paying an average of $10,428 in tuition in 2003; no comparable figures were given for past years.

Average costs for room and board were up 6 percent at public four-year colleges, 4.6 percent at private four-year colleges, and 1.6 percent at private two-year colleges. Total financial aid for the 2003 academic year was $89.6 billion, according to the College Board's most recent annual survey of college fees. Much of that—46.1 percent—was in the form of loans, some of which were unsubsidized. Get your kids to go find them.

COLLEGE TAX BREAKS

Washington has delivered some valuable tax breaks over the past few years to parents paying higher education costs. Here's a rundown of what's available.

- You can deduct up to $3,000 of college tuition and fees paid for you, your spouse, or any other person claimed as a dependent on your return. This is an "above-the-line" deduction, which means you don't have to itemize in order to take advantage of the break. However, the $3,000 figure is the annual maximum, regardless of how many students may be in your family. The other ground rules are as follows:

  - You don't get the deduction if you are unmarried with modified adjusted gross income above $65,000, or a joint filer with modified AGI above $130,000. There are no tricky phase-out rules here. You're either completely eligible, or you're completely ineligible. Period.

  - You're also completely ineligible if you're married and file separately from your spouse.

  - No deduction is allowed on the tax return of any person who can be claimed as a dependent on another's return. So your dependent college-age child can't claim the deduction when your own AGI (average gross income) is too high to qualify.

  - No deduction can be claimed for expenses paid with earnings from a Section 529 plan or withdrawals from a Coverdell

Education Savings Account. Also, you can't claim the deduction in the same year you claim the Hope Scholarship or Lifetime Learning tax credit for the same student.

SECTION 529 PLANS—STATE-SPONSORED COLLEGE SAVINGS PLANS

State-sponsored college savings plans, often called *Section 529 plans,* are a great deal, since withdrawals to pay the account beneficiary's qualified college costs are tax free. If you can afford to make substantial account contributions while your kids are still young, the tax advantages should sharply reduce the amount needed to fund their future college educations.

Most college savings plans now permit lump-sum contributions of well over $100,000. For gift-tax purposes, you can spread a large lump-sum contribution over five years. As you probably know, gifts made under the so-called $11,000 tax-free gift rule (ask your tax advisor) won't trigger any federal gift taxes, nor will they reduce your federal gift- or estate-tax exemptions.

But when contributing to a 529 plan, you can claim five years' worth of $11,000 exclusions up front. This means a married couple can make a lump-sum payment of up to $110,000 without any adverse gift-tax consequences.

$$(5 \times \$11,000) \times 2 = \$110,000$$

College savings plans typically offer several investment options, including equity mutual funds. Many plans also welcome out-of-state investors. They allow payouts for costs to attend any accredited college or university in the country. You should shop around to find the Section 529 college savings plan you like best. But keep in mind that your in-state program may offer state tax advantages that tip the scale in its favor.

Warning: Don't confuse *Section 529 College Savings Plans* with *Section 529 Prepaid College Tuition Plans.* They are both termed *Section 529 plans* because both are permitted by the same tax code section. The difference is

Section 529 Prepaid College Tuition Plans allow you to lock in the cost to attend certain in-state colleges, but you gain nothing if your account turns out to earn more than the rate of inflation for costs to attend those colleges.

Section 529 College Savings Plans allow you to benefit when your account earns more than the rate of inflation for college costs. Of course, if it earns less, you know what can happen.

Total assets in 529 plans doubled in 2002 to more than $20 billion. All 50 states and the District of Columbia offer plans, and most offer a wide variety of investment options. Many plans have beefed up their Web presences and now offer online account access. And maximum contribution limits have been significantly increased. The average is $240,000, with Louisiana having the lowest limit at $173,065, while South Dakota is highest at $305,000.

TABLE 9.1   Section 529 College Savings Plans

Section 529 College Savings Plans	Program Administrator	Total No. of Investing Options
ALABAMA		
Alabama College Education Savings Program (ACES) 866-529-2228–www.treasury.state.al.us	Van Kampen	4
ALASKA		
Manulife College Savings 866-626-8529–www.manulifecollegesavings.com	T. Rowe Price	18
ARIZONA		
Arizona Family College Savings Program 602-258-2435–collegesavings.azhighered.org	The AZ Commission for Postsecondary Education	4
ARKANSAS		
GIFT College Investing Plan 877-442-6553–www.thegiftplan.com	FAM Distributors	5
CALIFORNIA		
The Golden State ScholarShare College Savings Trust 877-728-4338–www.scholarshare.com	TIAA-CREF Tuition Financing, Inc.	5
COLORADO		
Scholars Choice 888-572-4652–www.scholars-choice.com	Citigroup Asset Management	5
CONNECTICUT		
Connecticut Higher Education Trust (CHET) 888-799-2438–www.aboutchet.com	TIAA-CREF Tuition Financing, Inc.	3

TABLE 9.1   *(Continued)*

Section 529 College Savings Plans	Program Administrator	Total No. of Investing Options
DELAWARE		
Delaware College Investment Plan 800-544-1655–www.fidelity.com/delaware	Fidelity Investments	11
GEORGIA		
The Georgia Higher Education Savings Plan 877-424-4377–www.gacollegesavings.org	TIAA-CREF Tuition Financing, Inc.	5
HAWAII		
Hawaii College Savings Program 866-529-3343–www.tuitionedge.com	Delaware Investments	5
IDAHO		
Idaho College Savings Program 866-433-2533–www.idsaves.org	TIAA-CREF Tuition Financing, Inc.	3
ILLINOIS		
Bright Start 877-432-7444–www.brightstarsavings.com	Citigroup Asset Management	4
INDIANA		
College Choice 529 Investment Plan 866-400-7526–www.collegechoiceplan.com	One Group Admin. Services Inc.	8
IOWA		
College Savings Iowa 888-672-9116–www.collegesavingsiowa.com	Vanguard Investments	4
KANSAS		
Learning Quest 529 Education Savings Program 877-882-6236–www.learningquest.com	Kansas State Treasurer	19
KENTUCKY		
The Kentucky Education Savings Plan Trust 877-598-7878–www.kentuckytrust.org	TIAA-CREF Tuition Financing, Inc.	2
LOUISIANA		
Student Tuition Assistance & Revenue Trust (START Saving Program) 800-259-5626–www.osfa.state.la.us	LA Tuition Trust Authority	1
MAINE		
NextGen College Investing Plan (Direct Program) 877-463-9843–www.nextgenplan.com	Merrill Lynch	4

TABLE 9.1 *(Continued)*

Section 529 College Savings Plans	Program Administrator	Total No. of Investing Options
MARYLAND		10
Maryland College Investment Plan	T. Rowe Price	
888-463-4723–www.collegesavingsmd.org		
MASSACHUSETTS		
U.Fund College Investing Plan	Fidelity Investments	11
800-544-2776–www.fidelity.com/ufund		
MICHIGAN		
Michigan Education Savings Program (MESP)	TIAA-CREF Tuition Financing, Inc.	3
877-861-6377–www.misaves.com		
MINNESOTA		
Minnesota College Savings Plan	TIAA-CREF Tuition Financing, Inc.	3
877-338-4646–www.mnsaves.com		
MISSOURI		
Missouri Saving for Tuition Program (MOST) (Direct Program)	TIAA-CREF Tuition Financing, Inc.	3
888-414-6678–www.missourimost.org		
MISSISSIPPI		
Mississippi Affordable College Savings (MACS) (Direct Program)	TIAA-CREF Tuition Financing, Inc.	3
800-486-3670–www.collegesavingsms.com		
MONTANA		
Montana Family Education Savings Program	College Savings Bank	1
800-888-2723–Montana.collegesavings.com		
NEBRASKA		
The AIM College Savings Plan	Union Bank & Trust Co.	24
877-246-7526–www.aiminvestments.com		
NEVADA		
Columbia 529 Plan	Columbia Funds	6
877-994-2529–www.columbiafunds.com		
NEW HAMPSHIRE		
Fidelity Advisor 529 Plan	Fidelity Investments	21
800-544-9999–www.advisorxpress.com		
NEW JERSEY		
NJBEST 529 College Savings Plan	NJ Higher Ed. Student Assistance Authority (HESAA)	11
877-465-2378–www.njbest.com		

TABLE 9.1 *(Continued)*

Section 529 College Savings Plans	Program Administrator	Total No. of Investing Options
NEW MEXICO		
The Education Plan's College Savings Program 877-337-5268–www.theeducationplan.com	Schoolhouse Capital	8
NEW YORK		
New York's College Savings Program 877-697-2837–www.nysaves.org	TIAA-CREF	4
NORTH CAROLINA		
NC National College Savings Program (Direct Program) 800-600-3453–www.seligman529.com	College Foundation Inc.	5
NORTH DAKOTA		
College SAVE 866-728-3529–www.collegesave4u.com	Morgan Stanley	20
OHIO		
CollegeAdvantage 529 Savings Plan 800-233-6734–www.collegeadvantage.com	The OH Tuition Trust Authority	18 for residents
OREGON		
MFS 529 Savings Plan 866-637-7526–www.mfs.com	MFS Investment Management	24
OKLAHOMA		
Oklahoma College Savings Plan 877-654-7284–www.ok4saving.org	TIAA-CREF Tuition Financing, Inc.	3
RHODE ISLAND		
CollegeBoundFund 888-324-5057–www.collegeboundfund.com	Alliance Capital Management	15
SOUTH CAROLINA		
FUTUREScholar 529 College Savings Plan (Direct Program) 888-224-5674–www.futurescholar.com	Bank of America	10
SOUTH DAKOTA		
CollegeAccess 529 Plan 800-628-1237–www.collegeaccess529.com	PIMCO	26

TABLE 9.1 *(Continued)*

Section 529 College Savings Plans	Program Administrator	Total No. of Investing Options
TENNESSEE		
Tennessee's BEST Savings Plan 888-486-2378–www.tnbest.org	TIAA-CREF Tuition Financing, Inc.	2
UTAH		
Utah Educational Savings Plan Trust (UESP) 800-418-2551–www.uesp.org	State Board of Regents	4
VERMONT		
Vermont Higher Education Investment Plan 800-637-5860–www.vsac.org	TIAA-CREF Tuition Financing, Inc.	3
VIRGINIA		
Virginia Education Savings Trust (VEST) 888-567-0540–www.virginia529.com	Virginia College Savings Plan	12
WEST VIRGINIA		
Smart 529 Plan 866-574-3542–www.smart529.com	The Hartford	12
WISCONSIN		
Tomorrow's Scholar 866-677-6933–www.tomorrowsscholar.com	Strong Financial Corp.	6
WYOMING		
College Achievement Plan 877-529-2655–www.collegeachievementplan.com	Mercury Advisors	5

SUMMARY

■ Set aside a separate savings plan for your children's education.

■ The best way to pay for college is having your kid win a scholarship. The next best is one of the state-sponsored college savings plans, often called *Section 529 plans*. They are a great deal, since withdrawals to pay the account beneficiary's qualified college costs are tax free.

■ Washington has delivered some valuable tax breaks over the past few years to parents paying higher education costs.

PART FOUR

INVESTING FOR YOUR RETIREMENT

Since more and more of the responsibility for investment selection and management has been handed to the participant, it is crucial that you have a full working knowledge of the types of retirement products and services available.

This next section concerns the goals of long-term investing specifically for retirement income. While everyone is still trying to rid themselves of the bad taste left in their mouths by the frightening "events" at Enron, Global Crossing, WorldCom, and Arthur Andersen, it's more important than ever to focus on how to safely utilize employer-sponsored, pretax plans to their fullest benefit. New legislation has made the use of retirement plans more tax-favorable than ever before, through increased allowable contributions and catch-up provisions.

CHAPTER 10

EMPLOYER-SPONSORED RETIREMENT BENEFITS

Thirty years ago, few people understood how their retirement plans worked. They just trusted that their company was going to pay them a certain amount of money per year at retirement without concern about where the money was coming from.

Prior to ERISA (Employee Retirement Income Security Act of 1974), a company could have a pension fund that wasn't really backed by anything. If the company went out of business, the pension evaporated. In the absence of any oversight of pension plans, there were abuses. Corporations lost money; retirees lost money. The system was out of control, so the federal government stepped in and mandated some restrictions. The government stated that it was unfair for somebody to work at a company for 20 or 30 years and then lose their retirement benefits. Further, the government informed employers that they had to put money aside so that if the company went bankrupt, employees were still guaranteed pensions. The irony, of course, is that the federal government is still doing with Social Security money what it told the private sector it couldn't do.

When ERISA was established in 1974, it changed the rules of investing forever. ERISA outlined rules and determined how much money must be allocated for pension funds based on the number of employees a corporation had. It created huge, rapidly growing pools of money and stipulated that anything done with this pool of money must be for the benefit of the employees.

The act did not tell corporations how to manage their money, but it did state that the trustees of a pension fund are fiduciaries and are, therefore, personally responsible for their actions. It mandated that they be guided by the *prudent investor rule.*

The prudent investor rule states that any investment selection may be made, provided that a review of the decision at a later date would determine that, with the information available at the time, the choice was a prudent one. It didn't give specifics, but it gave enough guidance so that corporations knew they'd better have an audit trail. Their decisions had better make sense, even to someone looking at them 10 or 20 years in the future. If any employee later claimed that he or she didn't get the pension he or she was entitled to, the corporation would be able to prove that, given the circumstances at the time, its actions were prudent.

Generally, the pension fund would be turned over to the CFO (chief financial officer) or to another top executive, where it was handled as a part-time job. Not surprisingly, business owners and corporate heads didn't want to be saddled with the fiduciary responsibilities of pension fund management. Their primary goal was to avoid being sued by their employees or embarrassed in front of their boards.

The pension fund administrator's job performance wasn't reviewed annually or semiannually as it would be for most employees, but quarterly—and the review was directly linked to fund performance. For instance, if the Dow Jones was up 10 percent but the administrator's fund was down 5 percent, it would not only be an embarrassment, but could lead to the administrator's being replaced.

When dealing with a quarterly time period, the administrator couldn't afford to lose, so pension funds became very conservative by sticking with predictable fixed-income investments. Most included a mixture of CDs, bonds, and fixed-income vehicles. Bonds were safe, and since safety was the name of the game, the plan administrator would usually put 70 percent of the money in bonds. If the administrator reported annualized returns of at least 6 or 7 percent every quarter, well, at least he wouldn't be embarrassed—and he would get to keep his job.

But attitudes changed. Shareholders and owners wanted to see their investments grow, and there wasn't much growth in fixed-income investments. The administrators recognized that they weren't qualified to manage equity investments, so they hired professional money managers to handle that portion of their funds.

The managers started breaking away from the banks and becoming professional asset managers. These money managers gave the people what they wanted: a very diversified, very conscious method of winning and losing to the market over short-term time periods—competing for every last basis point. Since turnover didn't have a tax effect, we saw an escalation in trading.

So far, so good—but, job security was still the name of the game, and for many pension administrators, it was too risky to let one manager handle the entire equity portion of their pension funds. What would happen if that one manager underperformed the market? To be safe, they'd bring in five or six managers and assume that each would take a different approach.

Then, in the 1980s, investment *styles* entered the equation, as did funds identified as growth, value, international, and so on. Corporations started tiptoeing into the international marketplaces. This was met with resistance at first because boards wanted to buy only U.S. stocks; but as it became apparent that companies such as Toyota or Sony were undeniably good investments, the resistance began to disappear.

It was a logical step, but still it took years to get U.S. companies to go global with their pension investments because international investments were still perceived as riskier than U.S. investments. The real clincher came when it was pointed out that foreign markets didn't move in correlation with the U.S. stock market, thereby ensuring broader diversification and adhering to the prudent investor rule. A prudent investor would certainly include international stocks in a diversified portfolio.

As pension plan administrators became more knowledgeable about volatility and more comfortable with investing in foreign equities, the equity ratios of pension funds increased—from 30/70 to 50/50 to 60/40. And new tools were designed to measure market volatility. These tools were all designed under the umbrella of total return and broad diversification.

The new approaches to pension plan management came even as the plans themselves were being eclipsed by a new investment phenomenon: the 401(k) plan.

AN ERA IS DEAD

The era of employees working at the same company for 40 years, then retiring with a gold watch and a full pension was passing. People started to change jobs more often, and corporations, eager to rid themselves of pension plan liability, began to move away from defined benefit plans and toward defined contribution plans, the 401(k) plan in particular. A *defined benefit plan* is a retirement plan in which the sponsoring company provides a certain guaranteed benefit to participants based on a predetermined formula. A *defined contribution plan* is an employer-sponsored plan in which contributions are made to individual participant accounts, and the final benefit consists solely of assets (including investment returns) that have accumulated in these individual accounts. Depending on the type of defined contribution plan, contributions may be made either by the company, the participant, or both.

The 401(k) plan seemed to be the ideal solution. These new plans allowed individuals to place pretax contributions into special investment accounts where the money would grow tax deferred until it was withdrawn during retirement. Employers could also contribute to employees' accounts, which was a great way for them to offer an additional benefit while drastically reducing both the cost and liability associated with traditional pension plans. Plus, they didn't have to worry about calculating retirement benefits.

The more the employer did to get employees to view their retirement plans as a component of their compensation, the greater the employees' participation. That greater participation, or investment, on behalf of the employees equates to improved owner–employee relations, loyalty, and vested interest in the profitability of the business. Moreover, the 401(k) plan was designed so that when employees changed jobs, they could take their retirement accounts with them.

These newly empowered employees, like the first wave of pension plan administrators, put all their money into fixed-income investments because they were thought to be safe. In the early days of 401(k) plans, 80 percent of employee contributions were invested in money market funds and bond funds.

That started to change when active mutual funds launched intense advertising campaigns aimed at the 401(k) market. Suddenly, retirement plans were offering 8 percent loaded funds to investors, a strategy that was easy for plan sponsors because the mutual fund was the easiest way to handle all the record-keeping responsibilities.

Educational campaigns were started to get people to invest in equity funds, which made more money. And then the greatest bull market in history began in 1982, and investors came to the conclusion that mutual fund returns would keep going up, up, and up—forever.

Suddenly, people couldn't get enough mutual funds. Tax efficiency and tax deferral didn't seem to matter to investors; they wanted returns—and plenty of them! People started looking beyond their retirement plans to fund supermarkets, where they could buy funds from any number of companies. There were thousands of offerings, all in one place.

At the same time, money management consultants, and nearly everyone else who worked with the pension market, stopped prospecting pension plans and started looking at the individual marketplace. They asked themselves, "How did we succeed with pension funds? We diversified them and came up with asset allocation, so let's do the same thing for the retail marketplace." Mutual fund wrap programs were born. Soon, a whole industry was built around evaluating mutual funds and creating portfolios of funds for individuals, the same way portfolios had been built for managers of pension funds.

In the quest to evaluate these funds, measurements of returns were scaled down to weeks, even days. Risk became undesirable; volatility was worse. If a consumer publication claimed a particular fund was "volatile," that was a negative statement. Of course, the lower the risk, the lower the expected return.

Attitudes that were ingrained in the institutional pension market were transferred to the individual investor market. The evolution started with the battle cry of: "Total return is the king! Risk is volatility in returns, and volatility is bad."

For an individual, risk is not volatility—it's not having enough money when you need it. Volatility in short-term returns isn't bad if the individual has a long-term time horizon. And if you need to accumulate a lot of money, you must accept volatility to achieve the higher rates of return. In that situation, volatility is your friend. Without it, you're never going to get there. If an individual has 15 years until the money is needed, what happens next month isn't that important. The risk is not the fluctuation along the way; the risk is that 15 years later, there won't be enough money for an investor to attain his or her goals. That's also the inherent risk in 401(k) plans.

It's not what you earn; it's what you keep.

What the pension fund administrators did to minimize market risk, or the risk of missing what the market was doing, was to diversify over as many capital markets as they could, using as many money managers as they could.

Today's individuals who are trying to accumulate wealth must control the amount of volatility or risk they're taking. They can do this by adding asset class funds to their portfolios. Time really determines how much risk an individual can take. That should be a major determining factor in asset allocation. If you need the money in five years or less, you can't take much risk. If you have in excess of five years, the game is different.

If you have a long enough time horizon, you can create wealth by holding a thousand stocks. It is also possible to accumulate wealth by holding one stock—which may be the company you started. One event, and one holding, has occasionally created tremendous wealth. That same holding or event can also wipe you out financially—examples are Enron, WorldCom, and Global Crossing.

Most people have lifestyle wants and needs that far exceed their current strategy in accumulating assets to achieve them—and they're going to be sorely disappointed as the time they had hoped to retire approaches. When it comes to retirement planning, these same people have overly ambitious goals, inadequate funding, and either no investment strategy or the wrong kind of strategy—as we have seen.

RETIREMENT CHECKUP

Pension miscalculations are a growing problem that affects people of all ages, not just at retirement age. Miscalculations can occur anytime someone changes jobs or takes a lump-sum cash-out. This is when the possibility for miscalculation arises. For the most part, pension mix-ups aren't intentional, but federal pension laws are incredibly difficult to interpret, even for expert number crunchers.

How would you know if there was an error that had been compounding for many years? How can you ensure that you'll get what's rightfully yours when retirement arrives? It's up to you to keep track of your own pension plan accounting.

Know your rights and monitor your retirement plan before the "golden years" creep up on you. Learn the details. Ask for a summary plan description. This will show how your pension is calculated. If you're invested in a workplace 401(k) plan, get a description of your program from the administrator of your benefits plan.

Also, an individual benefits statement will tell you what your benefits are currently worth and how many years you've been in the plan. It may even include a projection of your monthly check. Check for obvious errors, such as wrong years of service.

Save all your statements and compare the most recent to the last one you received. You should keep any pension documents your company gives you over the years. Also keep records of dates when you worked and your salary, as this type of data is used by your employer to calculate the value of your pension.

Here are seven common mistakes to watch for:

1. Company forgot to include commission, overtime pay, or bonuses in determining your benefit level.

2. Your employer relied on incorrect Social Security information to calculate your benefits.

3. Somebody used the wrong benefit formula (i.e., an incorrect interest rate was plugged into the equation).

4. Calculations are wrong because you've worked past age 65.

5. You didn't update your workplace personnel officer about important changes that would affect your benefits such as marriage, divorce, or death of a spouse.

6. The company neglected to include your total years of service.

7. Your pension provider just made a basic mathematical mistake.

Ask for professional help if you still think something might be wrong. Ask for the name of a qualified specialist (i.e., a Certified Pension Consultant) in your area. Call the American Society of Pension Actuaries at (703) 516-9300 or the National Center for Retirement Benefits at (800) 666-1000.

BEFORE YOU LEAVE YOUR JOB . . .

Find Out Your Retirement Savings Balance

Ask your employer for an accounting of *all* workplace savings plans: defined benefit pension plans, 401(k) plans, profit sharing plans, employer stock option plans, employee stock ownership plans (ESOPs), money purchase plans, thrift plans, or other after-tax savings plans.

Review Your Employer's Calculation of a Lump-Sum Distribution

If you are eligible for a lump-sum distribution from your employer's plan, ask for an explanation of how your distribution was calculated. Review it carefully. Then, consider rolling it over to a rollover IRA or a new employer's plan.

Manage Your Company Stock

If you own your employer's stock in your 401(k) plan or ESOP, ask your employer to calculate your cost basis. Then, review your withdrawal options with a tax expert who can explain the potential tax savings often referred to as *net unrealized appreciation.*

Investigate the Value of Unusual Assets in Your Employer-Sponsored Plan

If your workplace savings are invested in restricted stock or any other type of illiquid asset, such as a limited partnership, real estate, precious metals or artwork, work with a financial professional who can help you evaluate the appraisal of your share and oversee its proper distribution.

Get the Facts about Rolling Over

Request copies of your company's instructions and forms for rolling over savings to a rollover IRA or to a new employer's plan.

Inquire about Your New Employer's Rollover

If there is a waiting period before you are allowed to participate in a new employer's plan, roll your savings over to a rollover IRA to keep it tax deferred while you wait.

Choose a Knowledgeable Investment Advisor

Talk to a retirement specialist at a reputable firm about opening a rollover IRA. A knowledgeable financial partner will work with you to make your transaction go smoothly and may be able to help you avoid a costly delay.

Keep Track of Deadlines

Even if you receive a direct distribution of your 401(k) plan in the form of a check, you can still roll it over to a rollover IRA, avoid a penalty, and preserve the benefits of tax deferral if you act within 60 days.

SUMMARY

In the past, employees trusted that their company was going to pay them a certain amount of money per year at retirement without concern about where the money was coming from. That was then. Today you need to acquire a capital base large enough to make up for the loss of Social Security benefits you won't get, and from which you can earn income during your retirement years. To do this, you have to forgo present consumption. Money that is not being spent must be invested in such a way that it will grow over time. The current economic situation is forcing us to take risk. There are no guarantees in investing. The only guarantee now is that if you try to play it safe, you will not become financially independent. If you do nothing, you will fail.

CHAPTER 11

THE 401(k) PLAN

A 401(k) plan is a defined contribution retirement plan sponsored by companies for their employees. It allows for participant-directed investments in equities and fixed-income securities. The contributions are made pretax, and any earnings on those contributions compound tax-free until distribution in retirement. The nonprofit version of a 401(k) plan is the 403(b) plan offered by local and state governments.

HOW DOES YOUR 401(k) PLAN WORK?

Step 1. Read the Summary Plan Description

The Summary Plan Description provides a plain-English explanation of how the plan works and benefits the employees. In addition, a plan administrator is responsible for answering questions and providing information about the plan. Employees should understand eligibility requirements and vesting schedules, distribution rules, loan provisions, etc. You will be more likely to participate in the 401(k) plan if you understand how to use it to your advantage and how to get your money when you need it. Even an elementary understanding alleviates fear and heightens the sense of being in control.

Step 2. Increase Your Contributions

The 401(k) plans are one of the most effective wealth builders available, but they require fuel in the form of contributions. Increase the amount you contribute, even if you have to stretch your budget a little. A small increase in the amount of money invested and growing tax free can have a visible impact on your plan's value. (See Figure 11.1 for an example of how much difference a larger contribution can make.)

Step 3. Take Full Advantage of Matched Contributions

Don't turn down free money! Many employers offer matching contributions up to a percentage of what their employees contribute. There may be "profit sharing" or "nonelective" employer contributions that are made to each employee participating in the plan, regardless of elective contributions. Eligibility to share in these contributions is usually

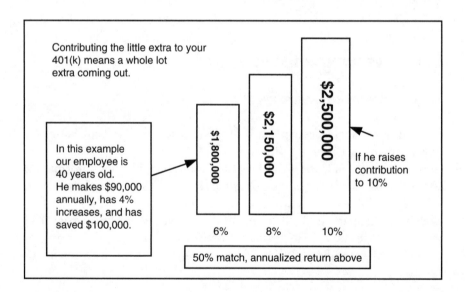

FIGURE 11.1
Contribution Increase

automatic, but you still need to fill out investment election forms. (See Figure 11.2 for how much difference a larger employee match can make.)

Matching percentages come in all sizes (e.g., 25 percent, 50 percent, 75 percent, etc). Matched contributions provide an automatic growth on your investment and supercharge the speed at which your 401(k) account can grow. For instance, at a 50 percent match, for every dollar you put into your 401(k) account, your employer puts in 50 cents. That's an instant return better than most stock market returns—even in just about any bull market. If you are eligible, sign up right away—any delay is costing you money!

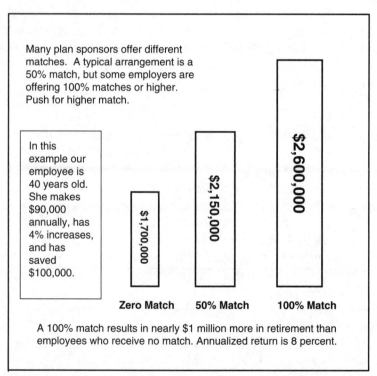

FIGURE 11.2
Increased Match

Step 4. Know How to Get Money out of Your 401(k) Plan Safely

Before you put money into a retirement plan, you want to know how you can get that money out. But, this topic goes much deeper than liquidity—the availability of your money. You should understand how your 401(k) investment can continue to build in your retirement. For example, by delaying accessing the funds for 10 years, the value of the 401(k) amount can triple. With longer life spans, retirees will need a source of income that can continue to grow, even as they withdraw funds from it. So, you may want to consider accessing your 401(k) plan at 72 rather than when you retire at 62, and relying on other forms of savings for the first 10 years of your retirement.

Some 401(k) plans permit you to withdraw money early in the event of a hardship. For plans that do not allow early withdrawals for hardship, sometimes you can borrow money from the account by taking a low-interest secured loan using your retirement savings as collateral. In many cases, though, this can derail your savings goals. Remember, no one ever got rich borrowing from himself.

Step 5. Understand Your Investment Choices

When you contribute to a 401(k) plan, investment results are your responsibility, not the responsibility of the plan sponsor. Such is the nature of a defined contribution plan (as opposed to a defined benefit plan, like a pension). This makes it vitally important that you understand your investment choices and make smart decisions. Take advantage of any educational program offered to acquaint yourself with the capital markets. (See Figure 11.3 for the typical investment options that your plan may have available for you.)

The problem is that limited available time does not permit employees to absorb and evaluate the vast amounts of information required to make astute investment decisions. Meeting their employment responsibilities must take priority. Often, these problems ultimately push the plan participant to choose expedient, short-term solutions that seem reasonable, but may not produce the desired results.

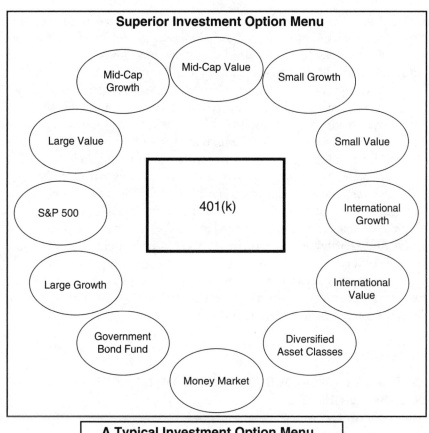

Superior Investment Option Menu

- Mid-Cap Growth
- Mid-Cap Value
- Small Growth
- Large Value
- Small Value
- S&P 500
- 401(k)
- International Growth
- Large Growth
- International Value
- Government Bond Fund
- Diversified Asset Classes
- Money Market

A Typical Investment Option Menu

Money Market

Bond Fund

Large Growth Fund

Large Value Fund

Small Company Fund

International Fund

Balanced Fund

FIGURE 11.3
Investment Options

The feature of switching gives the participant the freedom to transfer between investment options on a daily basis. To the detriment of available switching options, this could also facilitate turning investors into market timers, who would thus play a losers' game.

The best approach is to decide upon one strategy and stick with it. Most 401(k) plans have a long-term, systematic manner of monitoring any plan's investment progress. You should inquire into how your assets are to be monitored. If mutual funds are used as an investment vehicle, then you should be provided with their performance results periodically.

You may be able to run your own asset class strategy. An alternative is a balanced portfolio in which you combine elements of each asset class represented in your plan into a diversified portfolio. It will never involve an element of market timing. Balanced portfolios are often used by major funds and charitable endowments as well as individuals. They provide great flexibility.

You may consider obtaining specific investment counseling regarding an appropriate mix of investments and asset allocation for your individual objectives, retirement horizons, and risk tolerance.

WARNING INDICATORS THAT YOUR 401(k) ACCOUNT MAY BE IN TROUBLE

1. Your company is having financial difficulties and your deferrals are not getting into the plan in a timely manner.
2. You can't get any information on the investments in your plan.
3. You have asked for, but never received, a Summary Plan Description.
4. Most of the 401(k) assets are in a single investment managed or selected by the plan trustees.
5. Your money has been reallocated to different investments without your instruction.
6. Your statement doesn't match up to deductions taken from your paycheck.

What can you do if you find yourself in one of these situations? Start by asking questions through your manager or Human Resources department. If you get no results, contact the Pension and Welfare Benefits Administration division of the U.S. Department of Labor at (202) 219-8211 or www.dol.gov/dol/pwba/.

SUMMARY

- Read the Summary Plan Description, which provides a plain-English explanation of how the plan works and how it benefits you.

- Increase the amount you contribute, even if you have to stretch your budget a little. A small increase in the amount of money invested and growing tax free can have a visible impact on your plan's value.

- Take full advantage of matched contributions. Don't turn down free money! Many employers offer matching contributions as a percentage of what their employees contribute.

- Know how to get money out of your 401(k) plan safely. Before you put money into a retirement plan, you want to know how you can get that money out.

- Understand your investment choices. When you contribute to a 401(k) plan, investment results are your responsibility, not the responsibility of the plan sponsor. This makes it vitally important that you understand your investment choices and make smart decisions. Take advantage of any educational program to acquaint yourself with the capital markets.

CHAPTER 12

IRA VERSUS 401(k) PLAN—DO YOU HAVE TO CHOOSE?

Individual retirement accounts (IRAs) are just that: retirement accounts for individuals that are not tied to their employment, although the amount you can contribute *pretax* is tied to the amount of your earned wages. IRA contributions are no longer tax deductible if either you or your spouse is covered by another retirement plan, such as a corporate pension plan, SEP IRA accounts, Keogh plans, or 401(k) company-sponsored plans.

However, if your adjusted gross income in 2003 was less than $40,000 (single), or $60,000 (joint), you could still get a tax deduction for the full $3,000 IRA contribution, even if you or your spouse was covered by a qualified retirement plan. The $40,000 (single) and $60,000 (joint) adjusted gross income limits are being increased by $5,000 per year beginning in 2004 through 2005 (single) or through 2007 (joint).

There are special partial deduction rules above the limits, so consult your tax advisor if you are within $10,000 of the yearly limit.

Consider putting money into an IRA if:

- Your contributions are fully deductible—couples filing jointly with gross income of less than $60,000, singles who make less than $40,000, or anyone who is not covered by a pension, profit-sharing, or other tax-advantaged retirement plan.

- You qualify for a partial deduction and are sure that you will not need the money in your IRA before age 59½.

- Your tax bracket or age is such that a Roth IRA (discussed later in this chapter) is not a better choice.

- You are maxing out on your 401(k) already.

Contributing to an IRA is probably not worthwhile if:

- You are ineligible for a deduction, especially if you think that your tax rate when you retire will be higher than it is now.
- You can use other tax-favored retirement savings plans such as a 401(k) plan.
- You don't want to worry about the lifelong burden of paperwork required to document a nondeductible or partially deductible IRA for the Internal Revenue Service (IRS).

IRA CHECKLIST

The basic rules for contributing to any type of IRA (with the exception of educational IRAs, which are really not retirement accounts) are based on taxable compensation. This includes wages, salaries, tips, professional fees, commissions, and self-employment income. Your annual contribution to all IRA accounts cannot exceed $3,000 plus up to an additional $3,000 for a nonworking or low-earning spouse. The IRA is simply a tax shelter, because all the earnings that accrue in every type of IRA are completely tax deferred.

For example, say you accumulate $50,000 in a deductible IRA by the time you reach age 40. If your account averages a 10 percent annual return for the next 25 years, you'll generate $492,000 of earnings. And if you withdraw that as a lump sum and pay a 30 percent average tax rate, you'll net around $344,000. On the other hand, if you have that $50,000 in a taxable account, then your earnings are subject to an average tax rate of 30 percent, and you net only 7 percent per annum instead of 10 percent. At that rate, $50,000 earns about $221,000 over the next 25 years. So that's the benefit of compounding. You get an extra 3 percent provided by the IRA tax shelter.

IRAs are also a great place for a well-diversified portfolio of stock mutual funds because you want to strive for high returns to maximize the advantage of the tax-deferred compounding. Even though your stocks are riskier in the short run and there may be volatility over the long run, they may participate in the growth of the economy.

Since there are various types of IRAs available, it might appear that they could replace your 401(k). But, before you make any major decisions, understand all the facts.

Deductible IRA versus 401(k) Plan

A tax deduction on an IRA will generally have less of an effect than a pre-tax 401(k) deduction, because a 401(k) gives you the tax savings with each paycheck. With an IRA, you have to wait until you file your taxes to get the tax benefit. Meanwhile, your 401(k) tax savings have been earning all year long.

In addition, you cannot borrow money from your IRA. But, if you're a highly compensated employee and your 401(k) pretax contributions are limited (capped), you can still take advantage of the expanded contribution limits of an IRA for you and your spouse. Even if you are not eligible for a tax deduction, an IRA still provides an additional retirement savings opportunity since the earnings accumulate tax deferred.

A comprehensive booklet on 401(k) plans and IRAs is *How to Build, Protect, and Maintain Your 401(k) Plan* by Dale Rogers and Craig Rogers (Marketplace Books, 2004).

KEOGH PLAN

This term refers to a qualified retirement plan sponsored by a self-employed person or by a partnership. Prior to 1984, special rules existed for self-employed retirement plans. After 1984, the distinction between corporate retirement plans and self-employed retirement plans was eliminated. Now a sole proprietor or partnership can sponsor a 401(k) plan, a profit sharing plan, a pension plan, or any other retirement plan qualified under Internal Revenue Code Section 401.

A small company with no employees except the owner can adopt and maintain a 401(k) profit sharing plan. Annual limits for participants in such a plan can be as high as $40,000, plus any catch-up allowances if you are age 50 or more.

The name Keogh lingers on even though the distinctions have been eliminated. Be certain to get expert advice from a pension consulting firm *before* implementing such a plan. You may only need a Simplified Employee Pension (SEP) Plan.

SIMPLIFIED EMPLOYEE PENSION (SEP) PLAN

A SEP is like a giant IRA. SEPs were created by Congress so that small businesses could set up retirement plans that are a little easier to administer than normal pension or 401(k) plans. But anything designed by the government has a catch. The business must put exactly the same percentage of compensation in for employees as for the owner. In addition, every employee is 100 percent vested regardless of service, so, if you have employees, they can pull their money out of their IRAs the day after you put it in. Since these are IRAs, loan privileges are not available.

For larger limits and more flexibility, carefully examine and compare a qualified plan to a SEP. If large limits are not of interest, you will never have employees, and you will never want to have a loan privilege, the SEP is an excellent alternative.

EDUCATIONAL IRA

An educational IRA limits contributions to $2,000 per year, and while the earnings compound tax free, they have to be used for tuition or other allowable college costs. The IRS would penalize you if your child decided to buy a car with it instead. If the funds are used for any purpose other than education, income taxes and a 10 percent penalty are slapped on the earnings. Also, when you cash in an educational IRA, you become ineligible for new tuition tax credits during that calendar year.

Educational IRA versus 401(k) Plan

The value of an educational IRA is its tax-free feature, higher income limits for married couples, and the flexibility to use these monies for the expenses of education, public or private, kindergarten through graduate school. If the purpose of your savings is for education, a Coverdell Education Savings Account (ESA) (previously called the Education IRA) would beat the 401(k) plan.

The Coverdell ESA allows your money to grow tax deferred. You can open a Coverdell ESA for qualified elementary, secondary, and higher education expenses. You may invest up to $2,000 annually per child. Contributions are not deductible and earnings are tax deferred. Withdrawals may be tax free as long as they are used for qualified educational expenses. Contribution limits decline for singles with income between $95,000 and $110,000 and couples with income between $190,000 and $220,000.

An even better choice might be a Section 529 plan (see Chapter 9), also known as a *qualified state tuition program.*

The Economic Growth and Tax Relief Reconciliation Act of 2001 also provides a tax deduction for college tuition and a deduction for student loan interest. If you're considering using your home equity to pay college expenses, the double deduction could produce a very inexpensive loan.

ROTH IRA

The Roth IRA differs from other IRAs in that contributions are not tax deductible. Because of that, you can choose to contribute both to a traditional IRA and a Roth IRA in the same tax year, but your combined contributions to all your traditional and Roth IRAs cannot exceed the annual maximum limit in total.

The Roth IRA will be most valuable when it holds investments that compound at a high rate—such as stocks or stock mutual funds—for a long time. That's because the ultimate value of the compound investment returns will be distributed *tax free,* instead of being taxed at normal rates, as are distributions from regular IRAs and other retirement accounts.

Roth IRA versus 401(k) Plan

Using a Roth IRA means that you are betting that your tax rate in retirement will be equal to or higher than your current rate. [That is, you're counting on paying less in taxes now on the money that you put into a Roth IRA than you would pay on your 401(k) money after you retire.] We always recommend using your 401(k) to the maximum since matching contributions may be part of the plan.

Children's Roth IRA

A Roth IRA is an excellent investment account to open for children as soon as they have earned income. The extra years of compounding available to a child can produce a tax-free payoff that will give the child a big head start on lifetime financial security.

While a child must have earned income to open a Roth IRA, the IRA need not be funded with the child's earned income. It can be funded with money received as a gift—from parents, grandparents, etc. This gives the child the chance to "double up" by also saving the earned income in another account.

Roth IRA for Yourself

You can make a full $3,000 contribution to a Roth IRA if your adjusted gross income (AGI) is less than $160,000 for a joint return or $100,000 for a single return. If your AGI doesn't exceed $100,000, you'll be able to convert existing IRAs to Roth IRAs. To do this, you'll have to first withdraw your IRA assets and pay the taxes on the gains.

SPOUSAL IRA

While it's not actually called a "spousal IRA," non-wage-earning spouses can contribute up to $3,000 ($3,500 if age 50 or older) to their own Roth IRAs or traditional IRAs provided the other spouse qualifies and the couple files a joint federal income tax return. This IRA contribution is in addition to any IRA contribution the wage-earning spouse makes. The combined total amount eligible married couples (under age 50) may contribute to their IRAs is the lesser of either 100 percent of their combined compensation or $6,000 for 2004, $8,000 for 2005–2007, and $10,000 for 2008. This amount may be increased for cost-of-living adjustments thereafter. However, each spouse may not contribute more than the individual contribution limit to his or her IRA.

ROLLOVER IRA

A rollover IRA can be invested in mutual funds, stocks, bonds, or other securities, including CDs and Treasuries. This flexibility makes opening a rollover IRA a good opportunity to rebalance your retirement portfolio by rolling your savings into instruments not traditionally offered by employer plans (such as asset class funds). You can add additional money to your rollover IRA by making annual IRA contributions.

A rollover IRA is designed for people who are leaving a job or retiring and receiving money accumulated in a 401(k) account. Eligible distributions from such plans may be "rolled over" directly into a rollover IRA, tax free. Pretax 401(k) assets in a rollover IRA can generally be rolled back into another 401(k) plan in a different employer's plan down the road, if you choose.

Generally, there are two ways to roll over your 401(k) into a rollover IRA. A *direct rollover* is when your employer sends your vested 401(k) balance directly to the firm holding your rollover IRA without your receiving the payment. By directly rolling over the balance, your employer either wire transfers the money to the firm holding your rollover IRA, or sends a check made out to the firm holding your rollover IRA for your benefit. This method allows you to avoid the 20 percent mandatory withholding imposed by the IRS. A *60-day rollover* is when your employer sends your vested 401(k) balance to you. This can also be handled by a wire transfer or a check, where the check is made out to your name. With this method, companies are required to withhold 20 percent of your vested 401(k) balance for payment to the IRS. If you choose to deposit that money into a rollover IRA, you will have 60 days to do so, and you will be required to make up the 20 percent that was withheld out of your own pocket.

If you do that, you can receive credit for the 20 percent that was withheld toward your income tax liability when you file your tax return. However, if you don't have the cash to make up for the 20 percent withheld when making your new deposit, the IRS will consider that 20 percent as a distribution, making it subject to taxes and a possible 10 percent early withdrawal penalty.

If you already have a traditional IRA established, you can still roll your 401(k) into it. If you have made after-tax contributions to that established IRA, and you expect to roll your 401(k) assets back into a 401(k) plan in the future, you may want to consider keeping those assets separate to avoid commingling. On January 1, 2002, the rules regarding commingling were relaxed and no longer prohibit commingling.

If you have changed jobs several times in the past and have 401(k) plans at all of your previous companies, you can simplify your record keeping by combining those 401(k) amounts into one rollover IRA.

When you roll over your vested 401(k) balance, the remaining balance of any loan will be counted as a distribution, and it will be taxed as ordinary income. You may also incur a 10 percent early withdrawal penalty on the total balance of the loan if you are under age 59½. Some companies will allow you to finish paying back the loan before you roll it over, to avoid that tax burden.

Rollover to a Roth IRA

You also have the ability to move assets from your 401(k) plan into a Roth IRA if you prefer this to moving them to a traditional IRA, but you must use a rollover IRA in between. It involves a few steps, but here's how it works:

Step 1. Determine your eligibility. You can only convert to a Roth IRA if you have an adjusted gross income of $100,000 or less, for either single or joint filers. Additionally, you won't be eligible if you are married and filing separate tax returns unless you've lived apart from your spouse for the entire tax year.

Step 2. Assuming you're eligible to convert to a Roth IRA, you must first roll the assets into a rollover IRA.

Step 3. Once you establish and fund your rollover IRA, you can start converting money from your rollover IRA to your Roth IRA. [*Note:* Unlike a rollover IRA, once you convert to a Roth IRA, you can't roll the assets in it back into a 401(k) plan in the future.]

Be prepared for the tax bite when you convert to a Roth IRA. Taxes may be due on any deductible or pretax contributions and their earnings, as well as on earnings attributable to after-tax contributions. This is why some people who make Roth IRA conversions decide to convert just a portion of their eligible assets in a given year, and then convert the rest at a later time.

Conversion to a Roth IRA may be attractive if:

- You believe your tax rate will be the same or higher in retirement.

- You're able to pay taxes on the converted assets from a source other than your retirement savings.

- You can leave your converted assets in your Roth IRA for at least five years.

For some investors, moving assets from a 401(k) plan to a Roth IRA may serve as an effective income tax planning strategy. While the tax code requires you to begin taking minimum required distributions from a 401(k) plan and most other retirement accounts generally beginning by age 70½, no such requirement exists during the account holder's lifetime for Roth IRAs (regardless of your age).

In this chapter we have provided you with general descriptions of various IRAs. Before implementing any individual tax strategy, you should always consult your qualified tax advisor.

CHAPTER 13

WHO SAYS YOU CAN'T MAKE UP FOR LOST TIME?

As a result of legislation passed by Congress in 2002, you can now make up for lost savings opportunities if you find you are behind in your retirement planning. Under the Economic Growth and Tax Relief Reconciliation Act of 2001 (EGTRRA), you are now able to make larger contributions to IRAs and workplace savings plans [such as 401(k) plans or 403(b) plans], and that isn't the only change that may greatly benefit you. The new bill also allows you, if you're 50 or older, to make larger "catch-up" contributions annually to your workplace savings plan and your IRA.

The net effect? You have more opportunities to save money for your retirement—while keeping your hard-earned money out of Uncle Sam's pockets.

HOW EGTRRA AFFECTS RETIREMENT SAVINGS VEHICLES

Workplace Savings Plan Changes

Congress recognized long ago that many workers hadn't yet saved enough to support a comfortable retirement. In fact, according to the U.S. government's General Accounting Office, Social Security income accounts for just 37 percent (on average) of retirees' income. When you consider that, the need for more savings opportunities becomes glaringly apparent. That's why, with EGTRRA, contribution limits have been raised in everyone's workplace savings plans, regardless of age.

The new limit in 2004 for pretax contributions to 403(b), 457(a), or 401(k) plans is $13,000, and it will rise $1,000 a year through 2006, when the maximum pretax contribution will be $15,000. After 2006, the maximum amount will be indexed for inflation.

The catch-up amount increases by $1,000 a year through 2006 (when the catch-up amount will be $5,000). Larger contributions will, of course, generally lead to larger retirement accumulations.

Each year for the next six, the contribution limits increase incrementally. If you'll be 50 years old by the end of the year in which you plan to contribute, these limits allow you to "catch-up" on your savings. In Table 13.1, you can see how the limits increase over time.

Traditional and Roth IRA Changes

The very latest news is that Representatives Rob Portman (R-OH) and Benjamin Cardin (D-MD) introduced the Pension Preservation and Savings Expansion Act (H.R. 1776), on April 4, 2003. A modified bill was marked up in the House Ways and Means Committee (www.waysand-means.house.gov/legis.asp?formmode=item&number=100).

Under this bill, contribution limits to Roth IRAs would be changed to $5,000 ($6,000 if age 50 or over) starting in 2004. Direct rollovers from retirement plans to Roth IRAs would be permitted. The penalty for not making required distributions would be decreased from 50 percent to 20 percent.

The Bush administration has proposed sweeping changes to IRA tax policy that would greatly expand Roth IRAs and introduce a new Lifetime Savings Account with features similar to (and superior to) Roth IRAs.

TABLE 13.1   New Contribution Limits for 401(k), 403(b), and 457(b) Retirement Savings Plans

Tax Year	If You're Under Age 50	If You're Age 50 and Older
2004	$13,000	$16,000
2005	$14,000	$18,000
2006*	$15,000	$20,000

*Annual contribution amounts and catch-up contributions are indexed thereafter in $500 increments. Catch-up contributions are not indexed.

Both accounts would offer tax-free withdrawals with contribution limits of $7,500 each—with contributions to both allowed—for a total of $15,000. Also, income limitations on conversions and setting up Roth IRAs would be eliminated.

A modified version of the catch-up provisions will also apply to IRAs, but with lesser amounts until 2005, and larger amounts thereafter. Couple these two savings increases together, and the new limits can really make a big difference to your retirement nest egg.

However, the eligibility rules for Roth IRA contributions and conversions remain the same. To determine your eligibility for both types of IRAs, you should consult your tax advisor.

See Table 13.2 for more on the exact schedule of IRA increases.

Based on new tax laws, here are a couple of tips to consider:

- Project your estimated income and deductions during the next few years, focusing on which items you can control by either the timing of when you report them for tax purposes, or the amount you report. For example, it will probably be to your benefit to maximize deductions in a year when you know your income is slated to rise, perhaps through a bonus or a payment for a special consulting assignment, pushing you into a higher tax bracket.

- Take advantage of the opportunity to set aside more income in tax-deferred retirement plans. Consider ways to accelerate your deductions, taking them in earlier years when higher marginal tax rates are in effect (e.g., accelerating charitable gifts before year-end to allow the deduction this year).

TABLE 13.2 New Contribution Limits for Traditional and Roth IRAs

Tax Year	If You're Under Age 50	If You're Age 50 and Older
2004	$3,000	$3,500
2005	$4,000	$4,500
2006	$4,000	$5,000
2007	$4,000	$5,000
2008	$5,000	$6,000

SUMMARY

- The new proposed contribution limits in your IRAs will give you more opportunity to save. Plus, you can now make up for lost savings opportunities if you find you are behind in your retirement planning.

- The new limit in 2004 for pretax contributions to 403(b), 457(a), or 401(k) plans is $13,000, and it will rise by $1,000 a year through 2006, when the maximum pretax contribution will be $15,000. After 2006, the maximum amount will be indexed for inflation.

- The catch-up amount in 2004 is $3,000, and it increases by $1,000 a year through 2006 (when the catch-up amount will be $5,000). Larger contributions will, of course, generally lead to larger retirement accumulations.

- You may wish to consult a qualified advisor to take advantage of expanded limits.

CHAPTER 14

USE YOUR EMPLOYER'S MONEY

According to the Employee Benefit Research Institute's 2000 Survey of Defined Contribution Plans, about 84 percent of companies that provide 401(k) plans also offer to match employees' contributions at some level. The most common match is 50 percent of the first 6 percent of pay that the employee contributes. This means that the match from the employer cannot exceed 3 percent of any employee's compensation. However, if the employee contributes less than 6 percent of pay, the employer's contribution will go down proportionately. That means an employee who contributes only 3 percent of pay will receive a match of 1.5 percent of pay. A fair number of employers offer matches of 100 percent or even higher. When you contribute $1, they also contribute at least $1 to your account.

Figure 14.1 diagrams the flow of employee contributions.

Some plans have a fixed match with a formula and others are discretionary. Employers sponsoring a discretionary profit-sharing plan can put in from year to year whatever they wish to. A discretionary match can be very beneficial for the employee when the employer operates in good faith. In bad years, there may not be any match, but in good years, there should be a healthy match. By the time you know if the company has had a good year, it's too late. So put your money in regardless.

If you're eligible to take part in your company's 401(k) plan, learn about the plan and your investment options and determine how much you should be saving to reach your retirement goal. On average, 401(k) plan participants funnel only around 6.7 percent of each paycheck into their plans. It may seem obvious, but you can't fully appreciate how important your contributions are until you see the consequences of not fully funding your 401(k). A few extra dollars going into your 401(k) plan now means a whole lot extra coming out.

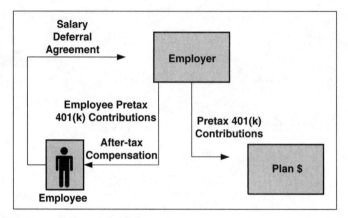

FIGURE 14.1
Employee Contribution Chart

Even if you don't receive the matching contributions but get just the tax advantage from Uncle Sam, it's still a great deal. You can put up to a maximum of $13,000 per year directly from your paycheck into your retirement account. The benefits of saving pretax dollars are huge. At present, if you are in the 28 percent tax bracket, putting in a $13,000 contribution represents $3,640 in tax savings. The result is that the $13,000 contribution really costs you only $9,360.

If—in addition to Uncle Sam's tax advantage—your employer makes contributions in the form of match or profit-sharing contributions, that makes your accumulation dynamic. In rare cases, in order to help employees, companies will make contributions for all employees, even those not contributing themselves.

READ YOUR PLAN'S FINE PRINT

Since these matched contributions are appearing more often as part of the overall compensation package, the 401(k) plan's design is critical to maximizing the value of a company's human resource dollar. Take the time to study your company's Summary Plan Description (SPD). Check to see if it specifies that your company's 401(k) plan has a *nondiscretionary* (mandatory) match; that means that the plan sponsor *must* make a contribution. Discretionary matches are usually based upon the company's being profitable.

Also, it's to your benefit to check out the definition of *compensation* in your SPD to determine the types of pay that will be matched. Regular pay, such as salary or hourly pay plus overtime, are the most common definitions. But compensation could also include commissions, bonuses, shift differentials, or special awards. Since matched funds have a ceiling of a specified percentage of your compensation, you want to be sure you're using the highest total in your computation. Increase your contribution accordingly to receive the full benefit of any matched money.

Learn how often and when matched money is deposited into your account. Many plans match your account only if you're still employed on specific dates—say, December 31, the last day of the year. You won't consider yourself very smart if you leave the company on December 29, only to find out that you were two days short of receiving the next quarterly, semiannual, or annual match contribution.

Matching in Company Stock

In many of the large plans (companies with thousands of employees), all or part of the employer's matched contribution is in the form of company stock. The belief is that employees who own shares in their company have a certain pride of ownership or interest in the company's well-being. And it demonstrates management's good faith in the company's future.

The bull market of the past 20 years masked the problems associated with owning company stock inside your 401(k) plan. As long as the market was going up, most companies' stocks soared in value along with 401(k) account balances, and employees were happy to have *free* shares of company stock contributed to their long-term retirement plans. Whether out of loyalty, ignorance, or convenience, more and more employees also opted to direct all or a large percentage of their own contributions to be invested in company stock.

According to the Profit-Sharing 401(k) Council of America, the single largest investment in 401(k) plans is employer's stock—39 percent of total assets. This high percentage of concentration and overweighting in a single equity resulted in an imprudent exposure to volatility and business risk.

When, in 2001, many publicly held companies dropped 40 to 60 percent of their value, 401(k) portfolios that weren't diversified over different asset classes suffered severe losses. Unlike defined benefit or pension plans, 401(k) contribution plans are *not* required by law to *diversify* their holdings— although there is now a rush to do that.

What happened at Enron is a glaring example of overweighting in one stock. About 63 percent of the employees' retirement money was invested in Enron stock. When Enron imploded, some $1 billion of savings disappeared. Now everyone is scrutinizing their portfolios to see if they are overweighted in one company and, to the extent they are, they're going to be shuffling assets around to reduce that exposure.

Of course, there are always two sides to every story. On one side of this issue are situations like the downfall of Enron, Global Crossing, or Lucent Technology. On the opposite side are the companies such as General Electric, Dell, Home Depot, and Microsoft, whose value grew by hundreds, if not thousands, of times over the last 10 years. For instance, $10,000 of Microsoft stock acquired in 1986 would be worth $5 million today!

A match in the form of company stock is *not* necessarily a bad thing. For every negative story related to company stock, a good one can be found. There's nothing wrong with owning company stock, so long as you accept the volatility.

Company Stock and Your Job

Most employees don't realize that they are placing a whopper of a bet on their employer when (1) their primary income depends on the company, (2) their benefits depend on it, and (3) all their 401(k) assets also depend on the value of its stock. The future security and value of each of these is tied together. Many of the companies whose shares have dropped 50 percent in value over the last 36 months have also downsized. So, not only did some participants lose significant value in their retirement plans, many lost their income and benefits as well.

In order to recover from a 50 percent loss, a 100 percent gain must occur. And, that's possible over time. But, if you're 59 years old, planning to retire, and had 60 percent of your 401(k) plan assets in Enron, you're sunk. You don't have the time to make up for losses that you sustained. (See Table 14.1 for the percentage amounts needed to regain such losses.)

TABLE 14.1 Regaining Your Loss

If You Lose This Much	You'll Need to Earn This Much to Break Even
10%	11%
20%	25%
30%	43%
40%	67%
50%	100%
60%	150%
70%	233%
80%	400%
90%	900%

Correct through diversification

The way to correct an overweighting in company stock is to diversify a percentage of your 401(k) assets into some other investment that tends to move dissimilarly to your company stock. This may seem like common sense, but, in fact, it was a dramatic breakthrough in investment methodology when Harry Markowitz developed his Nobel Prize–winning theory back in the 1950s.

Markowitz demonstrated that, to the extent that securities in a portfolio do *not* move in concert with each other, their individual risks could be effectively diversified away.

If you leave your company and you have shares of company stock in your 401(k) plan, you can either (1) transfer the stock to an IRA or liquidate the stock and transfer it to your new 40l(k) plan, or (2) take the stock at that time. If you take the stock, you will pay ordinary income tax on the stock's basis (what it cost you to buy it, not its appreciated value). The new capital gains tax rates often make it better to pay ordinary income tax on your stock's basis now and sell it later, when you will be taxed at a 15 percent rate, or possibly lower, depending on your income. This beats paying the ordinary income tax rate of up to 35 percent. If you elect to not take the stock, there will be no tax at that time, but you will pay ordinary tax on the full value of the stock when it is later distributed.

Company stock inside your 401(k) plan

- If you have the option to choose between a matching contribution of stock or cash, choose cash—for its liquidity as well as your ability to direct its investment. (Remember: you are already betting your wages on the future of your employer, and you may also be participating in their stock option plan!)

- If your plan sponsor requires that company stock must be held for a certain period, even after it is fully vested inside the plan, *rebalance* your percentage of stock ownership in your overall 401(k) plan as soon as possible.

- Evaluate your tax options concerning company stock if you leave your employer—whether you change jobs or retire.

SUMMARY

- Don't turn down free money! Understand the parameters of your company match.
- Know what types of pay will be matched.
- Be sure you are diversified when your match is company stock.

PART FIVE

ACTIVE INVESTMENT VEHICLES

These chapters explain the various actively managed investment vehicles and how they work. Maybe this is overly simplistic, but we think of these complicated products as nothing more than vehicles for transporting your money—the way a water truck is designed to carry water. Some do a good job; most don't.

There are many definitions you should know, but it doesn't necessarily mean you have to do anything with them. It just means that if someone else uses them, you should know what the consequences and the marketing motives behind them are.

CHAPTER 15

ACTIVELY MANAGED MUTUAL FUNDS

Think of an actively managed mutual fund as a financial intermediary that makes investments on your behalf. The mutual fund pools all its investors' funds together and buys stocks, bonds, or other assets on behalf of the group as a whole. Each investor receives a certificate of ownership and a regular statement of his or her account indicating the value of the shares of the total investment pool.

A mutual fund, in other words, is an investment company that makes investments on behalf of its participants who share common financial goals. Mutual funds continually issue new shares of the fund for sale to the public. The number of shares and the price are directly related to the value of the securities the mutual fund holds. A fund's share price can change from day to day, depending on the daily value of its underlying securities.

HOW MUTUAL FUNDS WORK

The manager of the mutual fund uses the pool of capital to buy a variety of stocks, bonds, or money market instruments based on the advertised financial objectives of the fund.

When you purchase mutual fund shares, you pay the *net asset value (NAV)*. This is the value of the fund's total investment, minus any debt, divided by the number of outstanding shares. For example, if the fund's investment value is $260,000, with no debt and 10,000 shares outstanding, then the NAV is $26 per share. The NAV is not a fixed figure because it must reflect the daily change in the price of the securities within the fund's portfolio.

A retail mutual fund includes thousands and often millions of shares. The NAV is calculated on a daily basis without commissions, in full and fractional units, with values moving up or down along with the stock and bond markets. The biggest mistake that first time investors make when buying an actively managed retail mutual fund is to look first (and sometimes only) at the prior performance of the fund or to pay too much attention to the current bond fund yield. Fund costs are an equally important factor in the return that you earn from a mutual fund. Fees are deducted from your investment. All other things being equal, high fees and other charges depress your returns.

Fees

Because of the large amounts of assets under management, investment companies are able to offer *economies of scale,* or competitive fee schedules, to their customers. The management fees charged depend on the complexity of the asset management demands. Foreign equity management requires substantially more research, specialized implementation, and greater transaction costs than the management of a U.S. government bond fund. Asset management fees reflect those differences. Equity mutual fund fees are higher than bond mutual fund fees.

Fee comparisons are particularly important. Remember to compare the proverbial apples to apples—in this case, similar equities to equity mutual funds, and similar bonds to bond mutual funds.

Keeping a Careful Eye on Costs

You can put more money to work for you in your investment by keeping a careful eye on costs. It's simply common sense—lower expenses translate to higher overall returns. The goal of the first time investor is to keep acquisition costs as low as possible.

Let's look at retail costs.

Sales charges

Sales charges (or *loads*) are commissions paid on the sale of mutual funds. In the past, all commissions were simply charged up front, but that has changed. There are now several ways that mutual fund companies charge fees.

The sales charge is subtracted from the initial mutual fund investment. A no-load fund does not have this charge, although other fees or service charges may be buried in its cost structure. Don't be misled: With the exception of true *no-load* funds, all mutual funds have a sales charge. Some are hidden; others are not. Let's talk about the ones that you can see. (Figure 15.1 diagrams how the no-load, front-end load, and back-end load funds operate.)

A *front-end load (A-share)* mutual fund charges a fee when an investor buys it. Loaded mutual funds can also be *back-end load*. These have a deferred sales charge and are sometimes known as *B shares*. This option has higher internal costs. If you decide to redeem your shares early, usually within five years, you pay a surrender charge.

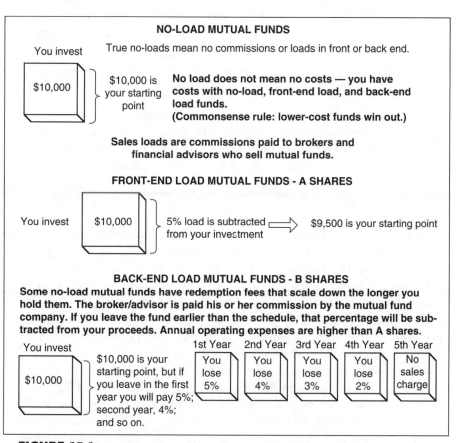

FIGURE 15.1
No-Load, Front-End Load, and Back-End Load Mutual Funds

A customer who redeems B shares in the first year of ownership would typically pay a 5 percent sales charge. This figure would drop by an equal amount each year. After six years, the shares could be redeemed without any charge. For large investments, you should never purchase B-share mutual funds, although there are brokers out there who will tell you it is better to invest in B shares, since you will not pay an up-front fee. If you invest a large amount, you will get a breakpoint inside an A-share mutual fund, and your annual costs will be lower.

- With A shares you pay the commission all at once.

- B shares have a contingent deferred sales charge. They are more popular with brokers because they receive the full commission while the customer thinks they have bought a no-load fund. What the investor doesn't realize is that every year an average of an extra 1 percent is added to the fund's operating expense to cover these commissions.

- C shares typically have even higher internal expenses and pay the selling broker up to 1 percent per year based on the amount of the assets. This fee comes directly from your investment performance.

The B and C shares may have no up-front fee, but there is a possible 1 percent deferred sales charge in year 1 (sometimes longer), and higher annual expenses (up to 1 percent extra per year). I would avoid them.

You will notice that the public offering price is different from the net amount invested. The offering price, known as the *ask price,* is greater than the fund's net asset value. The NAV is identified as the amount per share you would receive if you sold your shares.

No-load mutual funds do *not* mean *no cost.* B-share funds charge a redemption fee of up to 5 percent of the net asset value of the shares to cover expenses paid to the broker. Buying a no-load mutual fund is like doing your own plumbing work. You can save money if you know what you're doing, but if you don't have the required time and expertise, you can make a serious mistake. We highly recommend working with an investment advisor who can offer the same no-load funds. Another important fact to remember is that when you call the toll-free number of the mutual fund company with a question, you are serviced by an employee of the mutual fund company, and the advice you receive may be biased.

Investors who are truly devoted to learning about financial matters and who follow financial news, reading enough to keep themselves well informed, may be able to purchase funds for themselves. But most investors are not in this category and are well advised to seek professional guidance for their investments.

Operating Expenses

Fees pay for the operational costs of running a fund—employees' salaries, marketing, servicing the toll-free phone line, printing and mailing published materials, computers for tracking investments and account balances, accounting fees, and so on. A fund's operating expenses are quoted as a percentage of your investment; the percentage represents an annual fee or charge. You can find this number in a fund's prospectus in the fund expenses section, titled something like "Total Fund Operating Expenses." A mutual fund's operating expenses are normally invisible to investors because the expenses are deducted before any return is paid and are automatically charged on a daily basis.

Other Things You Should Know

Mutual funds do not escape share price declines during major market downturns.

Dividends

Dividends and capital gains (the profits from a sale of stock) are paid in proportion to the number of mutual fund shares you own. So even if you invest a few hundred dollars, you get the same investment return per dollar as those who invest millions. The problem is that you will have to pay taxes on this amount even if it is reinvested.

Prospectus and annual reports

Mutual fund companies produce information that can help you make decisions about mutual fund investments. All funds are required to issue a prospectus. You can now get a lot of the mutual fund prospectus information from the Internet. You can take a look at the funds' past performance and see what asset classes they really fall in. This legal document is reviewed and audited by the U.S. Securities and Exchange Commission.

Statements

Any mutual fund in which you participate will send you a year-end statement itemizing the income you've received. You should save this sheet along with other records of dividends, tax-exempt interest, and capital gains distributions, as well as records of the amounts received from the sale of shares for tax purposes.

Full-time professionals

When you invest in a mutual fund, you are hiring a group of active investment managers who try to make complex investment judgments and handle complicated trading, record-keeping, and safekeeping responsibilities for you.

Diversification

Diversification is only effective when applied to the various *asset classes*. Because retail funds are not academically defined, you may own a "diverse" portfolio of many stocks and/or bonds in the same asset class. A retail mutual fund is typically invested in 25 to 100 or more securities. This means you may be entirely invested, or heavily weighted, in just one asset class. It is only when you are invested in two or more asset classes that you can somewhat modulate your risk.

Low initial investment

Each mutual fund establishes the minimum amount required to make an initial investment, and then how much additional money is required when investors want to add more. A majority of mutual funds have low initial minimums, some less than $1,000.

Liquidity

One of the key advantages of mutual funds stems from the liquidity provided by this investment. You can sell your shares at any time, and mutual funds have a "ready market" for their shares. In addition, shareholders directly receive any dividend or interest payments earned by the fund.

Payments are usually made on a quarterly basis. When the fund manager sells some of the investments at a profit, the net gain is also distributed, but net losses are retained by the fund. Inside the mutual fund, when the dividends or capital gains are disbursed, the NAV is reduced by the disbursement.

Audited performance

All mutual funds are required to disclose historical data about the fund through their prospectuses—returns earned by the fund, operating expenses and other fees, and the fund's rate of trading turnover. The Securities and Exchange Commission (SEC) audits these disclosures for accuracy. Having the SEC on your side is like having a vigilant guard dog focused on the person who's responsible for your money. Remember, all mutual funds are registered investments. This does not mean that the SEC recommends them, but it does mean the SEC has reviewed them for abuse and fraud.

Automatic reinvestment

One of the major benefits of mutual funds is that dividends can be reinvested automatically and converted to more shares.

Switching

Switching, or an exchange privilege, is offered by most mutual funds through so-called family or umbrella plans. Switching from one mutual fund to another accommodates changes in investment goals as well as changes in the market and the economy. Again, this switching between mutual funds outside of your retirement or 401(k) plan has tax implications. For instance, when you redeem a Franklin Growth and Income Fund share and buy a Franklin NY Municipal Bond Fund share, you have to pay taxes on the gains if you earned any.

Low transaction costs

When an individual investor places an order to buy 300 shares of a $30 stock ($9,000 investment), he or she is likely to get a commission bill for about $204, or 2.3 percent of the value of the investment. Even at a discount broker, the commission is likely to cost between $82 (0.9 percent) and $107 (1.2 percent).

A retail mutual fund, on the other hand, is more likely to be buying 30,000 to 300,000 shares at a time! Its commission costs often run in the vicinity of one-tenth of the commission you would pay at a discount broker. Where your commission might be $0.35 per share, the mutual fund would only pay $0.05 per share or even less.

No risk of bankruptcy

A situation in which the demand for money back (liabilities) exceeds the value of a fund's investments (assets) cannot occur with a mutual fund. The value can fluctuate, but this variation doesn't lead to the failure or bankruptcy of a mutual fund company. In fact, since the Investment Company Act of 1940 was passed to regulate the mutual fund industry, no fund has ever gone under.

In contrast, hundreds of banks and dozens of insurance companies have failed in the past two decades alone. Banks and insurers can fail because their liabilities can exceed their assets. When a bank makes too many loans that go sour at the same time and depositors want their money back, the bank fails. Likewise, if an insurance company makes several poor investments or underestimates the number of claims that will be made by insurance policyholders, then it, too, can fail. But mutual funds are held in separate accounts and are not part of an insurance company's assets.

Custodian bank

A *custodian* is a separate organization that holds the specific securities in which a mutual fund is invested independent of the mutual fund company. The employment of a custodian ensures that the fund management company can't embezzle your funds or use assets from a better-performing fund to subsidize a poor performer.

FUND CLOSURES ON THE RISE

A record 226 mutual funds were shut down in 2001. Increased industry competition and growing investor impatience were cited as the primary reasons. Half of the funds closed were bond funds, and nearly one-third were funds investing overseas. However, bond or overseas funds generally have a hard time attracting investors, and that closure rate is not unusual.

New funds must attract and keep investors to stay solvent. In general, funds must have around $40 million in assets to be profitable, so the first few years are critical to a fund's continued longevity, regardless of its performance. A $40 million fund with a 1 percent expense ratio only provides $400,000 to meet trading and operating costs. As new industries, such as those related to biotech activities or the Internet, take hold, fund companies generally respond with a niche fund to satisfy the investor's demand. Although the 226 funds that were shut down were less than 1 percent of the funds available, it is a considerably larger number than we have seen in past years.

Investor impatience is considered to be the impetus for the close of almost all the equity funds. Stellar returns in 1999 and 2000 (over 170 funds posted triple-digit returns) increased investors' expectations and reduced their tolerance for poor performers. The overwhelming reason cited for exiting a fund was lack of growth in a booming market. With 36 months of declining markets behind us, many investors are expected to move funds into money market or fixed-income funds until a reversal is well established. As 2003 proved, this was exactly the wrong strategy! Our Ultra-Aggressive stock account was up over 40 percent.

HOW THE VARIOUS PARTIES TO A MUTUAL FUND WORK TOGETHER

After you have written your check to the retail mutual fund company, or selected your choice inside your 401(k) plan, the mutual fund company sends that check on your behalf to an organization functioning as a *transfer agent*. Here your investment is recorded and processed, and the real safeguards come into play. The agent transfers the money, not to the mutual fund's portfolio manager (the individual or firm that makes the investment decisions, technically known as the *investment advisor*), but to a *custodian bank*. Once that custodian bank receives the money, it notifies the mutual fund that new money is available for investment. The fund manager checks a daily account balance sheet, and "new" monies are invested according to the mutual fund's investment policy.

The Investment Company Act of 1940's requirement of independent custody for each mutual fund's assets has turned out to be the key provision that has sheltered the industry from potential trouble for half a century.

Separate custody means a mutual fund's parent company can go belly-up without any loss to the fund's shareholders, because their assets are held apart from other funds and apart from the parent fund.

Contrast this business structure with the far less restrictive setup between, say, individual investors and a real estate promoter, or investors and a stockbroker who may have direct access to her or his clients' accounts. In any number of notorious incidents, individuals in such positions have taken the money and run.

The tax-sheltered limited partnerships of the 1970s and 1980s were an excellent example of a terrible business structure. During those years, many unregulated and unregistered limited partnerships were formed, and investors sent their money directly to the limited partnership company. An unscrupulous promoter could simply write himself or herself a check. Financial scandals were numerous.

A money manager of a mutual fund has no direct access to the investors' cash. The fund manager only decides how to invest shareholders' money. The custodian who controls the underlying securities allows them to be traded or exchanged with other institutional investors only after getting proper documentation from the manager. The upshot of independent custody is that it's very difficult for a fund manager to use the money for personal purposes.

The Investment Company Act adds other layers of investor protection as well. Independent accountants must regularly audit every fund. Members of a fund's board of directors, who serve as modern-day trustees, negotiate prudent contract terms with the fund's service providers and generally oversee the operation. The SEC has the power to inspect funds and bring enforcement action against those who break the rules.

In addition, mutual fund firms have legions of compliance lawyers— essentially in-house cops—paid to make sure portfolio managers, traders, and others follow the rules.

A Code of Conduct

Under SEC rules, fund managers are required to abide by strict codes of conduct. The codes require advance reporting of personal securities transactions so that there can be no conflict of interest between a manager's personal trades and what she or he does with the fund's securities. Otherwise, managers could "front-run" their own funds, personally buying or selling securities before the fund traded them in, to the managers' gain and possibly the fund's loss. To avoid such potential for self-dealing— that is, favoring one fund at the expense of another—the SEC has set down strict guidelines for when funds in the same company trade a security between themselves rather than on the open market.

HOW TO READ A PROSPECTUS

A mutual fund is required by the federal government to provide a *prospectus* that describes its investment objectives, strategies, and risks. Any misstatements or omissions can lead to stiff penalties. Thus, prospectuses tend to be written in jargon-filled legalese and are difficult to read. A recent ruling now forces a fund to provide easy-to-comprehend interpretations of its prospectus. Be sure to check that the date is current—such documents must be updated at least once per year.

Following is a rundown of the parts of a mutual fund prospectus.

Investment Objective

At the core of the prospectus is a description of the fund's investments and the portfolio manager's philosophy. The objective should outline what types of securities the fund buys and the policies regarding the quality of those investments. If the fund has more than 25 percent of its assets in one industry or holds bonds rated below investment quality, these policies must be included in the prospectus.

A global equity fund, for example, earns a high level of total return through investments in world capital markets. A typical balanced fund strives to obtain income equally with capital growth, while the investment objective of a long-term municipal bond fund is to preserve capital by seeking a high level of interest income exempt from federal income tax.

Performance

This bottom-line information on how funds have fared over the last decade shows you what you would have earned in per-share dividends and capital gains distributions, and any increase or decrease in the value of that share during the year. The portfolio turnover rate reveals how actively the fund trades securities. The higher the turnover, the greater the fund's brokerage costs.

Risk

Different investors can tolerate various risk levels. In this section of the prospectus, the fund should describe the potential for risk. For instance, a fund that invests in only one portion of the economy may offer greater risk than a highly diversified fund, while a fund that invests in well-established companies may be less risky than one that favors start-up companies.

Other risks are associated with specific types of funds or securities. Bond funds are susceptible to interest rate changes, while fixed-income savings and investment vehicles are subject to inflation risks.

Fees

Management and accounting fees and the cost of printing and mailing reports to shareholders are internal charges that should be evaluated. Generally, a company that keeps its expenses—excluding sales fees—at 1 percent or less of its assets is considered a low-cost fund. A fund whose expenses are above 1.5 percent of its assets is viewed as high-cost.

Fees are required to be summarized in a table in the front of the prospectus. Other charges to consider are minimum fees for subsequent investments or fees for switching from one fund to another in the same family. This section of the prospectus will also tell you if features such as check writing or automatic investing are available.

Management

When you're putting money into a mutual fund, you're paying for professional management. Evaluate the fund management's investment philosophy and what asset class the fund is in.

Buying or Selling Shares

This information details how to get in and out of a fund and whether there's a charge for redeeming shares.

Additional information, such as securities in the fund's portfolio at the end of its fiscal year, is included in a Statement of Additional Information, also called Part B of the prospectus. Funds must provide this information free on request.

Other tools to evaluate mutual funds include news accounts and the fund's annual report. Make sure you are comparing *apples to apples.* Magazines measure funds during different time periods and use different criteria, which could affect a fund's ranking.

The SEC is recommending the creation of a clearly written one-page summary to accompany these documents and demanding the use of plain English. Fund companies may distribute a streamlined profile that includes a mutual fund's vital statistics, fees, investment objectives, a 10-year bar chart showing the fund's performance, a table comparing its performance to a market index, and a description of the risk involved in the investment.

This is a victory for investors, since, with the estimated 10,000 or more mutual funds to choose from, comparing possible investments can be overwhelming.

MAJOR TYPES OF MUTUAL FUNDS

In the current universe of approximately 10,000 retail mutual funds, there are funds that invest in growth stocks, or smaller growth stocks, or stocks that pay high dividends. Mutual funds that invest in corporate and government bonds are also available.

Retail Actively Managed Stock Funds

Stock mutual funds invest only in stocks. (They are also called *equity funds.*) Don't be confused by the names. These are not academically defined terms or asset class funds. These funds are active in management and follow the premise that the managers somehow can uncover mispricing or time the market. Since the overwhelming majority of funds fall in this camp, you must be able to recognize them.

Hopefully the picture is becoming clearer regarding how fund titles mislead investors. There are some strict rules being proposed. But when you hear *Fidelity Magellan* or *Putnam Voyager,* what does it really tell you? Are they going on a voyage? No. You don't have a clue as to what you're investing in. There is a proposed federal regulation that would require mutual funds to have at least 80 percent of their assets in securities that match the name of the fund, instead of the 65 percent now required. We emphasize this point to keep you from being misled by fund names.

Family of funds

Many retail mutual fund management companies offer a number of different types of funds under one roof, often referred to as a *family of funds.* A fund family might include a growth stock fund, an aggressive growth stock fund, a fund that invests in stocks and bonds, a tax-exempt bond fund, a money market fund, and perhaps many others. Most mutual fund families permit their customers to exchange from one fund to another within the group for a fee, should their personal investment objectives change.

Despite endless variations, there are basically three broad categories of mutual funds: those aimed at providing immediate income, those oriented toward long-term growth or appreciation, and those that stress tax-free returns. The retail fund's marketing department writes up the objectives and they are stated at the opening of the prospectus, indicating whether the fund emphasizes high or low risk, stability, or speculation. Retail funds generally fall into one of nine marketing categories: growth, growth and income, income, bond, money market, tax free, metals, foreign, and specialized.

Growth funds

This type of fund claims to stress capital appreciation rather than immediate income. Dividend payouts will typically be low.

A typical growth fund would be the Janus Fund. This is a fund that consists of U.S. large-cap stocks and has as its primary objective to equal the return of the large growth companies.

Aggressive growth funds

This is another marketing term. Aggressive growth retail funds invest in smaller, lesser-known companies. As the name implies, these funds are invested for maximum capital gains, capital appreciation, and performance.

This type of portfolio can be highly volatile and speculative. The old adage "high risk, high return" would fit. Don't confuse aggressive funds with small-cap asset class funds.

When you see that this asset class has outperformed growth funds, it doesn't mean that your fund has. You should be aware that these returns also come with higher volatility, meaning the roller-coaster ride has much bigger dips.

Balanced funds

Balanced fund is a marketing term for an actively managed retail fund portfolio that stresses three marketing goals: income, capital appreciation, and preservation of capital. This type of fund balances holdings such as bonds, convertible securities, and preferred stock as well as common stock. The mix varies depending on the active manager's view of the economy and market conditions.

The theory here is that the managers will have a better crystal ball than you at home, since they make big bucks and sit in front of a computer terminal all day looking at graphs.

Growth and income (value) funds

These are marketing names that describe actively managed retail funds that combine stocks and bonds; this type of retail fund makes a serious effort at capturing both modest income and a long-term rise in the stock market. These active managers are typically looking for their version of growth companies that pay high dividends. Their hope is these funds will have lower volatility and a more predictable and consistent return. But in recent years, *growth and income* has become synonymous with value fund, a fund that invests in distressed stocks that typically have higher dividend yields than growth stocks.

Income funds

The advertised investment objectives of income funds are safety and income, rather than capital appreciation, but we're skeptical. These actively managed retail income funds invest in corporate bonds or government-insured mortgages. If they own any stocks at all, these are usually preferred shares.

The danger is chasing higher yields and not looking at the risks. For instance, in the mid-1980s, fund managers paid a premium for high-yielding bonds, so when interest rates dropped and the bonds were called, the investors lost principal.

Utility funds

Actively managed retail utility funds invest in stocks in utility companies around the country. Like bonds, utility stocks generate high income. Utilities are marketed as defensive investments in case bad things happen. The concept here is that everyone needs electricity, gas, water, etc. The problem is that we may need them, but sometimes the amount of regulation on these companies and the cost of distributing energy can negate the benefit of constant demand. Utility funds need to be treated as risk-based investments as any stock mutual fund would.

Specialty funds

Specialty fund is a major marketing term that means nothing. Specialty funds are also called *sector funds* because they tend to invest in stocks in specific industries. Sector funds should be avoided unless you are a speculator. Investing in stocks of a single industry defeats a major purpose of investing in any mutual fund—you're giving up the benefits of whatever diversification you get. A sector fund would be something like a high-tech fund, an India fund, or a gold fund.

Specialty funds tend to carry much higher expenses than other retail mutual funds.

Gold funds

These actively managed retail mutual funds are highly speculative. The downside is that gold pays no dividends and can be highly volatile.

Global equity funds

U.S. international and global funds are actively invested outside of the United States. The term *international* typically means that a fund can invest anywhere in the world except the United States. The term *global* generally implies that a fund can invest anywhere in the world, including the United States.

Hybrid funds

Hybrid fund is just a marketing term for a fund that invests in a mixture of different types of securities. Most commonly, hybrid funds invest in bonds and stocks. These actively managed retail funds are typically known as *balanced* or *asset allocation funds*. Balanced funds generally try to maintain a fairly constant percentage of investment in stocks and bonds.

Asset allocation funds

Asset allocation fund is a marketing term that is used to sell a mix of different investment concepts according to the active portfolio manager's expectations of what sector of the market will be in favor. Depending on the manager, these could also be called *market-timing funds*. No one can accurately predict the actions of the market.

Principal-protected mutual funds (PPFs)

Offered by ING, Scudder, and other major investment companies, these too are actively managed retail funds that guarantee that investors will not lose any of their principal if they keep their money invested for a specified length of time.

Most of the roughly two dozen PPFs now on the market earmark a large slice of their portfolios for zero-coupon bonds (bought at less than face value, they pay off in full at maturity).

Many PPFs smack investors with loads, or sales charges, upwards of 5.75 percent. That's added to their generally high ongoing expense—an average of 1.5 percent a year, considerably more than other sorts of funds. By comparison, Vanguard Wellington Fund, a well-known domestic hybrid, currently charges investors 0.36 percent in annual expenses.

Another concern is the 5- to 10-year period for which you must hold a PPF before you can get back your guaranteed principal.

Retail Actively Managed Bond Mutual Funds

Bonds are essentially IOUs. When you buy a bond, you are lending your money to a corporation or government agency. A retail bond mutual fund is nothing more than a large group (pack) of bonds. Most retail bond funds invest in bonds of similar maturity (the number of years to elapse before the borrower must pay back the money you lend). The names of most bond funds include a word or two to provide clues about the average length of maturity of their bonds.

For example, a short-term bond fund concentrates its investments in bonds maturing in the next few years. An intermediate-term fund generally holds bonds that come due within 7 years. The bonds in a long-term fund usually mature in 10 years or so.

Retail global bond funds

These are actively managed retail bond funds that invest in foreign as well as in U.S. bonds.

Money Market Funds

Money market funds are the safest type of retail mutual funds if you are worried about the risk of losing your principal. Money market funds are like bank savings accounts in that the value of your investment does not fluctuate. This type of fund could be used to fill the part of an asset class.

Retail Index Funds

Think of these funds as whole baskets of stocks, representing the various stock market indexes. The S&P 500 Index Fund is by far the most common index fund for both institutional and individual investors. It tracks the performance of the Standard & Poor's 500 Index, a capitalization-weighted index of 500 large U.S. stocks. It is estimated that over 95 percent of all retail indexed monies are invested in S&P 500 Index funds.

Following is a list of the indexes:

- The *Wilshire 5000* includes all 5,000 stocks on the New York Stock Exchange Annex as well as over-the-counter (OTC) stocks. The Wilshire essentially takes the entire market as an index.
- The *Russell 2000* is sorted by capitalization size, beginning with 1,001 through 3,000 of the largest stocks. In other words, this index is composed of the 2,000 largest companies after disregarding the 1,000 largest. Typically quoted as a small company index, it is really more of a mid-cap index since there are 4,000 smaller companies in the United States.

- The *Nasdaq 100* is the National Association of Securities Dealers index of stocks traded over the counter via its automatic quoting system, Nasdaq. The Nasdaq 100 measures price changes in 100 of the largest OTC industrial stocks.

- The *S&P 500,* also known as *Standard & Poor's Composite Index* of 500 stocks, consists of the New York Stock Exchange-listed companies plus a few of the American Stock Exchange and over-the-counter stocks. Also, 7 percent of the companies are non-U.S. companies and investment companies that can be affected by currency translations. One of the downsides of the S&P 500 is that the companies are chosen by committee, rather than by market efficiency.

- *Morgan Stanley EAFE* (Europe, Australia, and Far East) *Index* is actually two subindexes of 1,000 stocks traded in Europe and the Pacific Basin; it is the most commonly used index for mutual funds that invest in foreign stocks.

Other types of index funds

Warning: Be cautious with the index hybrids we are about to discuss. Recent news indicates that some brokers are using these strategies to combat index investing and are advising their clients that they can trade these as they would a stock (which you now know doesn't work in the long run).

Anyway, these hybrids are called *SPDRs,* "spiders," for Standard & Poor's 500 Depositary Receipts, available on the American Stock Exchange. SPDRs combine the advantage of index funds with the superior trading and flexibility of common stocks.

SPDRs buy and sell shares only to adjust the changes in the composition of the S&P index without the need to meet investor redemptions as an index fund does. When individual investors want to take money out, they simply sell shares on the American Stock Exchange.

If you want an index other than the S&P 500, there's Standard & Poor's Mid-Cap 400 Depositary Receipts; and, globally, there are SPDRs called World Equity Benchmark Shares (WEBS) at select major international equity markets.

The ticker symbol for SPDRs is SPY; for the Mid-Cap, MDY, and for Diamonds (based on the Dow Jones averages), DIA.

For information on SPDRs, call 800-The-Amex or click on www.amex.com. On WEBS, call 800-810-WEBS.

Here is a list of companies that provide financial services:

Vanguard Group, 800-962-5160, www.vanguard.com

Charles Schwab and Co., 800-806-8481, www.schwab.com

Fidelity Investments, www.fidelity.com (you can ask for a rollover IRA kit, kit for retirees, mutual fund kit, brokerage kit, and retirement planning for small business)

Microsoft Money '98 Financial Office, www.pcmall.com/money98

National Discount Brokers, 800-888–3999, www.ndb.com

THE RATING GAME

The mutual fund rating game works in much the same way as the old dating game on television. Investors use ratings of actively managed retail mutual funds that are listed in newspapers and magazines as a guide to help them pick funds that are the right ones for their portfolios. Beware!

For example, a recent study[1] by Brown, Harlow, and Starks found that retail mutual fund managers increased the risk level of their portfolios right in the middle of the year if they were not ranked among peer group performance leaders. If they were successful and their funds' ranks improved, the managers would get bonuses and the fund would get increased assets from investors. If the gamble failed, then the fund performed worse than it would have if no changes had been made. But because funds are a winner-take-all industry, fund managers feel it's worth the gamble to take that kind of risk.

The mutual fund rating game is a loser's game.

A BAROMETER OF UPS AND DOWNS

When the stock market is said to be up 10 points, what is usually meant is that the venerable Dow Jones Industrial Average (DJIA) went up 10 points. The DJIA is based on the average prices paid for 30 blue-chip stocks.

[1] Kelly Brown, Van Harlow, and Laurel Starks, "On Tournaments and Temptations, An Analysis of Managerial Incentives in the Mutual Fund Industry," *Journal of Finance* (March 1996):85–110.

What Is the Dow Jones Industrial Average?

Most investors have never heard of 29 of today's companies in the widely watched Dow average. Only one stock, General Electric Co., remains from the original 12 chosen in 1896. The Dow reflects the U.S. economy. When the Dow average ended its first day at 40.94, 12 years before Henry Ford made his first Model T, the average included such stalwarts as U.S. Leather and Tennessee Coal & Iron.

If it hadn't changed, the average wouldn't be an accurate barometer of the economy. It's true that there are only 30 companies, but they are 30 of the best-known and largest companies:

3M Company	Home Depot
Alcoa Incorporated	Honeywell International
Altria Group	IBM
American Express	Intel
AT&T	International Paper
Boeing	Johnson & Johnson
Caterpillar	J.P. Morgan Chase
Citigroup	McDonald's
Coca-Cola	Merck
DuPont	Microsoft
Eastman Kodak	Procter & Gamble
Exxon Mobil	SBC Communications
General Electric	United Technologies
General Motors	Wal-Mart
Hewlett-Packard	Walt Disney

Note: Philip Morris changed its name to Altria Group in January 2003.

Narrow as it is, the Dow Jones Industrial Average is easily the most popular gauge of the U.S. stock market for the media. The public follows the Dow more than Wall Street does. All of today's television networks acknowledge the popularity of the Dow as a yardstick by citing it on their nightly news reports.

The Dow industrials are big brand names, and in that way they have become synonymous with the fortunes of U.S. stocks generally. Investors who want to know if stocks are up or down ask about the Dow just as customers ask for a soft drink or facial tissue. We ask for a Coke, or we ask for a Kleenex.

Rival stock market averages and indexes don't have the Dow's cachet. That was even more true in the 1930s. People watched the stocks, but in most people's minds, the Dow was an indicator of what the market was doing.

Dow Jones, publisher of the *Wall Street Journal,* helps ensure that the Dow industrials stay prominent. The biggest newspaper in the country, with a daily circulation of 1.8 million readers, the *Journal* usually features its average first when it is writing about the stock market. The *Wall Street Journal* promoted the Dow average, and once a generation or two was trained on it, it just became the easy thing to follow.

To understand the importance of the Dow Jones Industrial Average, investors must return to the closing years of the nineteenth century. Charles Dow was ahead of his time. When he decided in 1896 to create the industrial average, he sensed where the country was going. At the time, the NYSE did very little trading of industrial shares. They were too low-brow and were considered speculative—much as we would consider junk bonds today. The only stocks regarded as investment-grade were railroads and utilities. By giving investors a measuring instrument, Dow helped popularize stocks in general.

Big business was relatively unknown before 1880, when most companies were family owned. The next 25 years saw the creation of national businesses, companies such as General Electric and U.S. Steel. Charles Dow recognized the growing importance of manufacturing and the opportunities available to investors.

The Dow average's popularity grew because investors needed a way to compare their gains with the overall stock market. Professional money managers think of the Dow as a crude average because no allowance is made for the size of a company.

It's also possible that Dow Jones' editors will broaden the average by enlarging it beyond 30 names. After all, they expanded the original list of 12 companies to 20 in 1920, and enlarged the average to the current number of 30 companies in late 1928. It's not been a static index. They've added companies and taken companies out. Generally, when they update the index, they add a company that's a little more responsive to what's going on in the economy.

The Standard & Poor's 500 Index, the Value Line Composite Index, and the New York Stock Exchange Composite Index are ostensibly more accurate indexes and are also more widely followed. These are broader-based, which should make them somewhat more accurate in a large market. Since the DJIA consists of only 30 large companies, it may not truly reflect market performance.

Survivor Bias

In a typical year, about 1 actively managed retail mutual fund in 28 kicks the bucket. Each time that happens, the rating services like Lipper Analytical and Morningstar expunge the dead fund from their historical averages, wiping away that fund's returns for all previous years.

These are the funds with poor performance records. And though the rating services compute their category averages as if these funds never existed, they of course lived real lives and collected money from real shareholders who earned real returns (or, should I say, real bad returns). Though they are dead, their often horrifying performances continue to cast a shadow over the fund tables.

This statistical trip is called *survivor bias,* and the term is fitting for funds. The long-term "average" returns of fund categories, as now computed, ignore all the real-world investors who buy funds that crash and burn.

Mark Carhart, assistant professor of finance at the University of Southern California Graduate School of Business, in his 1995 dissertation, "Survivor Bias and Persistence of Mutual Fund Performance," writes of the explosion in new funds but the steady disappearance of others purged from databases.

Carhart precisely documents the havoc that "zombie" funds wreak on "average" category returns. Other researchers had already shown that survivor bias can skew fund averages, but Carhart has done them one better. He has painstakingly constructed a database of all diversified U.S. equity funds (at least those for which any records could be found) that existed at any time between January 1962 and December 1995.

Over the 34-year period he examined, out of a grand total of 2,071 stock funds that were ever open for business, 725 disappeared. Put another way: 35 percent of all stock funds went kaput, for an average annual mortality rate of 3.6 percent.

Counting only the survivors, as most performance tables do, the "average" fund returned 10.7 percent compounded annually from 1962 through 1995. That suggests the typical fund manager was at least earning his or her keep, since the S&P 500 Index returned "only" 10.6 percent compounded annually over the same period. (The S&P index, by the way, suffers almost no survivor bias, mainly because very few stocks drop out of the index for reasons of poor performance and because its average annual returns are not restated every time the membership of the 500 changes.)

The message: Buy an index fund and, history suggests, you've got a better than 3-to-1 chance of outperforming actively managed funds because managed funds charge higher expenses than passive funds.

Since equity mutual funds are made up of many individual stocks, the subject of the next chapter is individual stocks and how they work.

SUMMARY

- A mutual fund, in other words, is an investment company that makes investments on behalf of its participants who share common financial goals.

- Mutual funds continually issue new shares of the fund for sale to the public.

- The number of shares and the price are directly related to the value of the securities the mutual fund holds.

- A fund's share price can change from day to day, depending on the daily value of its underlying securities.

- The manager of the mutual fund uses the pool of capital to buy a variety of stocks, bonds, or money market instruments based on the advertised financial objectives of the fund.

- When you purchase mutual fund shares, you pay the *net asset value*. This is the value of the fund's total investment, minus any debt, divided by the number of outstanding shares.

- The biggest mistake that first time investors make when buying an actively managed retail mutual fund is to look first (and sometimes only look) at the prior performance of the fund or to pay too much attention to the current bond fund yield.

- The sales charge is called a *load* and is subtracted from the initial mutual fund investment. A no-load fund does not have this charge, although other fees or service charges may be included in its cost structure. Don't be misled. All mutual funds have operating expense charges.

- Retail stock mutual funds are not academically defined asset class funds. They are active in management and follow the premise that the managers somehow can uncover mispricing or time the market. Since the overwhelming majority of funds fall in this camp, you must be able to recognize them.

CHAPTER 16

INDIVIDUAL STOCKS

A stock is a security issued by a corporation or by a government as a means of raising long-term capital. The ownership is divided into a certain number of shares; the corporation issues stock certificates that show how many shares are owned. The stockholders own the company and elect a board of directors to manage it for them.

The capital that a company raises through the sale of these shares entitles the holder to dividends and to other rights of ownership, such as voting rights. Prices of stocks change according to general business conditions and the earnings and future prospects of the companies that have issued the stock.

If the business is doing well, stockholders may be able to sell their stock for a profit. If it is not, they may have to take a loss when they sell.

Large corporations may have many thousands of stockholders. Their stock is bought and sold in marketplaces called *stock exchanges*. A stock exchange occupies an important position in our country's financial system by providing a mechanism for converting savings into physical and portfolio investment. It also performs two major functions. It provides a primary or new-issues market, in which new capital can be raised by issuing financial securities. It also provides a secondary market for trading existing securities, which facilitates transferability of securities from sellers to buyers.

The shares of stock represent the value of the corporation. When the corporation has made a profit, the directors may divide the profit among stockholders as dividends, or they may decide to use it to expand the business.

Over the long term, stocks have historically outperformed all other investments. From 1926 to 2001, the stock market returned an average annual 10.7 percent gain. The next best-performing asset class, bonds, returned 5.3 percent.

OWNING A STOCK

Own a share of stock, and you are a part owner in the company, with a claim (however small it may be) on every asset, and every penny in earnings. Nevertheless, it's that ownership structure that gives a stock its value. If stockowners didn't have a claim on earnings, then stock certificates would be worth no more than the paper they're printed on.

Dividends are paid to the stockholders out of the corporation's profits. When profits are used to expand the business, the directors and stockholders may issue more stock to show that there is more money invested in the business. This new stock will be divided among the old stockholders as stock dividends. As a company's earnings improve, investors are willing to pay more for the stock.

Stocks are issued in two forms: *common* and *preferred.*

Common Stock

Common stock represents true ownership shares in a company. Stockholders share directly in growing company profits through increasing dividends and an appreciation in the value of the stock itself. As the holder of common stock, you are a part owner in the company issuing the stock. The purchaser of common stock not only receives a share of any dividends paid by the corporation, but also has the right to vote for corporate directors who, in turn, choose the corporate officers and set the corporation's policies. When a broker uses the term *stock,* he or she is normally referring to *common* stock. Common stock will be the bulk of investments in most mutual funds.

Preferred Stock

Preferred stock, like common stock, represents ownership or equity, and not debt. Preferred stockholders have a claim on profits that precedes—or is preferred to—the claim of the common stockholder. The preferred stockholder has a right to receive *specified* dividends (for example, 10 percent of the face value of the preferred share) before the common stockholder can be paid any dividend at all.

On the other hand, the preferred stockholder does not have the possibility of large gains open to the common stockholder. While the common stockholder may hope for rising dividends if the corporation prospers, the preferred shareholder will at most receive the specified dividend.

If the preferred stockholders share with the common stockholders in dividends beyond the specified percentage, the stock is called *participating preferred.*

Preferred stock may also be cumulative. That is, if there are no dividends given in a year, the preferred stockholders must be given double their dividend the next year. This is paid before anything is paid to the common stockholders. This principle continues for as many years as dividends are not paid.

More Stock Terminology

Sizing up a stock

The most common way academics size up a stock is to categorize companies by their market capitalization and call them micro-caps, small-caps, mid-caps, and large-caps, with "cap" being short for *capitalization.* As we have discussed earlier, different-sized companies have shown different returns over time, with the returns being higher the smaller the company. Most distinctions look something like this:

The majority of publicly traded companies fall in the micro or small categories.

Category	Market Cap
Micro-cap	Less than $300 million
Small-cap	$300 million to $1 billion
Mid-cap	$1 billion to $10 billion
Large-cap	Greater than $10 billion

Earnings per share (EPS)

Earnings, also known as *net income or net profit,* are the money that is left over after a company pays all its bills. For many investors, earnings are the most important factor in analyzing a company. To allow for apples-to-apples comparisons, those who look at earnings use *earnings per share*

(EPS). You calculate the earnings per share by dividing the dollar amount of the earnings a company reports over the past 12 months by the number of shares it currently has outstanding. Example, if Pet Corp. has 1 million shares outstanding and has earned $1 million in the past 12 months, it has an EPS of $1.00 ($1 million ÷ 1 million shares = $1).

Price/earnings (P/E) ratio

The *price/earnings (P/E) ratio* measures the stock's price divided by the company's earnings per share (EPS) over the past 12 months. If a company is earning $1 per share and the public is buying the stock at $10 per share, the market price is divided by the earnings. In this case, 10 is divided by 1; this tells us that the stock is selling at 10 times earnings. If you invest in this company and pay $10, theoretically you are paying 10 years' worth of earnings to own it. When the market is low, you will see a P/E around 10; in a bull market, the average is 25 to 30 times earnings.

Dividend payout ratio

This is the ratio of a company's indicated annual cash dividend per share to its earnings per share (EPS), and it can range from 0 to 100 percent. A utility that pays out $4 in dividends for each $5 of earnings would have a payout of 80 percent. The payout is greater than 50 percent for the average large industrial company and even higher for the typical utility. The higher the dividend payout, however, the less room there is for dividend increases, since less profit is available to reinvest for future growth.

Dividend yield

Dividend yield is the ratio of a company's annual cash dividends divided by its current stock price expressed in the form of a percentage. To get the expected annual cash dividend payment, take the next expected quarterly dividend payment and multiply that by 4. For instance, if a $10 stock is expected to pay a 25-cent quarterly dividend next quarter, you just multiply 25 cents by 4 to get $1 and then divide this by $10 to get a dividend yield of 10 percent.

This measures the annual dividend divided by the stock price. By way of another example, if a utility's dividend is $4 and its stock sells for $50 per share, the yield will be 8 percent. When the EPS (in general) is high, yields will be low.

Many newspapers and online quote services will include dividend yield as one of the variables. If you are uncertain whether the current quoted dividend yield reflects a recent increase in the dividend a company may have made, you can call the company and ask them what the dividend per share they expect to pay next quarter will be.

Sector

Standard & Poor's, a leading investment research firm, breaks stocks into 10 sectors and 59 industries. Generally speaking, different sectors are affected by different things.

Sector	Example
Basic materials	Nucor (steel); International Paper (paper)
Capital goods	Caterpillar (earth-moving equipment); Boeing (aircraft)
Communications	Verizon (local phone); Sprint (long distance)
Consumer cyclicals	Goodyear (tires); Sony (electronics)
Consumer staples	Anheuser-Busch (beverages); Procter & Gamble (household products)
Energy	Exxon Mobil (petroleum); Schlumberger (oilfield equipment)
Financial	Citigroup (banking); Wells Fargo (banking)
Health care	Merck (drugs)
Technology	Cisco Systems (Internet infrastructure); Nokia (cell phones)
Utilities	Southern Company (electric)

At any given time, some sectors are doing well while others are not.

WHERE IS THE STOCK TRADED?

The stock exchange is a marketplace in which member brokers (agents) buy and sell stocks and bonds of U.S. and foreign businesses on behalf of the public. A stock exchange provides a marketplace for stocks and bonds in the same way that a commodity exchange does for commodities.

To most investors, "the stock market" means the New York Stock Exchange. The New York Stock Exchange has been in existence for more than 200 years. Needless to say, it has come a long way since 24 merchants and auctioneers met at the site of the present exchange to negotiate an agreement to buy and sell stocks and bonds issued by the new U.S. government, along with those of a few banks and insurance companies. It wasn't until 1817 that the exchange adopted an approved constitution, whereby it named itself the New York Stock and Exchange Board. The exchange did not cross the million-share daily threshold until 1886. Its dullest day ever was March 16, 1830, when only 31 shares changed hands. In 1997, the exchange witnessed the first day in which 1 billion shares were traded.

There are also many other North American exchanges trading stock, from the American Stock Exchange (Amex) on down to the Spokane Stock Exchange. In addition, thousands of equities are not traded on any exchange, but rather are sold *over the counter (OTC)*. Prices for OTC stocks are readily available through Nasdaq, an acronym for the National Association of Securities Dealers Automated Quotations system.

Many unlisted industrial securities are more speculative than listed ones. There is a distinct difference between OTC stocks and exchange-listed equities, revolving primarily around eligibility requirements. Each stock exchange has listing requirements that must be met before a company may take its place on the exchange floor. For example, before a stock can be listed on the NYSE, the company must have at least 1 million shares outstanding (available to the public). Those shares must be held by at least 2,000 different stockholders, each of whom owns at least 100 shares. The company must also have earned a pretax profit of at least $2.5 million in the year preceding the listing, and the pretax profits in the two prior years must have been at least $2 million each year. The Amex and regional exchanges have similar (though less stringent) listing requirements, but no such limitations exist for OTC listings.

HOW DOES A STOCK EXCHANGE OPERATE?

Federal and state laws regulate the issuance, listing, and trading of most securities. The Securities and Exchange Commission (SEC) administers the federal laws. Stocks handled by one or more stock exchanges are called *listed stocks*. A company that wants to have its stock listed for trading on an exchange must first prove to the exchange that it has enough paid-up capital, is a lawful enterprise, and is in good financial condition.

How Stocks Trade on the Exchange

Probably one of the most confusing aspects of investing is understanding how stocks actually trade. Words such as *bid, ask, volume,* and *spread* can be quite confusing if you do not understand what they mean. They have two different meanings, depending on the exchange a stock trades on.

The New York Stock Exchange and the American Stock Exchange (composed of the Boston, Philadelphia, Chicago, and San Francisco exchanges) are both listed exchanges, meaning brokerage firms contribute individuals known as *specialists,* who are responsible for all the trading in a specific stock. This is known as an *open-auction market.* Volume, or the number of shares that trade on a given day, is counted by the specialists. These individuals control stock prices by matching buy and sell orders delivered by floor brokers shouting out their orders. The specialists change the prices to match the supply-and-demand fundamentals. The specialist system was created to guarantee that every seller finds a buyer, and vice versa. This process may sound chaotic, but specialists do succeed in their function of maintaining an orderly market and matching sellers to buyers.

In return for this service, the specialist charges the buyer an extra fee of 6.25 or 12.5 cents per share, depending on the price of the stock.

Over-the-Counter Market

The Nasdaq stock market, the Nasdaq SmallCap, and the OTC Bulletin Board are the three main over-the-counter markets. In an over-the-counter market, brokerages (also known as *broker-dealers*) act as market makers for various stocks. The brokerages interact over a centralized computer system managed by Nasdaq, providing liquidity for the market to function.

One firm represents the seller and offers an ask price (also called the *offer*), or the price the seller is asking to sell the security. Another firm represents the buyer and gives a *bid,* or a price at which the buyer will buy the security.

For example, a particular stock might be trading at a bid of $10 and an ask of $10.50. If an investor wanted to sell shares, she would get the bid price of $10 per share; if she wanted to buy shares, she would pay the ask price of $10.50 per share. The difference is called the *spread,* which is paid by the buyer. This difference is split between the two firms involved in the transaction. Volume on over-the-counter markets is often double-counted, as both the buying firm and the selling firm report their activity.

Placing an Order

A person who wishes to buy individual stock or an agent who acts on his or her own behalf places an order with a licensed representative. The representative gets a quotation (price) by telephone and relays the order to the floor of the exchange. The partner negotiates the sale and notifies the brokerage house. The entire transaction may take only a few minutes.

How do you place an order? What types of orders can you place? Let's look at the major types of orders.

- *Buy order.* This is the order you place when, obviously enough, you want to buy shares. Simply tell the broker how many shares you want to purchase.
- *Buy at market.* You instruct the broker to buy a specified number of shares at the prevailing market price.
- *Buy at a limit.* You instruct the broker to buy a specified number of shares, but only at a specified price or lower. For example, you might say, "Buy 100 shares of IBM at a limit of $50." In this case, you are willing to purchase shares of IBM only if you can do so at $50 or less.
- *Sell order.* This is an order you place when you want to sell shares.
- *Sell at market.* This is an order to sell your shares at the prevailing market price.
- *Sell at a limit.* This is an order to sell your shares only at the price that you specify or higher.
- *Sell at a stop limit.* You instruct your broker to sell your stock if it falls to a certain price. For example, you buy IBM at $50 and you instruct your advisor or broker to sell if it falls to $45. This is a *sell stop* at $45.

Shorting Stocks

Shorting a stock is the reverse of buying a stock. In effect, if you sell a stock by borrowing it from a broker, hoping that its share price will go down, you are "short" the stock. The idea is to buy the stock back later at a lower price and then return the shares to the broker and keep the difference. Although shorting is not the place for the first time investor, you should understand how it works.

The basics of the shorting transaction are straightforward. You first contact your brokerage house in order to determine whether it can borrow shares of the stock you want to short. When you receive the borrowed shares, you immediately sell them and keep the cash, promising to return the shares at some future time. The plan is to eventually repurchase the shares at a lower price and return them, keeping the difference yourself. But if the stock's price rises, you might have to buy back the shares at the higher price and thus lose money.

SUMMARY

- A stock is a security issued by a corporation or by a government as a means of raising long-term capital.

- The ownership of a stock is divided into a certain number of shares; the corporation issues stock certificates that show how many shares are owned. The stockholders own the company and elect a board of directors to manage it for them.

- The capital that a company raises through the sale of these shares entitles the holder to dividends and to other rights of ownership, such as voting rights.

- Prices of stocks change according to general business conditions and the earnings and future prospects of the companies that have issued the stock. If the business is doing well, stockholders may be able to sell their stock for a profit. If it is not, they may have to take a loss when they sell.

- The stock exchange is a marketplace in which member brokers (agents) buy and sell stocks and bonds of U.S. and foreign businesses on behalf of the public. To most investors, "the stock market" means the New York Stock Exchange.

CHAPTER 17

INDIVIDUAL BONDS

A recent survey indicates that more than 90 percent of the general public is in the dark when it comes to bonds. In fact, the majority of people who have actually invested in stocks and bonds don't really understand what makes a bond different from all other types of investments.

A *bond* is the legal evidence of a debt, usually the result of a loan of money. When you buy a bond, you are in effect lending your money to the issuer of the bond. The issuer agrees to make periodic interest payments to you, the investor holding the bond, and also agrees to repay the original sum (the principal) in full on a certain date, known as the bond's *maturity date.*

When the marketplace values a bond, the length of time to maturity is critically important. The longer the term to maturity, the longer the expected stream of interest payments to the bondholder. The market price of any bond represents the present value of this stream of interest payments discounted at the currently offered interest rates. As interest rates fluctuate, the present value of this stream of interest payments constantly changes. The longer stream of interest payments, which is found in long-term bonds rather than short-term bonds, creates higher price volatility for long-term bonds.

What "backs" the bond? In the case of many corporate securities, there is nothing more behind them than the full faith and credit of the companies that issue them. These bonds, usually called *debentures,* are probably the most common type of debt issued by industrial corporations today.

Public utilities generally issue bonds with specific assets as collateral against the loan. These are called *mortgage* bonds or *collateral trust* bonds. Some utilities, however, issue debentures, and some industrial corporations issue collateralized bonds.

WHAT ARE THE RISKS?

The main form of market risk for a bond is the risk that interest rates will change after a customer buys the bond—called *interest rate risk*. If market interest rates go up, the bond loses principal value; if market rates go down, the bond gains principal value. The longer the term of the bond, the more the price will be affected by changes in interest rates. Regardless of whether the U.S. government, a corporation, or a municipality issues the bond, the risk is similar. (See Figure 17.1 for a depiction of the inverse relationship between a bond's cost and its yield.)

Bonds are also subject to *call risk*—the risk that the bond issuer will choose to redeem (call) the bond before the maturity date. You would still get your principal, but would lose the return that would have been earned between the call date and the maturity date. The call provisions must be stated in the prospectus along with other special features—but a prospectus can be hard to understand.

A bond's current value is directly affected by changes in interest rates. The effect of higher interest rates on bonds is to lower their prices. Conversely, lower rates raise bond prices. The fluctuation is due to the fact that the price of the bond must offer a prospective purchaser current market rates.

Many brokers tell their clients to purchase bonds and bond funds as a part of their comprehensive investment portfolios. The clients are attracted because of bonds' perceived safety and high yields. But not all bonds and bond funds are the same. Investors are consistently lured by high yields into

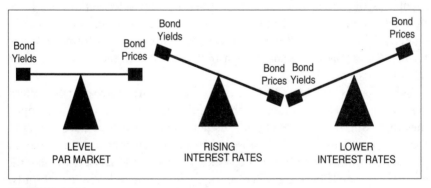

FIGURE 17.1
Bond Prices, Yields, and Interest Rates

high-risk bond strategies, only to lose principal. Remember the stock market crash in 1987? More money was lost in bonds that year than in stocks.

Why? As interest rates fluctuate, the *present value* (the worth of those dollars in today's market) of a bond's stream of interest payments constantly changes. And the longer the stream of interest payments, the higher the price volatility. The market value of a bond goes down when interest rates rise because its interest rate is fixed and cannot compete with newly issued bonds paying higher rates.

In terms of variability of total return, long-term bonds look more like stocks than short-term, fixed-income vehicles. Eugene Fama studied the rates of returns of long-term bonds from 1964 to 1996, a time frame long enough to illustrate that these bonds historically have had wide variances in their rates of total return, without sufficiently compensating investors with higher expected returns. Table 17.1 illustrates the historical statistics to support the theory.

The data indicate that long-term U.S. Treasuries have both lower average returns and higher price volatility than intermediate-term Treasuries. It implies that investors holding long-term bonds have not been compensated for the higher risk. In our opinion, the higher nominal yield of long-term bond funds is not enough to compensate the investor for their highly volatile NAVs.

Few investors look beyond the interest rate to find a bond's maturity date, perhaps not fully considering the implications of tying up money by choosing a long-term bond. This kind of investing decreases flexibility should the investor's investment objectives or needs change. And by investing in a long-term bond, you are betting that rates will not rise beyond what they are that day. If rates do go up, you've essentially lost out on earning a higher rate.

TABLE 17.1   Return Rates of Bonds

	Mean Return	Standard Deviation of Return
Short-term Treasury *bills*	5.98%	2.68%
Intermediate-term Treasury *notes*	7.35%	6.65%
Long-term Treasury *bonds*	7.01%	11.40%

Source: Dimensional Fund Advisors.

In the equity markets, volatility is calculated in terms of how much a stock's price gyrates during market swings (the beta measurement). Bonds, of course, have their own volatility measurements—duration and convexity—that are calculated by figuring in the bond's term, coupon, market price, and call provisions.

Think of bond volatility as a rubber band. Duration is how far the rubber band has stretched; convexity, how fast it snaps back. Long-term bonds are the rubber bands that have been stretched the farthest. When interest rates are headed down, everybody reaps the higher yields. But when rates rise, the rubber band snaps back with a vengeance. The market punishes long-term bonds, and the financial advisor winds up with some explaining to do.

Many financial advisors have been asking if now (after a couple of years of market downturn) is the time to get their clients back into the high-yield fixed-income market, reasoning that the market should soon rebound because it has taken such a beating. But getting beaten up doesn't ensure making a comeback.

Our economy began a steady grind upward in 1991. For 10 years, there was very little excessive inflation and a bull stock market, so risk became less of a concern. Until recently, many investors haven't even had to take a loss on a position, because for the last 10 years, all you had to do was hold the position a little longer and make a profit.

Until early 1998, the thinking was, "We've got a great economy and the companies are always going to service their debt." Credit spreads narrowed dramatically. For example, in 1997 we saw Chrysler trading only 60 to 65 basis points over the 10-year Treasury curve, or yield. Then, around August 1998, a number of events converged, including the "Asian flu" and the collapse of some of those currencies, and the Russian default on the GKOs (the Russian equivalent of Treasury bills) and suspension of payments on them. Suddenly credit spreads started to widen. In August 2003, Chrysler paper was 270 points over the 10-year Treasury curve!

Unfortunately, this can't-lose attitude also found its way into the psyche of the bond market. It's what behavioral psychologists call a *cognitive bias*, meaning that selective historical information is used to support the prediction of the course of future events. It has its foundation in hindsight, but so do remorse and regret. And, while this method of thinking is compelling, common, and normal, it can, nevertheless, cause you to leap to the wrong conclusion.

In 1998, Long Term Capital Management gave us one of the best examples of a cognitive bias by betting heavily on things returning to a historical norm; but they didn't, and disaster followed. LTCM, which was run by a couple of Nobel laureates, was shorting Treasuries and buying long positions in corporate bonds, trying to eliminate interest rate risk and only taking the risk of the credit. Contrary to historical performance, both strategies headed in the wrong direction. Treasuries became more and more expensive, and the credit of the spread product they had was becoming cheaper and cheaper.

To compound the event, by October 1998, there were no bids for bonds—zero bids! In contrast, even after the devastating events of September 11, 2001, there were bids in the bond market. But during October 1998, it didn't matter what you wanted to sell; nobody was buying. Investors finally recognized that credit risk was something they needed to pay attention to, and that they should get higher yield for that risk. The original belief or bias was that the capital markets would always be there to provide monies. The problem is that the media has lumped everything together, so when it talks bond funds, it's talking emerging market debt as well as junk bonds, Treasuries as well as corporate bonds. Historically, when you played in the junk bond market and you guessed right, you'd get huge returns. You need to think of junk bonds as dividend-paying equities, as opposed to bonds, because they move in tandem with the perception of earnings capabilities of their companies.

It's important to make this distinction, because a first time investor should be more worried about return *of* principle than return *on* principle. For instance, if you'd invested in @Home Cable because of its high yield, you would have lost your entire investment. Every time you hear a junk bond with an ultra-high yield, you need to think of the Sirens from Greek mythology whose beautiful voices lured sailors into the rocks and disaster, and beware.

And don't think long-term bonds are the answer either. Having your money tied up for 15 years or longer at a fixed rate does not allow you to roll with the punches as interest rates go up and down. If you're buying 100-year Disney bonds, and interest rates change before that bond matures (as they always do), you may have either a large gain or a very large loss, depending upon the direction of interest rates.

Consider the decade of the 1950s, the worst decade for long-term bond investors, with an average annual loss of −0.1 percent if you reinvested the interest income, or substantially lower if you did not reinvest. This practical example of the interest rate risk of long-term bonds illustrates what can happen when interest rates rise. The volatility of long-term bonds, particularly over long time periods, approaches the volatility of common stocks. Clearly, long-term U.S. Treasury bonds don't have the price stability that many fixed-income investors are seeking.

KINDS OF INDIVIDUAL BONDS

There are three main categories of bonds: U.S. government or one of its agencies, corporate, and municipal. While these three types have some different characteristics, they share a basic structure.

U.S. Government Notes and Bonds

The U.S. government issues both Treasury notes (maturities of 2 to 10 years) and bonds (maturities greater than 10 years). U.S. government securities are considered to have no credit risk, and their rate of return is the benchmark to which all other rates of return in the market are compared. The government auctions U.S. government securities on a regular quarterly schedule.

In a normal yield-curve environment, U.S. government notes typically have yields 50 to 250 basis points higher than those on T-bills and the same spread lower than a U.S. government bond (100 basis points equals 1 percent).

Individual Corporate Bonds

Corporations of every size and credit quality issue corporate bonds, from growth companies to small companies with low ratings. Corporate bonds are not easy to evaluate, especially those with longer maturities when call provisions may apply and the credit outlook is less certain. Corporate bonds may be backed by collateral and are fully taxable at the federal, state, and local levels.

Yields are higher on corporate bonds than on a certificate of deposit (CD) or government-issued or insured debt. The coupon is fixed, and return of principal is guaranteed by the issuer if the investor holds it until maturity.

If the investor sells the bond prior to maturity, the bond will be subject to market fluctuation. Investors who want to be able to check the prices of their bonds in the newspaper should buy listed bonds, preferably those listed on the New York Stock Exchange.

The fully taxable nature of corporate bonds (as opposed to municipals or Treasuries) has an effect on yield. When buying an AAA-rated corporate bond, you are buying a security that has more risk than a U.S. government bond. For the risk you are taking, you should receive an additional 25 to 50 basis points in yield.

Municipal Bonds

What are municipal bonds? Very simply, they are investment instruments used to finance municipal government activities. They are not always guaranteed by the municipality, but are backed by the full faith and credit of the *issuing* authority.

Caution: Tax free certainly does not mean risk free; some are callable and they have been known to fail. Before a first time investor buys these instruments, he or she should consult with an expert.

Municipal bonds have high trading costs. This is because there are large bid/ask spreads and significant market impact costs in the municipal marketplace. These additional costs eliminate the benefits of using an enhanced trading strategy, such as the matrix pricing strategy we use in our government and corporate bond portfolios. The turnover required would simply be too costly. Because of their high trading costs, municipal bonds are only suitable for buy-and-hold investors who want to hold longer-maturity bonds or high-yield municipals.

Municipal bond funds

Municipal bond funds are nothing more than a large grouping of various municipal bonds. Most municipal bond funds invest in municipal bonds of similar maturity (the number of years before the borrower, in this case the municipality, must pay back the money to you, the lender).

Unlike with individual issues, active retail mutual fund managers can switch bonds from time to time within a fund. A bond fund is always replacing bonds in its portfolio to maintain its average-maturity objective.

All investors should consider the following information before making a bond purchase:

- *Security description.* Type of bond, purpose of the bond, and the issuer.
- *Rating.* For example, AA is better than A.
- *Trade date.* The date the bond is purchased in the market.
- *Settlement date.* The date on which the purchaser pays for the bond and interest starts accruing.
- *Maturity date.* The date on which the purchaser will be repaid the principal and last interest payment.
- *Interest payment dates.* Dates on which interest payments are made, usually semiannually.
- *Coupon.* Fixed annual interest rate (interest income) stated on the bond.
- *Price.* Dollar price paid for the bond. (An offer price is the price at which the individual investor buys the bond; the bid price is the price at which the individual can sell the bond.)
- *Current yield.* The coupon divided by price, giving a rough approximation of cash flow.
- *Yield to maturity.* Measure of total return on the bond at maturity.
- *Par amount.* Face amount of the bond when it was issued, normally $1,000.
- *Accrued interest.* The amount of interest income (coupon income) earned from the date of the last coupon payment to the settlement date.
- *Basis for calculating interest payments.* Whether the bond uses a 360- or 365-day basis to calculate interest payments.

BOND RATING SERVICES

There are two major independent rating services: Moody's and Standard & Poor's. Investment-grade ratings range from AAA to BBB (Standard & Poor's), or Aaa to Baa3 (Moody's). Lower-rated bonds are considered speculative. Ratings are intended to help you evaluate risk and set your own standards for investment.

The price of any bond fluctuates in harmony with the rise and fall of interest rates in general and the stability of the underlying corporation or agency issuing the bond. Grades AAA through BBB are considered investment grade, although many advisors will confine their attention to bonds rated A or above. Ratings attempt to assess the probability that the issuing company will make timely payments of interest and principal. Each rating service has slightly different evaluation methods.

SUMMARY

- A *bond* is the legal evidence of a debt, usually the result of a loan of money.

- When you buy a bond, you are in effect lending your money to the issuer of the bond.

- The market price of any bond represents the present value of this stream of interest payments discounted at the currently offered interest rates.

- A bond's current value is directly affected by changes in the interest rates. The effect of higher interest rates on bonds is to lower their prices. Conversely, lower rates raise bond prices.

- There are three main categories of bonds: the U.S. government or one of its agencies, corporate, and municipal. While these three types have some different characteristics, they share a basic structure.

CHAPTER 18

ANNUITIES

In general, there are two types of annuities: fixed and variable. A fixed annuity provides a specific income for life. With a variable annuity, payouts are dependent on investment return, which is not guaranteed. Variable annuities offer the choice of several investment divisions such as stocks, bonds, and money market funds, which can cause the rate of return to fluctuate according to market conditions.

In both fixed and variable annuities, you do not have to pay income tax on the accumulated earnings until payouts start. But keep in mind that withdrawals are partially taxable and, if you are under age 59½, may be subject to a 10 percent tax penalty.

Warning: An annuity is not inherently good or bad. An annuity is nothing more than a tool that can be used in certain limited situations. The best uses are to supplement conventional retirement benefits or to hold as a reserve until other payouts are exhausted.

FIXED ANNUITIES

The word *fixed* is used to describe the type of annuity referred to by the interest rate paid by the issuing insurance company. The fixed annuity offers security in that the rate of return is certain. Typically, with a fixed annuity the insurance company declares a current interest rate and sets the interest rate. The insurance company promises to pay at a lower rate than the rate it expects to earn on its investment.

The difference in rates is sometimes referred to as the *spread.* It allows the insurance company to recover its administrative costs and to profit.

The fixed aspect of the annuity also offers security in that the annuity holder does not take responsibility for making decisions about how the money should be invested. Also, the amount of the benefit that will be paid out of the annuity when the contract is annuitized (i.e., the income payout option phase) is fixed. The settlement options that the annuitant receives from the insurance company are the same each year during the annuitization phase. If the annuitant chooses a settlement option based on life expectancy, the same amount will come to that annuitant each month for the rest of his or her life without any investment decisions or risk on the participant's part.

VARIABLE ANNUITIES

Variable annuities are often called *mutual funds with an insurance wrapper.* A variable annuity combines the best aspects of a traditional *fixed* annuity (tax deferral, insurance protection for beneficiaries, tax timing of controlled income options) with the benefits of the traditional mutual fund type of portfolio (flexibility in selecting how to invest funds and the potential for higher investment returns).

Let's say you are a 35-year-old investing $10,000 in a low-cost tax-deferred variable annuity, and you're fortunate enough to be in the right asset classes, which allow your annual return to average 12 percent. By your sixty-fifth birthday, you could accumulate more than $240,000. If you are able to add $5,000 per year all along the way, your $160,000 of total invested capital, compounding tax free, could balloon to more than $1,282,558. If you continue working and don't retire until age 70, your variable annuity could hold more than $2,224,249. That's what is made possible by investing in a variable annuity.

Variable annuity investors control their contract options. They dictate the amount, frequency, and regularity of their contributions; how their contributions are invested; and when the money is disbursed. The investor pays a premium to the insurance company, which then buys *accumulation units,* similar to mutual fund shares, in an investment fund. The IRS imposes no limits on the annual nonsheltered amount that an individual may contribute to a variable annuity funded with after-tax dollars. In other words, you can put in as much money as you can afford. This is particularly important when it comes to supplementing retirement assets beyond the annual tax-free contribution limitation.

The variable annuity investor directs those funds in subaccount portfolios consisting of stocks, bonds, or cash money market funds. Diverse investment options make it possible to structure an investment portfolio to meet a variety of needs, goals, and risk tolerances. These investments may be managed by a mutual fund company or by the insurance company. With the important advantage of tax-free rebalancing, investors can adjust their portfolios at any time. This allows an investor's advisor to carefully plan and manage the asset allocation strategy based on changing needs or market conditions, without having to worry about generating current tax.

Unlike a mutual fund, an annuity does not pay out earnings or distribute any capital gains, so these are compounded on a tax-deferred basis. The ability to reallocate assets without current tax ramifications, combined with the tax-deferred compounding of potential earnings, makes variable annuities a highly competitive investment vehicle.

A variable annuity's rate of return is not guaranteed, but rather is determined by the performance of the investments selected.

Today's variable annuity managers, along with their affiliate mutual fund managers, seek diversification, consistent performance, and competitive returns by maximizing a portfolio's return and also minimizing the level of risk. Variable annuity investments are often balanced by investing a percentage of assets in the annuity fixed-income option to provide a less volatile investment return. These fixed annuity investments tend to smooth out extreme fluctuations; investors won't profit as much from a good year in the market with such an annuity, but neither will they suffer as great a loss of income during a bad year.

Payouts from variable annuities reflect the investment experience of the underlying portfolios. The amount of variable payments is not guaranteed or fixed and may decline in periods of market decline. However, if the annuitant dies during the accumulation phase (i.e., prior to receiving payments from the annuity), the investor's designated beneficiary is guaranteed to receive the greater of the account's accumulated value or the full amount invested less any withdrawals and applicable premium taxes. Some annuities also offer *enhanced death benefits,* such as options that would enable a client to receive a step up every six years until age 75, to lock in gains. Also, in most states, this built-in benefit generally bypasses the delays and costs of probate.

When withdrawals do begin, taxes are generally paid only on the amounts withdrawn that represent a gain at ordinary tax rates, while the remainder of the account value can continue to grow tax deferred. However, if the investor takes funds from the variable annuity before age 59½, there is the additional 10 percent IRS penalty on the withdrawal of any gain.

Most variable annuities offer a free annual withdrawal provision that gives the investor access to up to 10 percent of the annuity value yearly without paying any surrender charges. Any distributions in excess of that 10 percent are subject to the surrender charges. No-load variable annuities that do not impose a surrender charge are 100 percent liquid but, like all annuities, may be subject to a 10 percent federal penalty for withdrawal prior to age 59½.

Despite their inherent advantages, not all variable annuities are created equal. They can vary widely in terms of costs and available investment options. Because of their insurance benefits, variable annuities generally cost more than traditional taxable investments, such as mutual funds. There may be front-end charges (loads), management fees, and sometimes back-end surrender charges for early withdrawals from the policy. These charges and the length of time that they apply to the policy vary widely across the industry. The average policy probably has a 6 to 7 percent first-year surrender charge that declines 1 percentage point per year. Some have *rolling surrender charges*, which means that each investment made has a new surrender charge schedule. For example, if you invested $1,000 every year, each $1,000 contribution would have a new surrender charge schedule. I would avoid these if possible.

In addition to portfolio management fees, variable annuities charge a fee to cover the issuing insurance company's administrative costs and mortality and expense (M&E) charges. According to Morningstar Benchmarks, annual M&E charges for the current industry average are around 1.3 percent and are increasing.

The higher the overall costs, the longer it takes for the benefit of tax deferral to compensate for those costs. A no-sales-load, low-cost variable annuity shortens that breakeven holding period. Variable annuities are designed to be held as long-term investment vehicles, so a breakeven of 10 to 15 years may be affordable for only those investors with that type of time frame. The time horizon is measured not by when you will retire, but according to the time at which you need to start withdrawals.

A variable annuity receives varying interest on the funds placed inside the annuity depending upon the choice of investment options. In addition, the holder of the variable annuity assumes the risk associated with the underlying investments made at the time of the investment decision. Understanding how returns are credited on money invested in the framework of variable annuities can be a little more complicated than in the case of a fixed annuity.

One of the main differences between a fixed annuity and a variable annuity is that the variable annuity is considered to be a security under federal law and, therefore, is subject to a greater degree of regulation. Anyone selling a variable annuity must have acquired securities licenses. Any potential buyer of a variable annuity must be provided with a prospectus—a detailed document that provides information on the variable annuity and the investment options.

In a variable annuity, the annuity holder may choose how to allocate premium dollars among a number of investment choices including stocks, bonds, a guaranteed account, income, growth fund, and various funds called *subaccounts*. Any funds placed in the guaranteed account of a variable annuity are credited with a fixed rate of interest in much the same manner as funds in a fixed annuity contract. There's a guaranteed interest rate and a current interest rate, and the current rate changes periodically. If it drops below the floor set by the guaranteed rate, then the annuity holder receives at a minimum the guaranteed rate.

The variable annuity typically offers the annuity holder several different subaccounts in which to invest all or a portion of the premiums paid into the annuity. The terms *subaccount, flexible account,* and *flexible subaccount* are certainly interchangeable. When an annuity holder purchases a variable annuity, he or she determines what proportion of the premium payments, usually on a percentage basis, will be allocated or paid to the different variable subaccounts. Once a percentage is determined, it remains in effect until the annuity holder notifies the insurance company of a desire to alter the allocation arrangement. Many variable annuities offer an option called *dollar cost averaging,* which provides a method of systematic transfer of dollars from one fund to another inside the variable annuity.

The accumulation phase is the period of time from the purchase of the annuity until the annuity holder chooses to begin receiving payments from the annuity. It is during this period that the annuity builds up and accumulates the funds that will provide the annuity holder with future benefits. This works for both the fixed annuity and the variable annuity.

Warning: In the past, annuities—both fixed and variable—were used to limit taxation. But today, because of the lower interest rate environment and new tax rules, the advantage has been lost. In most cases, buying an annuity makes no financial sense unless you are in the top tax bracket.

The number one complaint that we have noticed recently at our local Better Business Bureau has been the aggressive sale of annuities. We've gone to some of the meetings. Here is what we've found.

Annuities are pushed because of the high commissions they pay their brokers—typically three or four times the commission of a mutual fund, even a load mutual fund. For example, we've seen annuities used inside an IRA. Let us ask you a question: Why would you ever want to tax shelter a tax shelter? Whether these are sold because the salesperson is uninformed or they are sold intentionally, the result is the same: The salesperson gets a large commission, and the owner gets a product that may or may not be of any real benefit.

You must be aware of many aspects of this product.

- *Be aware of the commission.*   Look for an annuity that's moderate on the commission. The selling broker or agent can pick an annuity that pays him or her from about 4 percent all the way up to 25 percent.
- *Look at what they call "surrender charges."*   This is another way the broker can be paid. You need to know what the broker is making on the sale of this annuity. Obviously, if the broker is paid a 20 percent commission, the investor is going to have a huge surrender charge, and you will be required to hold the annuity for many years before the surrender charge disappears.
- The annuity has an expense ratio in addition to what the mutual funds charge.   The expense ratio is typically 1 to 3.5 percent.
- *Can you get your money out?*   It doesn't matter what rate you are making if you can't get your money out. You can borrow against the annuity, but normally only up to the surrender value.

If you must buy a commercial annuity—there are some that are available free of commissions, called *no-load.* You can find them at Vanguard or TIAA-CREF. Both of these are fine. They typically have a low 0.65 percent operating expense in addition to the mutual fund's operating expenses. Because they have no surrender charges, you can leave any time, and whatever gains you've made are real.

DEFERRED ANNUITIES

A deferred annuity is an interest-bearing contract between an investor and an insurance company. When an investor purchases a deferred annuity, the insurance company pays interest that is tax deferred until withdrawal. The investor may withdraw the money at regular intervals or at a specific time in a lump sum or through random withdrawals.

One feature of a deferred annuity that is unique and is not found in any other investment vehicle is that the annuity provides a stream of income that an annuitant cannot outlive. Dollars inside the annuity remain tax-deferred until withdrawal, which is at the complete discretion of the owner of the annuity.

For example, if you have $10,000 to invest in a deferred annuity that is earning 5 percent per year, at the end of the first year your annuity will be worth $10,500. That full amount will be available to earn interest the following year. If, instead, you invest in a currently taxable investment that is also earning 5 percent and your marginal tax rate is 28 percent, then at the end of the year, only $10,360 will be available for reinvestment. The remaining $140 will be paid to the government for income tax on the $500 you earn. This may seem like a small sum of money, but if this process continues for 10 years, the difference between the value of the tax-deferred annuity and that of the currently taxable investment will be $2,046! (Of course, taxes must still be paid when the earnings inside the annuity contract are distributed. If the annuity were cashed in after 10 years, the income tax would be $1,761, assuming a 28 percent rate and no penalty taxes.)

IMMEDIATE ANNUITIES

An *immediate* annuity is one that begins paying benefits very quickly, usually within 1 year of the purchase date. By nature, it is almost always a *single-premium* purchase. The immediate annuity can be useful for an individual who has received a large sum of money and must count on these funds to pay expenses over a period of time.

METHODS OF PURCHASE

Single-Premium Annuity

A single-premium annuity is purchased with one premium. Usually the loan premium is fairly large. The single-premium option may be used to purchase either a fixed annuity or a variable annuity. A single-premium annuity requires an initial lump-sum deposit (generally a minimum of $1,000 to $5,000) and does not accept any future contributions.

As an example, Jovita Fontanez recently received a settlement from an insurance claim—a lump sum of $150,000. She does not need the money currently, so she uses the funds to purchase a single-premium annuity for $150,000 and chooses to receive benefits at her retirement age by electing one of the income settlement options.

Other types of individuals might be athletes, actors, or artists who receive large payments at one time. They purchase single-premium annuities that begin paying benefits when their careers end. Or it might be a business owner who recently sold her company. Once a single-premium annuity has been purchased, the annuity holder can choose to begin receiving the benefit payments from the annuity at any time. If it is an immediate annuity, benefit payments will usually begin within 1 year of the annuity's purchase. However, if the annuity is a deferred annuity, the annuity holder may delay the receipt of benefits for several years.

Flexible-Premium Annuity

A flexible-premium annuity allows payments to be made at varying intervals and in varying amounts. Flexible-premium annuities can accept future contributions and often require a smaller initial deposit. This type of annuity is usually used for accumulating a sum of money that will provide benefits at some point in the future. As with a single-premium annuity, the flexible-premium annuity can purchase either a fixed or variable annuity.

ANNUITY STAGES

There are two phases of an annuity: the asset-building, or accumulation, phase and the payout, distribution, or benefit phase.

A variable annuity is generally more appropriate for a customer with a longer time horizon to allow a substantial accumulation of wealth through equity investments on a tax-deferred basis.

In the accumulation phase, you buy units similar to those of mutual fund shares. But unlike a mutual fund, the annuity does not pay out income or distribute any capital gains, so the customer accumulates unit values over a period of years. These also grow tax deferred, making the compounding effect even more dramatic.

During the payout phase, the insurance company starts making a series of payments consisting of principal and earnings for a defined period to the annuitant or to the main beneficiary. Taxes are assessed only on the portion of each payment that comes from earned interest (except with qualified contracts).

The following are payout options:

- *Lifetime income.* The entire account value is converted to a monthly income stream guaranteed for as long as the annuitant lives.

- *Lifetime income with period certain.* Income stream is guaranteed for a specified number of years or for as long as the annuitant lives, whichever is longer.

- *Refund life annuity.* The entire account value is converted to a monthly income stream guaranteed for as long as the annuitant lives. If the annuitant dies prior to the principal amount's being annuitized, the balance is paid to the beneficiary.

- *Joint and survivor.* The income stream is guaranteed for as long as either annuitant lives (e.g., you or your spouse).

- *Fixed period certain.* The entire account value is fully paid out during a specified period.

- *Fixed-amount annuity.* Equal periodic installments are withdrawn until the account balance is exhausted.

Unlike regular life insurance, which pays out a lump sum upon premature death, the lifetime payout option protects you against the danger of outliving your money. Once a guaranteed income option is elected, the investor cannot withdraw money or surrender his or her contract.

The single exception to this is the immediate annuity, which does not actually pass through an accumulation phase, but moves immediately after it is purchased into the annuitization phase.

PARTIES TO AN ANNUITY

Generally, there are four potential parties to an annuity contract: the owner, the annuitant, the beneficiary, and the issuing insurance company. The rights and duties of each of these entities will be discussed in a general overview.

The *owner* purchases the annuity, and the *annuitant* is the individual whose life will be used to determine how payments under the contract will be made.

The *beneficiary* is the individual or entity that will receive any death benefits, and the *issuing insurance company* is the organization that accepts the owner's premium and promises to pay the benefits spelled out in the contract.

The most common situation involves only three parties, since the owner and the annuitant are most often the same individual. Thus, the three parties are the owner-annuitant, the individual or beneficiary, and the insurance company.

The Owner

Every annuity contract must have an owner. Usually the owner is a real person, but there's no requirement that the owner be a real person as there is with the annuitant. In most instances where the owner and the annuitant are the same person, the owner pays money in the form of premiums into the annuity during the accumulation phase.

Also, the owner has the right to determine when the annuity contract will move from the accumulation phase into the payout or annuitization phase and begin making payments. Most annuity contracts do not specify a maximum age past which annuity payments cannot be deferred.

The Annuitant

According to the Internal Revenue Code, the annuitant is the individual whose life is of primary importance in affecting the timing and the amount of payout under the contract. In other words, the annuitant's life is the measuring life. The annuitant, unlike the owner and the beneficiary of the annuity contract, must be a real person.

The Beneficiary

Similar to the conditions of a life insurance policy, in the annuity contract, beneficiaries receive a death benefit when the annuitant dies prior to the date upon which the annuity begins paying out benefits. In effect, the payment of the death benefit allows the owner to recover her or his investment and pass it along to the beneficiaries if the annuitant does not live long enough to begin receiving annuity contract benefits. The death benefit is generally equal to the value of the annuity contract at the time of death.

The beneficiary has no rights under the annuity contract other than the right to receive payments of the death benefit. He or she cannot change the payment settlement options, alter the starting date of the benefit payments, or make any withdrawals or partial surrenders against the contract. The owner, under most annuity contracts, has the right to change the beneficiary designation at any time.

In a very general sense, the insurance company that issues the annuity contract promises to invest the owner's premium payments responsibly, credit interest to the funds placed in the annuity, pay the contract death benefit in the event of the death of the owner prior to annuitization of the contract, and make benefit payments according to the contract settlement options selected by the contract owner.

The Internal Revenue Code requires that all annuities contain certain provisions in order to be eligible for the tax benefits associated with the annuity contract, but there is considerable variation among companies. For example, all companies have a maximum age beyond which they will not issue an annuity contract. If an individual is 80 years old, he or she will not be able to purchase an annuity contract from a company whose maximum age is, say, 75.

The financial strength and the investment philosophy of the issuing company should be examined. To evaluate the financial strength, you could look at the AM Best Companies, Moody's, Standard & Poor's, or Duff and Phelps.

The rating services examine the items connected with the insurance company that are important in gauging the effectiveness and probability of the company's performance in the future. It includes a list of information evaluating the company's profitability and capitalization and its liquidity. In addition, rating services examine the company's investment strategy and marketing philosophy as well as its business practices and history.

PREMIUM PAYMENTS

Most annuity contracts require each premium payment to be at least a certain minimum amount. For example, under a deferred annuity the contract might require a minimum monthly premium of $50, while another annuity might require a minimum single premium of $5,000.

SETTLEMENT OPTIONS

A settlement option in the annuity contract is the method by which the annuity owner selects to receive payments of benefits under the annuity contract.

Most annuity contracts allow the settlement option to be changed with proper notice to the insurance company. Although not a complete list, following are the most common settlement options: life annuity, life with period certain guaranteed, refund life annuity, joint survivor annuity, fixed-period annuity, and fixed-amount annuity.

MAINTENANCE FEES

The annual contract maintenance fee generally ranges from $25 to $40.

INSURANCE-RELATED CHARGES

Many fixed annuity contracts levy a charge against partial or full surrender of the contract for a period of years after the annuity is purchased. This charge is usually referred to as a *surrender charge* or a *deferred sales charge.* It can range from 0.5 to 1.5 percent per year of the average account value.

There are also no-load annuities that do not have surrender charges. The surrender charge is usually applicable to a surrender made for an annuity for a certain number of years. Typically, a surrender charge is a percentage decreasing with each passing year, similar to vesting. For example, a fixed annuity contract might provide the following surrender charges: year 1, surrender/withdrawal charges, 8 percent; year 2, 7 percent; year 3, 6 percent; year 4, 5 percent; year 5, 4 percent; year 6, 3 percent; year 7, 1 percent.

LOANS

Most annuity contracts do *not* offer the option of taking a loan against the annuity value.

DEATH BENEFITS

There are certain standard provisions common to most annuity contracts.

- They require distribution after the death of the owner to be made in a particular manner as described by the Internal Revenue Code.

- If the annuitant dies, the value of the death benefit is the greater of the amount originally invested in the contract or the annuity's account value.

- The death benefit is (sometimes) guaranteed never to be lower than the total amount invested in the annuity. In this sense, annuities look a bit like life insurance.

INTEREST RATES

Typically, a fixed annuity contract will offer two interest rates: a guaranteed rate and a current rate. The guaranteed rate is the minimum rate that will be credited to the funds in the annuity contract regardless of how low the current rate sinks or how poorly the insurance company fares. Typically, the guaranteed rate is 2.5 to 3 percent.

The current interest rate varies with insurance companies. On the anniversary of the purchase of the annuity, the company notifies the owner of the new current rate. If, for some reason, the interest rate drops below the guaranteed rate, a bailout provision allows the contract holder to fully surrender the annuity contract and not incur any surrender charges under the annuity contract. The name for this is a *bailout provision* or *escape clause.*

For example, an annuity offering a bailout clause allows the contract to be surrendered if the current interest rate drops 1 percent below the interest rate of the previous period. Assuming that the prior interest rates were 6.5 percent, if the current rate for the next period falls below 5.5 percent, the annuity holder could surrender the annuity contract completely and not be subject to any contract charges. The 10 percent penalty tax on premature withdrawals may still apply to a surrender under the bailout provision.

RETURN

Fixed annuities offer an interest rate closely tied to the medium- or long-term maturities rather than the typically lower rates of short-term maturities associated with products such as CDs. The current rate, which is actually the annualized rate, is usually guaranteed for one year, although other options may be available. At the end of the guaranteed period of the current or initial rate, the annuity will renew with a new rate that is the best rate the company can offer under the current economic conditions. The minimum guaranteed rate also applies, usually the lowest rate possible regardless of where the current rates are. And that rate is also tax deferred.

As we have discovered, because annuities have many different features, there are a number of factors to examine. For example, you should ask if there are penalties for early withdrawals. Are there graduated withdrawal charges over a period of years? How much can you withdraw at any one time without a penalty?

In addition, if you are considering the purchase of an annuity, you should ask these questions:

- Are there front-end or back-end load charges or annual administrative fees? How much are they, and how will they affect your return?
- What is the current interest rate, and how often does it change?
- What is the minimum interest rate guaranteed in the contract?
- Is there a bailout option that permits you to cash in the annuity, without withdrawal penalties (there may be tax penalties), if the interest rate drops below a specific figure?

WHAT IS A SUBACCOUNT?

Subaccount is a term that describes the actively managed retail mutual fund portfolio held inside a variable annuity.

Variable annuities offer anywhere from 5 to 35 subaccount investment options. Mutual fund account managers select individual securities inside the subaccounts; the investor then selects the most appropriate subaccount based on the security selection for her or his portfolio. If this sounds exactly like a mutual fund, that's because it is. The same, or *clone,* as they're commonly called, mutual funds tend to have the same managers for their variable annuity subaccounts, so the same criteria exist for choosing a mutual fund as for choosing a subaccount—and the same benefits also exist, such as professional money management, convenience, economies of scale, and diversification. Subaccount exchanges do not create taxable events and do not entail sales or transfer charges. Most companies do set limits, usually 12, on the number of annual exchanges before a transfer fee is charged.

The variable annuity, however, gives the added benefit of tax-deferred wealth accumulation. Subaccounts usually include a list of the primary investment objectives, and it's relatively easy to determine what the fees are charged for. It is required for a subaccount to specify the primary group of securities held as well as the issuing insurance or mutual fund company.

Investment Flow of a Subaccount

All investment funds flow through the insurance company into the various subaccounts, depending on those chosen by the investor or investment advisor.

Each subaccount has a specific investment objective. Combined with other subaccounts, this gives the investor a chance for diversification and the ability to select different portfolios to meet asset allocation and diversification needs. Subaccount managers purchase stocks, bonds, or cash which are valued daily as an accumulation unit, another name for fund shares of the mutual fund.

Accumulation units—shares—are purchased by the contract owner at the *accumulation unit value* (AUV), which is very similar to the mutual fund equivalent known as net asset value (NAV), without commissions, in full and fractional units.

Types of Subaccounts

Subaccounts may be divided into several broad categories: asset classes seeking aggressive growth; asset classes seeking more stable growth; asset classes seeking low volatility utilizing fixed-income bonds; a combination of these; and asset classes featuring money market rates. Inside each of these classes, categories are broken down further.

Fixed-income accounts are established to decrease risk for those in need of meeting current income requirements. Fixed-income subaccounts include government agency bonds; corporate rate bonds; high-yield, foreign government corporate bonds; and certain fixed-income choices.

Equity or stock investing would be in funds for growth of principal.

Since variable annuities are long-term investments, the equity subaccounts will be most important to review. The following discussion addresses any questions you still may have about subaccounts and mutual funds, how they work, and what makes up a mutual fund.

How Mutual Funds and Subaccounts Work

The manager of the mutual fund uses the pool of capital to buy a variety of stocks, bonds, or money market instruments based on the advertised financial objectives of the fund. The mutual fund manager uses the investment objectives as a guide when choosing investments. These objectives cover a wide range. Some follow aggressive policies, involving greater risk in search of higher returns. Others seek current income and little risk.

When you purchase mutual fund shares, you pay the *net asset value* (NAV), which is the value of the fund's total investment minus any debt, divided by the number of outstanding shares. For example, if the fund's investment value is $26,000, it has no debt, and there are 1,000 shares outstanding, then the net asset value is $26 per share. In a regular mutual fund, which includes thousands and often millions of shares, the NAV is calculated on a daily basis, with values moving up or down along with the stock or bond markets.

The NAV is not a fixed figure because it must reflect the daily change in the price of the securities in the fund's portfolio. In contrast, a variable annuity issues shares at the *accumulation unit value* (AUV). The only difference between the two is that inside a mutual fund you will sometimes pay higher than the NAV for shares that have front-end commissions, and in annuities this is not an option.

COSTS

It's simply common sense that lower expenses generally translate to higher overall returns. The goal of the smart investor is to keep his or her acquisition costs as low as possible. There are four basic kinds of costs: sales charges, operating expenses, M&E charges (mortality and expense charges), and transaction charges.

Sales Charges

Sales charges (or loads) are commissions paid on the sale of mutual funds. All commissions used to be simply charged up front, but that's all changed. There are now several ways in which mutual fund companies charge fees.

Annuities and mutual funds are similar if you compare the B-share mutual fund option. This option has no front-end sales charges, but has higher internal costs. If you decide to redeem your shares early, usually within the first five years, you pay a surrender charge. This is very similar to annuity investing.

Some sales charges, as in B shares, are levied on the back end as a contingent deferred sales charge. The load is charged when the investor redeems shares in the fund. A customer who redeems shares in the first year of ownership typically pays a 5 percent sales charge. The amount drops by an equal amount each year. After six years, the shares can be redeemed without further charge. For large purchases, you should never purchase B-share mutual funds. There are less-than-ethical brokers out there who will tell you it is a better deal to invest in B shares since you will not pay an up-front charge.

Class C shares typically have even higher internal expenses, but pay the selling broker up to 1 percent per year based on assets. This fee comes directly from your investment performance and is paid to the selling broker. C shares may have no up-front fee, possibly a 1 percent deferred sales charge in year 1 (sometimes longer), and higher annual expenses (up to 1 percent extra per year).

No-load mutual funds do *not* mean *no cost*. Some no-load funds charge a redemption fee of 1 to 2 percent of the net asset value of the shares to cover expenses mainly incurred by advertising. Fee comparisons are particularly important. Every dollar charged comes directly from the performance of the subaccount. Remember to compare the proverbial apples to apples—in this case, similar equities to equities subaccounts and similar bonds to bonds subaccounts.

Operating Expenses

These are fees paid for the operational costs of running a fund. These costs can include employees' salaries, marketing and publicity, servicing the toll-free phone line, printing and mailing of published materials, computers for tracking investments and account balances, accounting fees, and so on. A fund's operating expenses are quoted as a percentage of your investment; the percentage represents an annual fee or charge. You can find this number in a fund's prospectus in the fund expenses section, titled "Total Fund Operating Expenses" or "Other Expenses." A mutual fund's operating expenses are normally invisible to investors because they're deducted before any return is paid, and they are automatically charged on a daily basis. Beware, though, a subaccount can have a very low management fee, but have exorbitant operating expenses. A fund that frequently trades will have more wire charges, for instance, than a fund that does not.

Mortality and Expense (M&E) Charges

An annual charge, 1 to 1.5 percent of the daily asset value of each subaccount, is charged for the mortality risk that arises from the obligation to pay guaranteed death benefits or guaranteed lifetime income payments to annuitants.

Transaction Charges

Transaction charge is another term for execution costs. Total transaction costs (or the cost of buying and selling stocks) have three components: (1) the actual dollars paid in commissions; (2) the market impact, that is, the impact a manager's trade has on the market price for the stock (this varies with the size of the trade and the skill of the trader); and (3) the opportunity cost of the return (positive or negative) given up by not executing the trade instantaneously.

For example, when an individual investor places an order to buy 300 shares of a $30 stock ($9,000 investment), she or he is likely to get a commission bill for about $204, or 2.3 percent of the value of the investment.

Even at a discount broker, commissions are likely to cost between $82 (0.9 percent) and $107 (1.2 percent). A mutual fund, on the other hand, is more likely to be buying 30,000 to 300,000 shares at a time! Its commission costs often run in the vicinity of one-tenth of the commission you would pay at a discount broker! Where the commission might have been $0.35 per share, the mutual fund could pay only $0.05 per share or even less! The commission savings can (and should) mean higher returns for you as a mutual fund shareholder.

You should be aware that a variable annuity's rate of return is *not guaranteed*, but rather is determined by the performance of the investments selected. As the value of the stocks in the portfolio varies, each unit will be worth more or less.

More and more variable annuity companies are offering asset class investing to provide a less volatile investment return. As we have already pointed out, these asset classes tend to smooth out extreme fluctuations; investors won't profit as much from a good year in the market with such an annuity, but neither will they suffer as great a loss of income during a bad year.

Any distributions in excess of the 10 percent premature distribution penalty tax, which was set up to discourage the use of annuity contracts as short-term tax-sheltered vehicles, imposed by the Internal Revenue Code are subject to the surrender charges. No-load variable annuities that do not impose a surrender charge are 100 percent liquid; but, like all annuities, they may be subject to a 10 percent federal penalty for withdrawal prior to age 59½.

Warning: Annuities can vary widely in terms of their costs and available investment options.

Because of their insurance benefits, variable annuities generally cost more than traditional taxable investments, such as mutual funds. There may be front-end charges (loads), management fees, and sometimes back-end surrender charges for early withdrawals from the policy. These charges and the length of time they apply to the policy vary widely across the industry.

The average contract probably has a 6 to 7 percent first-year surrender charge that declines 1 percentage point per year. Some have *rolling surrender charges*, which means that each investment you make has a new surrender charge schedule. For example, if you invested $1,000 every year, each $1,000 contribution would have a new surrender charge schedule. I would avoid these if possible.

The higher the overall costs, the longer it takes for the benefit of tax deferral to compensate for those costs. A no-sales-load, low-cost variable annuity can help shorten that breakeven holding period. In general, variable annuities are designed to be held as long-term investment vehicles, so a breakeven of 10 to 15 years may be affordable for those investors with that type of time frame.

THE DEATH BENEFIT

Obviously, no one can predict if you will die when the market is up or down. But the *standard* death benefit provided by variable annuities guarantees that if the policyholder dies while still saving for retirement, his or her heirs will receive the greater of either the amount of money invested or the policy's value at the time of death. Many variable annuities go even further and offer *stepped-up* benefits that actually lock in investment gains every year.

This means that if an investor buys a variable annuity today with $100,000 but dies when it's worth only $80,000, then the insurance company is on the hook for the difference of $20,000. A variable annuity is, in effect, insuring the heirs against a market downturn, and the investor is paying for that benefit. Mortality expense charges finance the whole support function, including commissions on commission products, the processing of paperwork, customer service, and the guarantee of insurance benefits.

WHAT CAN YOU DO TO BECOME BETTER INFORMED?

Monday issues of the *Wall Street Journal* carry the variable annuities listings. Notice the subheadings that indicate names of insurance products and investment subaccounts. Instead of focusing only on past performance or unit price, look at the total expense column (the last column listed). Total expense includes management-, operations-, and insurance-related expenses. You will see that these costs wander all over the board, as high as 2.79 percent and as low as 0.79 percent. Now check the prospectus of the annuity you are considering in order to uncover any up-front costs or surrender charges.

Not all variable annuities are shown in the *Journal;* only ones that have three years of performance numbers are listed.

SUMMARY

- There are two types of annuities—fixed and variable.
- The concept of an annuity is to defer taxation on the investment earnings.
- Annuities have investment applications for high-net-worth individuals.
- Annuities are *sold*, not *bought*—meaning there has to be an incentive to the selling agent or broker. This means you must examine the commissions and fees before purchasing this product.
- The best advice is to stay away unless there is a compelling need based on your individual circumstances.

CHAPTER 19

SEPARATE ACCOUNTS

TERMS USED FOR DIFFERENT TYPES OF ACCOUNTS

This chapter is designed to give you basic information and definitions of the various types of separate accounts.

■ The terms *separately managed account, individually managed account,* and *managed account* are synonymous and are used interchangeably. For the purposes of this book and to avoid confusion, we're going to use the term *separate accounts* to refer to all three terms.

■ *MDA (multidiscipline account)* is a popular term right now, specifically within Smith Barney. Acronyms are used to describe packaging together investment disciplines in predetermined percentages— often with lower investment minimums. An *MDA manager* is really a sponsor. A *program sponsor* is the investment advisor—the entity responsible for establishing and maintaining the program.

(Sponsors generally do not recommend an unlimited number of managers. They typically restrict each style category to three or four managers with the total recommended list not exceeding 40 to 50 manager names. Our experience is that the sponsor recommended lists turn over approximately 20 percent in a normal year.)

■ *MSA (multistyle account)* is Cerulli Associates' umbrella term for the growing list of acronyms used to describe the packaging together of investment styles in predetermined percentages—often with lower investment minimums.

■ *UMA (unified managed account)* is a centralized platform for brokerages to support and service their financial consultants' fee-based businesses—a type of platform for wirehouse advisors.

- *Client-directed, fee-based account* is an account in which the client directs the investments on a discretionary basis and can trade as much as he or she wants, but is only charged one fee. These accounts are rising in popularity and usually contain trading restrictions to control the frequency of trading.

- *Broker-directed account* or *personally advised account* is an account in which the stockbroker directs the investments on a discretionary basis. There is no independent money manager.

- *Guided managed account programs* are brokerage accounts that use their research departments to put together "buy" lists and give broker-advisors a choice of one or two securities in each category for the clients.

- *Fee-based brokerage account* is used interchangeably with *guided portfolio account*, where the broker manages on a discretionary basis.

- *Wrap fee account*—the original wrap account was an individually managed account run by a professional money manager on a discretionary basis for the client.

NAMES OF WIREHOUSE PROGRAM PLATFORMS

Proprietary Consultant Programs

This category is composed of discretionary fee-based separate account assets managed by a brokerage firm's internal asset management unit and gathered "off-platform" (i.e., outside of a brokerage's own consultant wrap program) via its retail rep force. High-net-worth investors are targeted, with account minimums of $100,000 to $250,000 or more. A bundled asset-based fee covers money management, trading, and custody.

Mutual Fund Advisory Programs

These programs are designed to systematically allocate investors' assets across a wide range of mutual funds. Services include client profiling, account monitoring, and portfolio rebalancing. An asset-based fee of 1.25 percent, for example, is charged instead of commission. Account minimums typically range between $10,000 and $50,000.

Fee-Based Brokerage Programs

These are programs in which active traders pay a flat asset-based fee (usually about 1 percent) for all trading activity instead of a commission for each individual trade. Historically, there has been no advisory element to these programs. However, to combat the growing popularity of online trading, many of these programs are now incorporating advice. These programs offer both mutual funds and individual securities, but individual stocks dominate.

Rep as Portfolio Manager Programs

These are programs in which the brokers act as money managers for their clients by taking full responsibility for selecting a portfolio of securities. Your authors are grateful that only a small number of brokers are approved to participate in these programs.

Proprietary Programs

These are managers inside the broker-dealers' own companies. Raymond James and Merrill Lynch, for example, have their own proprietary programs in separate account management: Merrill Lynch has Investment Management; Raymond James has Eagle Asset. Within Eagle, for example, there are 10 different strategies, including an aggressive strategy, a small-cap strategy, and a bond strategy—but the strategies are *proprietary*.

Both firms also have *nonproprietary programs* in which they do the due diligence and hire outside independent money managers—but, in the case of Raymond James, for instance, all managers, both inside and outside, use the same platform that Eagle is using. Raymond James's nonproprietary program is called Investment Advisory Services. It has about 30 different outside independent money managers, for whom Raymond James performs due diligence on inside managers for the various asset class boxes, does the reporting on private accounts, and handles the trading. Overall, Raymond James serves as the investment advisor to the account and uses the independent outside money managers as its sub-advisors. If this sounds confusing it's because it is. It just the way they speak on Wall Street.

What is a sub-advisor?

A *sub-advisory program* is defined as one where clients' assets are invested among a sanctioned roster of money managers, in a separate account, as determined by the sponsoring brokerage firm. Some current examples include Legg Mason, Salomon Smith Barney, and Janney Montgomery Scott.

The sub-advisor is the money manager. For example, under IAS, which is the Investment Advisory Services division of Raymond James, the client signs an investment advisory agreement with Raymond James, and Raymond James serves as the *investment advisor,* and an independent money management firm serves as the *sub-advisor.* In other words, the Raymond James investment advisory program hires the money manager as a sub-advisor to their program. Raymond James has the ultimate fiduciary responsibility, the reporting responsibility, and the trading responsibility.

Under sub-advisory program processes, separate account investors have a single contract with a brokerage firm that covers the scope of the program, including the brokerage firm's arrangement with the money manager. That program is discretionary, but it is the investment manager that has the discretion, not the sponsoring broker-dealer. It is usually the broker-dealer's responsibility to pick the money manager for the client, though sometimes it remains the client's decision.

What is open architecture?

Like separate account sub-advisory programs, *open architecture separate accounts* are invested in a separate account run by an asset manager. There are, however, several crucial differences between the two.

Most separate account providers offer versions of both the separate account sub-advisory and open architecture models. One brokerage firm, for example, has between 50 to 60 money managers in its sub-advisory program, but also includes as many as 1,500 institutional money managers in an open architecture version of its separate account program.

A major difference between sub-advisory and open architecture separate accounts is in pricing. Unlike a sub-advisory program, which bundles together all pricing components such as trading, clearing, or management, investors in most open architecture separate account programs have more options to pay for their services. There is generally an arrangement where they can elect to pay some sort of directed brokerage commissions or fee plus ticket charges instead of straight asset-based fees.

This means clients in an open architecture program can pay for money management through either fees or commissions. Some open architecture programs, like A.G. Edwards Private Advisory Services Program, allow multiple pricing options; others, like Merrill Lynch, do not.

The open architecture structure is the older of the two program designs, but there are now more sub-advisory than open architecture programs. They also dominate in terms of assets.

Platform sub-advisors are outside money managers in a broker-dealer's program.

TAMPs are turnkey asset management programs. Independent practitioners including independent advisors, CPAs, banks, and insurance agents use these TAMP programs for their separate account services. TAMPs manage all the components in the investment management process, including developing an investment policy statement, creating an asset allocation and style study, and manager selection and rebalancing. Large-cap equity is the dominant asset class in most programs.

Caution: The best way to think about separate accounts is to remember they are simply actively managed individual accounts trying to beat an index by finding inefficiencies in the market. There are only a few models and everybody either fits this one or that one. The manager can vary the model a little, such as by taking a core S&P 500 fund and sprinkling in a few stocks—so look for a manager with a good track record.

SUMMARY

- A separate account is an investment vehicle that owns individual stocks and bonds.
- The appeal of a separate account is to high-net-worth investors who have expectations of individual investment and tax management of their portfolios.
- Though a separate account may represent stocks in an asset class, these are not asset class funds.

CHAPTER 20

OTHER INVESTMENTS

COMMODITIES/FUTURES

Commodities are normally sold as a futures contact. Most futures transactions involve exchange of contracts on goods not yet produced. Originally, all commodities were agricultural products. Today, they include currencies, petroleum, metals, cotton, and lumber.

When you speculate in commodity futures, you're not buying a piece of paper that says you own an intangible piece of a company; you're buying a contract to purchase a tangible bushel of corn or several hundred pounds of coffee.

Commodities prices move because of shifts in supply and demand. High prices lead companies to overproduce, leading to excess supply and stockpiling. As a result, inventory builds up, demand dries up, and prices fall.

Commodities tend to zig when the equity markets zag. They appear to flourish during times of soaring inflation and volatile interest rates and languish when the economy is stable. But you only make money when you sell.

STOCK DERIVATIVES—OPTIONS AND FUTURES

Options and futures are *derivative* securities, meaning their value is derived from that of another security or commodity. Options and futures both are very risky because they often carry an incredible amount of leverage. For instance, each options contract on an individual stock controls 100 shares of that stock for a fraction of the stock's current value. This can make for huge upward moves, but this is offset by the risk of losing 100 percent of the money put into the option. If an investor owns an option and the underlying stock is not within the given price range within the given time period, the option expires, worthless.

REAL ESTATE

One of the best *long-term* investments people can make is in their home, though they seldom view it as an investment or a tax shelter.

During the 1970s, when inflation was rampaging in a way the United States had never before experienced, real estate investment became the darling of investors and speculators alike. Interest rates lagged behind the inflationary upticks, mortgage money was available, and repayment could be made in ever-cheaper dollars. In fact, tax savings subsidized out-of-pocket costs.

Euphoric investors caught the scent of fast profits and snapped up properties regardless of costs, and often regardless of quality. The prevailing wisdom dictated that inflation would inevitably push prices higher, and another investor would willingly pay an even fatter price later on. This delivered nice capital gains to countless sellers. In those glorious days, everyone investing in real estate became an instant financial genius.

Of course, the bubble burst, as it always does. The real estate frenzy slowed to a crawl in the early 1990s, as inflation fell. Prices remained high, but there were precious few buyers. There was no market for many of those looking to turn over these assets. Short-term loans or balloon payments came due as the ability to refinance at favorable rates or make large lump-sum payments weakened. And once again, investor dollars moved back into equities.

Real Estate Syndication

On the surface, real estate syndication looks like an ideal vehicle for those who'd like to join the parade but don't care for hands-on exposure. Such deals *need* inflationary pressures to boost profits at resale. Most never pan out.

The syndicator generally assumes the role of general partner, meaning he or she manages the properties, collects rent, and eventually sells them.

Theoretically, the general partner's risk is unlimited, but the general partner usually puts no cash into the project and receives an acquisition fee, often a management fee, a share of the cash flow from the properties, and a share of any capital gains realized at sale. Real estate is subject to cyclical swings. I would avoid this type of investment.

Real Estate Investment Trusts

Real estate investment trusts (REITs) are like a mutual fund of real estate investments. A typical REIT invests in different types of property, such as shopping centers, apartments, and other rental buildings.

REITs are a specialized form of equity that allows investors to own a portion of a group of real estate properties, although most investors think of them as an alternative to bonds. REITs have become increasingly popular over the past decade. Granted special tax status by the Internal Revenue Service, REITs pay out at least 95 percent of their earnings in the form of dividends to shareholders, often offering healthy dividend yields of the same magnitude as bonds. Even better, as REITs acquire more property and increase the value of the properties they own, the value of the equity increases as well, providing a nice total return.

REITs trade as securities on the major stock exchanges. You can research and purchase individual REITs. Even better is to buy a mutual fund that invests in a diversified mixture of REITs. Some real estate writers have criticized REITs. REITs are a good alternative for people who want to invest in real estate without all the hassles and headaches that come with directly owning and managing rental property. You can easily buy REITs in a retirement account investment (you can't do so with rental properties). For more information on REITs, check the Web site of the National Association of REITs (NAREIT).

OTHER TANGIBLE ASSETS

This category includes the many attractive and exciting acquisitions that appeal to an investor's aesthetic sense and desire to have a tangible asset. They are frequently sold as having an investment value, but that value mostly resides in the buyer's subjective gratification of ownership.

Some of the popular assets represented in this sector are collectibles, art, antiques, diamonds and gemstones, and coins. The speculative nature of these types of investments is compounded by their lack of liquidity. This category does best during periods of high inflation and investor fear, and languishes in stable markets. The main point to remember about tangible investments is that their value is primarily "in the eye of the beholder."

Investing in Gold

Gold is a monetary asset traded as a commodity. Its value today in the exchange is related to its use as an industrial and ornamental metal. It is also held by countries as a part of their international reserves and sometimes used to finance the balance of payment deficits. Prior to 1972, many countries operated a gold coin standard system under which gold was used as the basis of a country's domestic money supply. However, the gold standard gave way to a domestic monetary system based on paper money.

Gold commodities pay no dividend and a speculator makes money strictly on the appreciation of the asset. What we've experienced is that money is only made on these trades by the trader or the organization selling the commodity.

SUMMARY

- The appeal of the "investments" covered in this chapter is that they are tangible.
- With the exception of REITs, these other investments have no earnings and pay no dividends.
- The only growth with all these investments comes from the speculative nature of a future market.

CHAPTER 21

COMPANY STOCK OPTIONS

Here's an investment vehicle that is often misunderstood—the company stock option. At face value, stock options are a great benefit to both the employer and employee. Employees see their efforts on behalf of the company directly benefiting them as shareholders.

Well-documented problems with corporate governance as well as the suggested new financial reporting of stock options by issuing companies may diminish their appeal and ultimate usage as a long-term incentive. Because the fallout from Enron has yet to be determined, and as a result of stock opinions that have already been issued, employees would be well advised to focus on the wealth they can produce.

For whatever reason—possibly because of the lack of time at work and at home—most people rarely focus on planning how to get the maximum out of their stock options. Failure to plan with cash flow, investments, tax ramifications, and wealth accumulation in mind can squander the opportunity to build significant wealth and lead to a disgruntled employee. The following is a short course in understanding company stock options.

Upon receiving stock options as part of his or her compensation package, an employee needs to know what types of options have, in fact, been granted to him or her under the company's plan. In addition, the employee needs to understand all the terms and provisions of the stock option plan. Failure to do so means a lost financial opportunity.

We want to thank Jeff J. Saccacio, a CPA and a director at myCFO, Inc., in Irvine, California, for his contribution in writing this chapter.

TYPES OF OPTIONS

There are two types of stock options: incentive stock options and non-qualified stock options.

Incentive Stock Options

An *incentive stock option (ISO)* is a right granted by a company (*issuer*) to an employee (*holder*) to purchase one or more shares of the company's stock at a given time (at the date of grant and/or over a specified period of time) at a predetermined purchase price. Continued appreciation of the company stock, following the grant date, will allow holders of the ISO to obtain stock worth substantially more than their cost.

The issuer may only grant ISOs to *employees* and only for an exercise term of no more than 10 years. Also, no more than $100,000 worth of stock (valued at the time of grant) may be exercisable for the first time in any one year and at an exercise price not less than the fair market value at the time of grant. The option must be exercised while employed or within three months following termination of employment.

Nonqualified Stock Options

Nonqualified stock options (*NQSOs*) are more flexible than ISOs. NQSOs may be granted to an employee, independent contractor, or director. An NQSO also grants the holder a right to purchase one or more shares of the company's stock at a given time .As with an ISO, any appreciation of the stock following the grant date will allow the holders to obtain the stock at substantially more than they paid for it. There are no limits on the amount of stock that can be optioned, its exercise price, or the term of exercise.

VESTING SCHEDULES

When an employer grants a stock option, it rarely can be exercised immediately. Typically, the options must *vest* over a specified time period to tie (i.e., "handcuff") the employee to the company. Vesting means that the employee earns the right to exercise the options over a period of time. As an example, a grant of 5,000 stock options with a five-year vesting period would mean that the holder would earn the right to exercise those options at the rate of 20 percent each year. In other words, at the end of year 1, the holder would be able to exercise 1,000 options; at the end of year 2, 2,000 options; and so forth.

Understanding the vesting schedule is very important to employees. They must know how many unvested options they are walking away from if they leave the company. Such knowledge could arm them with the information they need to negotiate some sort of compensation for the value of the lost stock options with new employers. At a minimum, it allows them to more fully understand the cost of new employment.

EXPIRATION PERIOD

When a company grants an option to buy stock, it's generally only open for a specified period of time. The expiration period differs from a vesting period, because it is the date beyond which the holder cannot exercise options, even if they are vested. If the holders are not actively planning the exercise of the options, they may unknowingly let the options lapse and lose valuable wealth. Or, they may box themselves into a corner where they must either exercise the options or face losing some or all of them. The impact on cash flow and the tax consequences of the exercise can become magnified in such an event, dampening the wealth the employee recognizes.

Let's say that on December 10, 2003, Employee A is granted 5,000 options that vest over a five-year period, but the expiration date is ten years from today, December 10, 2013. Let's say he goes through five years and has the right to exercise all 5,000 options, but decides, for whatever reason, not to exercise them. He has put away somewhere in a desk drawer the little sheet of paper that explains his right to exercise the options and any reminders his employer has sent him. If he doesn't remember that the right to exercise those options expires on December 10, 2013, and he goes past that date, even though he is vested, those options will expire. He will lose a valuable right.

Post-Separation Expiration

An employee also needs to understand what happens to options that are vested under the plan when he or she leaves the company. For example,

Employee B has options to buy 5,000 shares of stock and they vest ratably over a five-year period. Let's say she gets an offer and decides it's worth it for her to leave the company. She leaves in year 3 and has vested in only 3,000 of her 5,000 stock options. Not only is she leaving 2,000 option shares on the table, but the employee also needs to know what the stock option plan says with regard to the 3,000 vested options if she leaves the company.

Many plans accelerate the exercise deadline upon departure, leaving the individual with a deadline date that is sooner than would otherwise have been available to exercise the options.

It's very conceivable that the company's stock option agreement may state that if an employee leaves the company, the expiration date on the right to exercise vested stock options is no longer December 10, 2013 (using our example above). It quite honestly could be something much sooner, even six months or a year after the employee leaves the company. In addition, the character of an ISO can change upon departure, leaving the holder with a nonqualified stock option.

SURVIVOR IMPLICATIONS

Most option holders fail to consider what will happen to their options if they die prior to exercising them. Typically, in a stock option program, the period of time in which to exercise a stock option is compressed, perhaps dramatically, after the holder dies. In estate planning, not only must there be liquidity for all the normal concerns such as paying taxes and supporting a spouse, but also to provide for the exercising of any outstanding stock options, especially if the acquisition of the stock is expected to play a significant role in the financial well-being of a surviving spouse and heirs. Insurance can play a key role here in providing the cash necessary to finance the exercise.

TAXES

Generally, no immediate tax consequence results from the *grant*, or the *exercise*, of an ISO. Instead, the employee will be taxed on the gains when he or she sells the stock at long-term capital gains tax rates The Internal Revenue Code provides such favorable income tax consequences for the option holder if certain conditions are met. To qualify, the employee must hold the stock for at least two years from the date the stock option is granted, and for at least one year from the date when the option is exercised (referred to as the *2 Year/1 Year Rule*). If the employee sells the stock before that time, the stock is converted to a nonqualified stock option, with the gain taxed as ordinary income—like salary or interest income. Currently, the top federal tax rate on the ISO gain is 15 percent (20 percent for sales of stock before May 6, 2003)—instead of the top rate of 35 percent for ordinary income: a savings of 20 percent!

For example, a company awards an executive an ISO with an exercise price of $10 a share. At some point in the future, the executive exercises the stock when it is worth $50 a share. The difference between what is paid for the stock and the current fair market value is called the *spread*. In this example, there is an immediate $40 dollar increase in wealth to the employee. The $40 spread is not subject to income tax, and the employee now owns the stock. If the sale meets the requirements of the 2 Year/1 Year Rule, the employee delays paying any income tax until the sale of the shares, receiving a 20 percent tax savings. That original spread, plus any future appreciation, is taxed only when the employee sells the stock.

On the other hand, the employee must recognize the spread as income at the time he or she exercises an NQSO, which is taxed at a maximum ordinary federal income rate of up to 35 percent. This is a major disadvantage to the employee, in that he or she is deemed to have received taxable income when the options are exercised, but has not actually received any cash from which to pay the income taxes. This is especially relevant if you decide to hold the stock for a really long time. Of course, the employee can dispose of some shares to pay the tax, but this waters down his or her ownership in the company and participation in any future increase in its value.

To continue using the prior example of the nonqualified stock option worth $10, if the employee exercises the option when the stock is worth $50, the $40 spread becomes part of his or her income for that year's taxes. So not only is the spread taxable before the stock is sold, it's considered compensation—just like salary. Instead of being capped out at a maximum tax rate of 15 percent, it's subject to a tax rate as high as 35 percent.

Overlooked Tax Consequences

In terms of managing tax liability and accumulating wealth with as little drag from income tax as possible, an ISO is seemingly ideal. However, there is one additional tax drawback: exposure to the *alternative minimum tax*. There are certain tax benefits vis-à-vis deductions and the ability to exclude certain income from taxation—such as the spread on the ISO—in computing the tax the regular way (i.e., tax preferences).

Each year the government requires taxpayers to perform a second tax computation adding back these preferences (including the spread), to come up with an alternative minimum tax. To the extent that a taxpayer's alternative minimum tax is greater than the regular tax, the taxpayer must pay that amount. So when subject to the alternative minimum tax, the tax benefits of an ISO are negated, resulting in immediate income tax.

Tax calculations should be performed regularly to determine the tax, cash flow, and financial consequences of exercising stock options. Often the option exercise can impact the efficacy of other tax strategies the holder is putting in place currently or on the immediate time horizon. Thus, multi-year tax projections must be performed. Although the option holder wants to minimize the tax and out-of-pocket cash cost of the option exercise, he or she can't let this obscure the true economic value of acquiring the stock.

INVESTMENT CONSIDERATIONS

You may have heard the saying, "Don't let the tax tail wag the dog." That is, don't let tax considerations blur the overall economics of a transaction. The goal should be to accumulate the most wealth after expenses (only one of which is taxes). This rings true with employer-granted stock options.

Remember that stock options give you an opportunity to sit on the sidelines and evaluate when and to what extent to harvest your benefit. That is, you have the right to acquire something (the appreciation on the stock or the spread) that doesn't require you to risk any capital until you purchase it. It's upside with no money down. However, you will have two issues to consider. The first is how long to let it go before you put your money down and acquire the stock (you can, after all, wait until just prior to the end of the expiration period). The second is whether it is worth it to acquire the stock and hold onto it for a while.

The first issue focuses on how much profit on your stock options shares is enough. Once you hit that spread, you should be willing to exercise your options, acquire the shares, sell them, and diversify the proceeds from the sale. This will lock in your profit and eliminate the risk of having large amounts of wealth in one concentrated stock position. You must, however, factor taxes being paid at ordinary income rates into the equation.

The second issue is a little dicier, as you are betting the stock acquired through the exercise of the options is better than available alternatives. The analysis takes into account the fact that holding it for greater than 12 months produces a substantial tax benefit—taxation at 15 percent capital gains rates. This benefit must be weighed against the risk of holding a concentrated stock position and being exposed to stock market fluctuations.

FINANCING THE EXERCISE PRICE

Once the options holder decides to get off the sideline and into the game, he or she needs to know how to pay for the stock options—through cash, borrowing, cashless exercise, or swapping. Although the first two methods are self-evident, an options holder could concurrently exercise the right to acquire the stock and sell as many shares as necessary to pay the exercise price and the tax cost of exercise. That's a *cashless exercise.*

For example, let's say the exercise price for each share of stock is $2 and Employee C has 10 options. Let's assume the fair market value of each option is $5. It would cost $20 to acquire all 10 shares. If all 10 shares are acquired, they will be worth $50. A cashless exercise means that if Employee C were going to exercise all of them, she would exercise them, and then immediately would sell 4 of the 10 shares to pay for the exercise price. In other words, it costs $20 to exercise all 10 stock options, but if she doesn't have the $20, she can exercise all those stock options and immediately and concurrently tell her stockbroker to sell 4 of the shares, which are trading at $5 a share, and use that $20 to pay the exercise price. The holder would end up with 6 shares worth a total of $30. If the employee desires, additional shares could be sold to pay the taxes resulting from the exercise of the options.

Another financing method is *swapping.* Employee D acquires shares of employer stock using his current holdings, without out-of-pocket cash cost. For example, if the holder owns 4 shares of stock that are now worth

$5 a share, and has a stock option to acquire 10 more shares at $2, he could exchange the 4 shares of stock to exercise the 10 options. The holder would then own 10 shares worth a total of $50. However, the tax basis of these 10 shares is the same as the original 4 shares he used to finance the purchase.

Note: Swapping is *not* considered a taxable event. The IRS won't treat the transaction as if the 4 shares were sold.

SUMMARY

Option holders should collaborate with their tax advisors and financial advisors to understand all key dates, provisions, taxes, and investment and financing issues of their stock option plans to incorporate them into their wealth accumulation and tax planning. Taking the time to truly under-stand the value of this employer-provided incentive could make the dif-ference between financial security and an opportunity lost.

- Know the type of options you have and the key dates: grant date, vesting dates, exercise date, expiration date.
- Know the effects of employment separation on your options' key dates.
- Know the consequences to your heirs if you have unexercised options at your death.
- Determine your investment and wealth accumulation goals regarding your options.
- Understand the investment and tax consequences under alternative scenarios before exercising the options.
- Time the exercise of options to properly manage tax liability and cash flow costs.
- Examine financing alternatives and the consequences of each on other elements of your cash flow planning and wealth accumulation.

CHAPTER 22

CONCLUSION

By now you must realize that investing doesn't require a master's degree or five undisturbed hours in a brokerage firm or a pile of money. The idea of investing has become a lot less mysterious and intimidating. It's just a process to follow. You now have the knowledge that will enable you to achieve your financial goals.

1. PAY YOURSELF FIRST AND ELIMINATE DEBT—BECOME AN INVESTOR

Pay yourself before anybody else! As selfish as that might sound, it is a *sound* approach. Perhaps the most important piece of advice is to pay down your consumer debt and then pay the equivalent of those monthly interest payments to your investment program.

Next, go from building a "savings" program to building an investment program. Start small, but be consistent. Put the money into a savings vehicle where you can't spend it. You'll be encouraged by how quickly your weekly or monthly contributions add up. Challenge yourself to increase the amount frequently. Start as a saver first, then build your savings into an investment program.

2. PARTICIPATE IN RETIREMENT PLANS AT WORK

Things have changed dramatically in the last few years. Participate in your company's 401(k) retirement plan. Realize that investment results are your responsibility, and not that of the sponsor of the plan. This makes it even more important for you to understand your investment choices and make smart decisions. Some employers will match your contribution. That's like found money.

3. ELIMINATE INVESTMENT NOISE, CLUTTER, AND NONSENSE

Look past all the hype and maintain realistic expectations. Don't panic and sell if your mutual fund prices go down. In fact, it's wise to expect fluctuations and ride them out. Use a drop in the stock market as an opportunity to average your cost downward (dollar cost averaging). Upgrade your knowledge about investing. Education is the key to simplifying all the investment advice and products available and to knowing how to apply them to your personal situation.

4. TAKE TIME TO UNDERSTAND INVESTMENT THEORY

Follow the principles developed in Modern Portfolio Theory. Now taught in virtually every graduate business school in the country, Modern Portfolio Theory instructs investors, no matter what size their wealth, how to achieve higher returns through asset allocation while minimizing risk by diversifying investments.

5. BUILD YOUR INVESTMENT PROGRAM

Identify how much money you can leave untouched for five years in an investment portfolio except for emergencies or income needs. This is the dollar amount you should start with. Then you need to:

- Consider using one of the model portfolios that most closely aligns with the risk you want to take as your target investment allocation.

- Select the asset class mutual funds that best incorporate the concepts that we have discussed on a cost-effective basis. In Part Two, we've shown you how to do it and listed many of the currently available retail asset class funds.

- Diversify. To the extent that you take advantage of effective diversification, you will increase the expected rate of return of your portfolio over time. We learned from Harry Markowitz, a Nobel Prize winner in economics, that while almost all diversification is good, there is effective diversification and ineffective diversification. If your investments move together, then this is ineffective diversification. It's as if you didn't diversify. If your investments do not move in tandem, you can accomplish effective diversification of your portfolio. This is because the overall risk of the portfolio can be less than the average risk of its components.

- Rebalance at least annually. By systematically rebalancing your original portfolio at least annually, you will gradually sell those asset classes that have gone up while buying those that currently have lower returns. This approach eliminates the negative results of being driven by emotions.

6. GET HELP

The most important thing to do is find an investment advisor who understands asset class investing. For many investors, having a qualified investment advisor on their financial team to make sure they stay on track will add substantial value. Financial planners, brokers, or financial advisors will make rebalancing much easier to complete.

7. ADD TIME!

Become a long-term investor. Time smoothes out market volatility while giving companies a chance to multiply your savings. Then, if your rate of withdrawal in retirement is equal to or below your rate of return, you will never run out of money. Lengthen time horizons for investments. The problem is that every investor has expectations of having immediate performance, and those expectations are not compatible with being a long-term investor. Instead of running down the road in hopes of finding the pot of gold at the end of a rainbow, why not be standing where the next rainbow appears?

8. TEACH YOUR FAMILY ABOUT INVESTING

Providing for family is at the heart of everyone's financial concerns. But who said it was up to you alone? Don't operate in a vacuum, leaving those you care about in the dark. There is no better way to provide for your loved ones' futures than to teach them to help themselves.

THE END

There we are. We're finished. Some parts of the book were very difficult to write without getting into the mathematics and deeper explanations, but the idea was to expose you to these new concepts and get you thinking that you can win at this investing game. Use these steps to build a secure retirement. So that's it. We've covered the basics of being a first time investor, but really we've taken you to a much higher level. We're trying to get through the noise and make it as easy as possible to do, as well as to understand.

Best of luck!

APPENDIX A

RETAIL ASSET CLASS MUTUAL FUNDS

To date, there are several progressive mutual fund families offering retail asset class mutual funds to the public. These funds are very similar to the institutional asset class funds, but still face many of the inherent problems of being available to the retail public. For investors with portfolios of less then $100,000, these can add substantial value over traditional retail mutual funds.

We have shown you how to build your own portfolio using these asset class mutual funds. It is a good place to get started if you have less than $100,000 to invest. However, as we discussed earlier, these retail asset class mutual funds are still subject to many of the problems that retail mutual funds experience in general.

Fund Name	Investment Objective	Fund Family	Phone
Advance Capital I Bond	Corporate-High Quality	Advance Capital I Group	800-345-4783
ASM	Growth-Income	ASM Fund	800-445-2763
Biltmore Equity Index	Growth-Income	Biltmore Funds	800-462-7538
BT Investment Equity 500 Index	Growth	BT Funds	800-943-2222
California Investment S&P 500 Index	Growth-Income	California Investment Trust Group	800-225-8778
California Investment S&P MidCap	Growth	California Investment Trust Group	800-225-8778
Colonial Small Stock A	Small Company	Colonial Group	800-248-2828
Composite Northwest 50 A	Growth	Composite Group of Funds	800-543-8072
Dean Witter Value-Added Market Equity	Growth-Income	Dean Witter Funds	800-869-3863
Domini Social Equity	Growth-Income	Domini Social Equity Trust	800-762-6814
Dreyfus-Wilshire Large Company Growth	Growth	Dreyfus Group	800-645-6561
Dreyfus-Wilshire Large Company Value	Growth	Dreyfus Group	800-645-6561
Dreyfus-Wilshire Small Company Growth	Small Company	Dreyfus Group	800-645-6561
Dreyfus-Wilshire Small Company Value	Small Company	Dreyfus Group	800-645-6561
Fidelity Market Index	Growth-Income	Fidelity Group	800-544-8888
First American Equity Index A	Growth-Income	First American Investment Funds	800-637-2548
First American Equity Index B	Growth	First American Investment Funds	800-637-2548
Galaxy II Large Company Index	Growth-Income	Galaxy Funds	800-628-0414
Galaxy II Small Company Index	Small Company	Galaxy Funds	800-628-0414
Galaxy II U.S. Treasury Index	Government Treasury	Galaxy Funds	800-628-0414
Gateway Index Plus	Growth-Income	Gateway Group	800-354-6339
Gateway Mid-Cap Index	Growth	Gateway Group	800-354-6339
Gateway Small Cap Index	Small Company	Gateway Group	800-354-6339

Fund	Objective	Family	Phone
Jackson National Growth	Growth	Jackson National Capital Management Funds	800-888-3863
MainStay Equity Index	Growth-Income	MainStay Funds	800-522-4202
Monitrend Summation	Growth-Income	Monitrend Mutual Funds	800-251-1970
Nations Equity-Index Tr A	Growth	Nations Funds	800-321-7854
Peoples Index	Growth-Income	Dreyfus Group	800-645-6561
Peoples S&P MidCap Index	Growth	Dreyfus Group	800-645-6561
Portico Bond Index	Corporate-High Quality	Portico Funds	800-228-1024
Portico Equity Index	Growth-Income	Portico Funds	800-228-1024
Principal Preservation S&P 100 Plus	Growth-Income	Principal Preservation Portfolios	800-826-4600
Schwab 1000	Growth-Income	Schwab Funds	800-526-8600
Schwab International Index	Foreign	Schwab Funds	800-526-8600
Schwab Small Cap Index	Small Company	Schwab Funds	800-526-8600
Seven Seas Matrix Equity	Growth	Seven Seas Series Fund	617-654-6089
Seven Seas S&P 500 Index	Growth-Income	Seven Seas Series Fund	617-654-6089
Seven Seas S&P Midcap Index	Growth	Seven Seas Series Fund	617-654-6089
Smith Breeden Market Tracking	Growth-Income	Smith Breeden Family of Funds	800-221-3138
Stagecoach Corporate Stock	Growth-Income	Stagecoach Funds	800-222-8222
STI Classic International Equity IndexInv	Foreign	STI Classic Funds	800-428-6970
T. Rowe Price Equity Index	Growth-Income	T. Rowe Price Funds	800-638-5660
U.S. Large Stock	Growth-Income	U.S. Large Stock	800-366-7266
United Services All American Equity	Growth-Income	United Services Funds	800-873-8637
Vanguard Balanced Index	Balanced	Vanguard Group	800-662-7447
Vanguard Bond Index Long-Term	Corporate-General	Vanguard Group	800-662-7447

(Continued)

Fund Name	Investment Objective	Fund Family	Phone
Vanguard Bond Index Short-Term	Corporate-General	Vanguard Group	800-662-7447
Vanguard Bond Index Total Bond	Corporate-High Quality	Vanguard Group	800-662-7447
Vanguard Index 500	Growth-Income	Vanguard Group	800-662-7447
Vanguard Index Extended Market	Small Company	Vanguard Group	800-662-7447
Vanguard Index Growth	Growth	Vanguard Group	800-662-7447
Vanguard Index Small Cap Stock	Small Company	Vanguard Group	800-662-7447
Vanguard Index Total Stock Market	Growth-Income	Vanguard Group	800-662-7447
Vanguard Index Value	Growth-Income	Vanguard Group	800-662-7447
Vanguard International Equity Emerging Market	Foreign	Vanguard Group	800-662-7447
Vanguard International Equity European	Europe	Vanguard Group	800-662-7447
Vanguard Quantitative	Growth-Income	Vanguard Group	800-662-7447
Victory Stock Index	Growth-Income	Victory Group	800-539-3863
Woodward Equity Index Ret	Growth-Income	Woodward Funds	800-688-3350

APPENDIX B

FORMULAS

CASH AND EQUIVALENTS

The first asset class we've chosen to examine is cash and equivalents. Most investors will use a money market fund as part of their fixed-income asset classes. In research completed by Eugene Fama, the best indicator of future interest rates is today's interest rates. The expected rate of return for a money market fund is very simple to calculate then. It is the current yield of that money market instrument. The formula for our money market fund estimate would be as follows:

$$R_{mm} = t_{90}$$

where:

R_{mm} = Money market expected return

t_{90} = Observed 90-day T-bill return

ONE-YEAR HIGH-QUALITY CORPORATE

The second fixed-income asset class is a one-year fixed-income portfolio. This portfolio's expected rate of return will not be just the one-year maturity if you utilize a matrix pricing strategy. This strategy, as outlined in Chapter 6, is able to capture a trading premium over and above the 90-day Treasury, which is its benchmark.

The expected rate of return is illustrated as follows:

$$R_f = t_{90} + P_t$$

where:

R_f = One-year fixed-income expected return

t_{90} = Observed 90-day T-bill return

P_t = Observed premium of one-year fixed-income strategy over 90-day T-bill

FIVE-YEAR U.S. GOVERNMENT

The five-year U.S. government institutional asset class portfolio utilizes the matrix pricing strategy illustrated in Chapter 6.

The expected rate of return is illustrated as follows:

$$R_g = t_{90} + P_t$$

where:

R_g = Five-year U.S. government expected return

t_{90} = Observed 90-day T-bill return

P_t = Observed premium of five-year U.S. government strategy over 90-day T-bill

U.S. LARGE COMPANY STOCKS

In calculating the expected rate of return for the U.S. large company stock asset class, we've utilized the S&P 500 Index as our benchmark. The expected rate of return for the five-year period is based on the risk-free investment plus the risk premium associated with market risk. Investors are rewarded for taking this market risk. This risk premium can be estimated historically by determining the excess returns the S&P 500 Index earned over five-year government bonds. Investors with a five-year time horizon would have five-year government bonds as their risk-free investments. To be enticed to take the additional market risk of the S&P 500, a premium would have to be earned to compensate for this risk.

To determine today's expected S&P 500 Index, you simply observe the current yield to maturity for five-year government bonds and add the market risk premium. To calculate this premium, you subtract the arithmetic average return of the S&P 500 for the longest period available, 1926 through 1993, less the arithmetic average return of the five-year government bond.

The expected rate of return is illustrated as follows:

$$R_{us} = t_{5yr} + P_e$$

where:

R_{us} = U.S. large company stocks expected return

t_{5yr} = Observed five-year zero-coupon Treasury bond return

P_e = Observed premium of S&P 500 Index over five-year zero-coupon Treasury bond

U.S. SMALL COMPANY STOCKS

With small company stocks, we have an additional risk premium for which we're rewarded over the U.S. large companies. It's very logical if you stop and realize that no one in their right mind would buy small companies, if they had the same returns as large companies. Small companies are subject to downturns in times of recession and often go out of business. The risk is substantially higher. You need to be rewarded for the risk.

To calculate this risk premium, you subtract the arithmetic average return of the U.S. small company stocks for the longest period available, 1926 through 2002, less the arithmetic average return of the S&P 500. To determine today's expected U.S. small company returns, you simply observe the current yield-to-maturity for five-year government bonds, add the market risk premium, and add the small company stock premium.

The expected rate of return is illustrated as follows:

$$R_{sc} = t_{5yr} + P_e + P_{sc}$$

where:

R_{sc} = U.S. large company stocks expected return

t_{5yr} = Observed five-year zero-coupon Treasury bond return

P_e = Observed premium of S&P 500 Index over five-year zero-coupon Treasury bond

P_{sc} = Observed arithmetic small company (9th and 10th decile) return over the S&P 500 Index premium

INTERNATIONAL LARGE CAPITALIZED STOCKS

Investors demand a return for the risk they take. In calculating the expected rates of return, we want to utilize as long a time series of information as possible. Unfortunately, in the international markets, the time series of information available is much less than in the U.S. market. We had some major events that changed things dramatically internationally: World War I, World War II, etc. For our benchmark indexes, we have used Morgan Stanley's EAFE.

To calculate the expected rate of return we use a relative equity premium, the observed equity premium of the S&P 500 Index multiplied by the relative risk of international large company stocks as contrasted with the S&P 500 Index. To determine today's expected international large company stock returns, you observe the current yield to maturity for five-year government bonds and add the market risk premium adjusted for relative risk.

The expected rate of return is illustrated as follows:

$$R_{il} = t_{5yr} + \left(\frac{\sigma_{il}}{\sigma_{us}} \right) P_e$$

where:

R_{il} = International large company stocks expected return

t_{5yr} = Observed five-year zero-coupon Treasury bond return

σ_{il} = Standard deviation of international large company stocks

σ_{us} = Standard deviation of S&P 500 Index

P_e = Observed premium of S&P 500 Index over five-year zero-coupon Treasury bond

INTERNATIONAL SMALL COMPANY STOCKS

The international small company stock returns are calculated in the same manner as for the international large company stocks. We've used the following as our composition:

$$R_{is} = t_{5yr} + \left(\frac{\sigma_{is}}{\sigma_{us}} \right) P_e$$

where:

R_{is} = International small company stocks expected return

t_{5yr} = Observed five-year zero-coupon Treasury bond return

σ_{is} = Standard deviation of international small company stocks

σ_{us} = Standard deviation of S&P 500 Index

P_e = Observed premium of S&P 500 Index over five-year zero-coupon Treasury bond

Well, you made it through so far! We now have calculated the expected rates of return for each of the asset classes. Onward to the next step.

STANDARD DEVIATION

Let's examine the risk of each portfolio by calculating the standard deviation. The formula for standard deviation is illustrated below:

$$\sigma = \sqrt{ \frac{(X_1 - \overline{X})^2 + (X_2 - \overline{X})^2 + K + (X_N - \overline{X})^2}{N} }$$

Standard deviation = square root of variance

$$\text{Variance} = \frac{(X_1 - \overline{X})^2 + (X_2 - \overline{X})^2 + K + (X_N - \overline{X})^2}{N}$$

where:

$\overline{X}$ = Average value of the variable for the period observed

N = Number of observations[1]

[1] Purists will divide by N - 1 instead of N to ensure that the estimate of variance is an unbiased estimate of the true or underlying variance.

To determine the standard deviation for each of the asset classes, we have used their historical standard deviation. In any statistical measure, you want to use as much information as is available for as long a time period as possible, unless you have some valid reasons for discarding time series information. Many publications tend to use relatively short periods in calculating the standard deviation, such as 3, 5, 10, or even 15 years. These relatively short periods of time don't allow you to really understand the true risk components. For example, over the last 10 years, bonds have had their best decade ever. The 1980s was a decade during which it was almost impossible for the stock market not to look good. During 1973 and 1974, we had our worst financial recession since World War II, but most studies ignore this period.

CORRELATION COEFFICIENTS

The most important component of investing is correlation coefficients. Common sense dictates that you don't "put all your eggs in one basket." By combining assets with low correlation, we can lower the overall portfolio risk while enhancing the risk-adjusted rates of return.

The formula to determine the correlation coefficients between two asset classes is:

$$\text{Covariance between } X \text{ and } Y = \text{average of } (X - \overline{X})(Y - \overline{Y})$$

$$\text{Correlation} = \frac{(X_1 - \overline{X})^2 + (X_2 - \overline{X})}{(\sigma_X)(\sigma_Y)}$$

Table B.1 illustrates the correlation coefficients for each of the asset classes we are considering for our portfolio.

Now that we've calculated the expected rates of return, the standard deviations, and the correlations of each of our asset classes, we have to determine the optimal combination of investments that gives us the highest rate of return for each level of risk. Our portfolio expected rate of return is simply the average weighted expected return for each of the asset classes. The risk for a portfolio is determined by calculating its standard deviation. Because the asset classes do not move in tandem, the standard deviation is not the weighted average, but the following formula.

TABLE B.1   Correlation Coefficients

	MMF T-bills	*Fixed*		*U.S.*		*International*	
		One-Year Fixed	Five-Year Notes	Large Co. Stocks	Small Co. Stocks	Large Co. Stocks	Small Co. Stocks
Money Market Fund	1.000						
One-Year Fixed	0.852	1.000					
Five-Year Treasury Notes	0.198	0.622	1.000				
U.S. Large Company Stocks	−0.106	0.153	0.253	1.000			
U.S. Small Company Stocks	−0.010	−0.043	0.096	0.666	1.000		
Int'l. Large Company Stocks	−0.005	−0.053	−0.009	0.575	0.456	1.000	
Int'l. Small Company Stocks	−0.027	−0.114	−0.096	0.278	0.263	0.883	1.000

$$\text{Portfolio variance} = w_1^2 s_1^2 + 2w_1 w_2 r_1 r_2 s_1 s_2 + w_2^2 s_2^2$$

where:

w_1, w_2 = Proportion of the portfolio invested in assets 1 and 2

s_1, s_2 = Standard deviations of returns on assets 1 and 2

r_1, r_2 = Correlations between returns on assets 1 and 2

Once expected returns, standard deviation (risk), and correlation coefficients (dissimilar price movements) have been determined, theoretical "optimal portfolios" can be calculated for every level of risk.

APPENDIX C

BUDGET

SWEAT THE SMALL STUFF!

If you're like most people, you tend to think about money in a grand sense. You view your personal finances on a macro scale (the cost of a house, the cost of a car, the cost of an expensive vacation) instead of on a micro scale (the price of lunch, the cost of a pack of cigarettes). This is a bad habit, because in planning for the big stuff, you overlook the total cost of all the little items that nibble away at your pocketbook every day.

While most Americans are overextended on their mortgages and drive cars they can't really afford, these major expenses, despite the enormous drag on finances that they represent, aren't what keep us living paycheck to paycheck. It's the small stuff. That $1.50 per day spent on coffee, the $5.50 on lunch, and the $3.50 for a magazine quickly add up to hundreds of dollars a month and thousands of dollars a year. Don't forget about banking and ATM fees. Pay attention to those fees and avoid them whenever possible.

Although a few dollars a day might seem insignificant in light of your mortgage or car payments, just $2 a day adds up to $730 per year. If you can save just $10 a week from your grocery bill and put it into your 401(k) plan instead, you've just found another $520. Add that to the daily cost of a fast-food lunch, and you've got several thousand dollars that can go into your 401(k) plan this year, and the year after.

That's it. No magic tricks, no get-rich-quick schemes. Just live within your means. To make this happen, you need to review your finances, put together a prudent financial plan, and stick to it.

First, create a visual record of your personal wherewithal. Here's a detailed data sheet for you to use as a template.

1. *Family census.* List names, residential and business addresses, contact data (phone, fax, e-mail), names of children, ages and dates of birth for all family members, and Social Security numbers. Are children married? Grandchildren? Health status? Special needs?

2. *Net worth statement.* Determine ownership for all assets—that is, ownership by client, spouse, or partner; joint ownership (define, such as community property); trust (define); other (define, such as accounts held for minors). Request copies of all statements.

3. *Checking, savings, money market, CDs (show maturity date).*

4. *Stocks, bonds, mutual funds (list or provide brokerage or custodial statements).* Include data on U.S. savings bonds. Obtain tax basis for all securities.

5. *Annuities (fixed and variable).* Obtain copy of policy and recent quarterly and annual reports. Determine owner; annuitant; primary and contingent beneficiaries; tax status.

6. *Life insurance.* Request copy of policy, original proposal, last annual report. Determine type of policy, face amount, the insured, owner, beneficiary (primary and contingent), premium payments, adequacy of payments (how long will the policy carry given current assumptions?), purpose of the coverage, cash values if applicable (current value, surrender value, loans outstanding). Include data on group insurance and any coverage tied to employer benefits or business arrangements such as buy/sell agreements. Determine all sources of death benefits.

7. *Real estate.* Include primary residence, vacation home, and rental properties. Identify owner, purchase price, current value, mortgage terms and current balance, cash flow from rental properties.

8. *Partnership investments.* Obtain a copy of recent quarterly or annual report. Determine cash flow, tax benefits, estimated values, liquidity, if any.

9. *Business interests.* List name; type of business; form of ownership (C-corp., S-corp., sole proprietor, partnership, LLC); percentage of ownership; value of interest; buy/sell agreement or succession plan.

10. *Personal assets.* Include description (car, boat, aircraft); value; debt. List value of other assets such as jewelry and household furnishings.

11. *Retirement plans.* Obtain statements for all pension/profit-sharing plans; IRAs; 401(k) plans; 403(b) plans; 457 plans; deferred compensation plans, etc. Specify primary and contingent beneficiaries.

12. *Stock option plans.* Obtain complete description, type of options, number of shares, exercise price, current stock price, vesting.

13. *Education planning.* Include Section 529 plans, Education IRAs, other.

14. *Tangibles.* List type of asset (precious metals, gems, coins); date of purchase; original investment; current value.

15. *Other insurance.* Obtain copies of homeowner, rental, auto, umbrella liability policies; personal and group disability policies; long-term care policy.

16. *Copies of legal documents and other key documents.* Include will(s); trusts (including revocable or irrevocable living trusts, charitable trusts); durable powers of attorney for assets and health care; divorce decrees, alimony and child support agreements; prenuptial agreements; stock purchase agreements; business buy/sell agreements; family limited partnerships; most recent tax return.

17. *The advisory team.* Provide the name, address, and contact information for other key advisors such as a CPA or other tax advisor; attorney, banker, trustees, insurance agents, brokers, etc.

18. *Anything else you think is important to your life and future.*

Next, prepare a budget of your expenses. The goal here is to reduce them and, thereby, increase the amount of money you have available to invest.

For some people, just the mention of the word *budget* conjures up images of spending limitations and being unable to afford life's little (and big!) luxuries. This self-defeating image couldn't be further from the truth. Yes, it is true that careful management of your finances may stop you from making purchases that you can't truly afford and racking up big debts, but the real truth about budgets is something that most consumers simply overlook. *Budgets are a tool for growth!*

The companies that operate within their budgets succeed. Those that do not, fail. Now, putting that in terms of your personal life, think about yourself as the CEO of your future. Your life is a business that you run. You have income and you have expenses. You have long-term goals and short-term needs. If you plan well and stick to your budget, you will significantly increase your chances of success. Unsuccessful investors don't plan to fail; they just fail to plan.

Budgeting does not require fancy spreadsheets or expensive software. It begins with a humble pencil and paper. For one week, carry a pencil and paper with you and keep track of how much money you spend. Write it all down—not just every dime—every penny. Whether you spend 60 cents for a donut or $11.23 for groceries, write it down.

At the end of the week, take out your piece of paper and add up the numbers. You'll be amazed at where all of your money has gone. If you take a good look at that list, you're likely to notice that you spent a significant amount of money on items that you didn't need and/or you'd be willing to do without. When you add up the numbers, you will truly develop a newfound awareness of how extraneous purchases drain away your hard-earned dollars.

To truly take control of your future, you need to take a close look at your lifestyle.

- Is your monthly long-distance telephone bill out of control?
- Do you spend too much money on fast food?
- How much is that cable bill?
- How about those magazine subscriptions?
- Do you look at the price on the sign in front of the gas station before you pull in and fill up?

It is quite likely that more than a few of your monthly expenses could be eliminated without making any detrimental changes to your lifestyle. Certainly, you have to strike a balance between enjoying your life today and saving for tomorrow, but a little prudence can go a long way.

Debra Pankow, family economics specialist at North Dakota State University, compiled the data for household expenditures for the average U.S. consumer unit (families, households, or individuals; see Figure C.1). Since inflation has been virtually flat since then, the data should still be pretty close to the mark.

While everyone has different needs, interests, and expenses, generally speaking, you would do well to spend less than the average in every category except "Pension." [Think of "Pension" as your 401(k) plan and other retirement investments.]

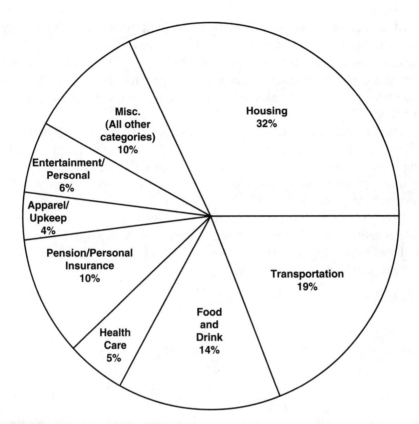

FIGURE C.1
Household Expenses

Pay off credit card debt as fast as you can. Credit cards are a consumer's worst nightmare. After house payments and car payments, monthly credit card payments account for the next most significant chunk of monthly expenses for many consumers. The high credit allowances that most cards offer are designed to convince consumers to rack up mountains of debt that will take years to pay off.

According to American Consumer Credit Counseling, Inc., a consumer with an $8,000 credit card balance making the minimum monthly payment at 18 percent interest will pay $15,432 in interest and take 25 years, 7 months to pay off the debt. That means the $8,000 purchase will cost you $23,432 by the time your balance is paid off. For the credit card companies, it's a great strategy that has paid big dividends.

Make a commitment to stop using your credit cards unless you already have the money to pay for your purchases in cash, but don't happen to have the cash with you at the moment. This way, you never buy anything that you can't afford and you never pay interest. Ideally, don't have more than two credit cards. The more cards you have, the more likely you are to use them.

Then, identify the cards charging the highest interest rates and pay them off first. If you can't afford to pay off the balances all at once, start by making a commitment to send in more than just the minimum required monthly payment. In the meantime, if you can get a lower interest rate by consolidating your credit card debt onto a single card, do it.

Going through this process is extremely empowering, with potential side benefits of sleeping better at night, having more patience and energy, and generally being in a better all-around mood. One thing is certain—it will put you back in control of your future.

GLOSSARY

The beginning of wisdom is to call things by their right names.

Active management: The practice of picking individual stocks based on fundamental research and analysis in the expectation that a portfolio of selected stocks can consistently outperform market averages.

Advisor: One who gives investment advice in return for compensation.

Aggressive growth: This term doesn't mean anything except to Wall Street marketing departments, which want to describe an investor as someone who is being aggressive in the way he or she grows his or her money.

Analysis: Process of evaluating individual financial instruments (often stock) in hopes of determining whether they are an appropriate purchase.

Annual interest income: The annual dollar income for a bond or savings account is calculated by multiplying the bond's coupon rate or savings account's interest rate by its face value.

Asset allocation: A mixture of investments among various classes of financial assets. The goal is to create an efficient portfolio that provides the highest return for a given amount of risk and reduces risk by placing portions of the portfolio in asset classes that move up or down in value in an inverse relationship to one another.

Asset class: Assets composed of financial instruments with similar characteristics.

Asset class mutual funds: Funds composed of financial instruments with similar characteristics. Unlike managers of index funds, asset fund managers actively manage costs when buying and selling for funds.

Asset mix: Investable asset classes within a portfolio.

Average return: The arithmetic mean is the simple average of the returns in a series. But what does that really mean? To illustrate: Suppose you give a broker $1,000 and one year later it's worth only $500. Then the year after that, it's worth $1,000 again. After two full years, how much money have you made? Nothing, right? You're right back where you started. But that broker can legally claim that your average annual return was 25 percent! Here's how the broker does the math: In year 1 the return was minus 50 percent—but in the second year, by going from $500 to $1,000, it was plus 100 percent. When you add the two returns together you get plus 50. Divide it by the two years and the annual average rate of return is 25 percent! Whereas if you were invested in a more conservative program, you might get a 10 percent return per year. If you got 10 percent in year 1 and year 2, your average annual return would be 10 percent, less than the 25 percent in the example above ($10 + 10 = 20 \div 2 = 10$). Averages are deceiving. If I put my head in an oven and my rear end in a freezer, on average, my body would be comfortable!

Balanced index: A market index that serves as a basis of comparison for balanced portfolios. The balanced index used in the Monitor is comprised of a 60 percent weighting of the S&P 500 Index and a 40 percent weighting of the SLH Government/Corporate Bond Index. The balanced index relates unmanaged market returns to a balanced portfolio more precisely than either a stock or a bond index would alone.

Balanced mutual fund: This term can be applied to any kind of portfolio that uses fixed income (bonds) as well as equity securities to reach goals. Many "boutique" investment managers are balanced managers, because this permits them to tailor the securities in a portfolio to the specific clients' cash flow needs and objectives. Balanced portfolios are often used by major mutual funds. They provide great flexibility.

Basis point: One basis point is 1/100 of a percentage point, or 0.01 percent. Basis points are often used to express changes or differences in yields, returns, or interest rates. Thus, if a portfolio has a total return of 10 percent versus 7 percent for the S&P 500, the portfolio is said to have outperformed the S&P 500 by 300 basis points.

Bear market: A prolonged period of falling stock prices. Wall Street defines a bear market as a drop of at least 20 percent over two back-to-back quarters. We also define a bear market as a 6- to 18-month period when the kids get no allowance, the wife gets no jewelry, and the husband gets no kisses.

Beginning value: The market value of a portfolio at the inception of the period being measured by the customer statement.

Benchmark: A standard by which investment performance or trading execution can be judged. The most widely used performance benchmark is the total return of the S&P 500.

Beta: Beta is the linear relationship between the return on the security and the return on the market. By definition, the market, usually measured by the S&P 500 Index, has a beta of 1.00. Any stock or portfolio with a higher beta is generally more volatile than the market, while any with a lower beta is generally less volatile than the market.

Boiler room (sometimes called a *bucket shop*): Brokerage firm that uses high-pressure telephone techniques to get investors to buy stocks.

Bond rating: Method of evaluating the possibility of default by a bond issuer. Standard & Poor's, Moody's Investors Service, and Fitch's Investors Service analyze the financial strength of each bond's issuer, whether a corporation or a government body. Their ratings range from AAA (highly unlikely to default) to D (in default). Bonds rated B or below are not investment grade. Institutions that invest other people's money may not, under most state laws, buy them.

Bonds—long-term, short-term, and high-yield: Debt instruments that pay lenders a regular return. Short-term bonds are five years or less. High-yield bonds pay lenders a higher rate of return because of perceived risk.

Book-to-market ratio: Size of company's book (net) value relative to the market price of the company.

Book value: The current value of an asset on a company's balance sheet according to its accounting conventions. The shareholders' equity on a company's balance sheet is the book value for that entire company. Many times when investors refer to book value, they actually mean book value per share, which is the shareholder's equity (or book value) divided by the number of shares outstanding. Theoretically, the book value is what a company could be sold for (liquidation value). This book value number is sometimes used by active managers as a guide as to whether or not the shares are undervalued.

Broker: An individual with a Series 7 license entitled to buy and sell securities, especially stock, on behalf of clients and charge for that service.

Broker-dealer: A firm employing brokers among other financial professionals.

Bull market: A prolonged period of rising stock prices. Some on Wall Street define a bull market or bull leg as a rise of at least 15 percent over two back-to-back quarters. We define it as a random market movement causing an investor to mistake him- or herself for a financial genius.

Business day: A day when the New York Stock Exchange is open for trading.

Call option: A call option gives the investor the right, but not an obligation, to buy a security at a preset price within a specified time. A **put** gives the investor the right to sell a security at a preset price within a specified time. Calls and puts are therefore essentially bets on whether the underlying security will rise or fall in price. The option holders gain or lose in proportion to changes in the values of the new indexes, which in turn reflect the net asset value performances of the funds that comprise the indexes.

Cap—small-cap, large-cap: The stock market worth of an individual equity. Large-cap stocks can be found on the New York Stock Exchange. Small-cap stocks are often listed on the Nasdaq.

Capital appreciation or depreciation: An increase or decrease in the value of a mutual fund or stock due to a change in the market price of the fund. If you bought a stock at $50 and it has risen to $55, you have a 10 percent return from the appreciation of the original capital you invested. If the price of the stock fell to $45, it would have a depreciation of 10 percent. Dividend yield is the other component of total return, but not included in appreciation.

Capital preservation: Investing in a conservative manner so as not to put capital at risk.

Cash: Investment in any instrument (often short-term) that is easily liquidated.

Churning: Excess trading of security accounts for the purpose of generating commissions for the brokers at brokerage firms.

Commission: A transaction fee commonly levied by brokers and other financial intermediaries.

Commission of payment received: Payment received for the sales agent for selling an investment product. The commission is split with the broker and the firm.

Commissions: Fees charged for buying or selling securities.

Compound annual return: *Geometric mean* is another expression for compound annual return. The geometric mean is more appropriate when one is comparing the growth rate for an investment that is continually compounding.

Compounding: The reinvestment of dividends and/or interest and capital gains. This means that over time dividends and interest and capital gains grow exponentially. For example, $100 earning compound interest at 10 percent a year would accumulate to $110 at the end of the first year and $121 at the end of the second year, etc., based on the formula:

$$\text{Sum} = \text{principal} \times (1 + \text{interest rate})^n$$

where n is the number of periods (n is the exponent)

Conservative: There is no precise definition of the term. Generally, the term is used when the mutual fund manager's emphasis is on the below-market betas.

Correction: A correction is a reversal in the price of a stock, or the stock market as a whole, within a larger trend. While corrections are most often thought of as declines within an overall market rise, a correction can also be a temporary rise in the midst of a longer-term decline.

Correlation: A statistical measure of the degree to which the movement of two variables is related.

Coupon: The periodic interest payment on a bond. When expressed as an annual percentage, it is called the *coupon rate*. When multiplied by the face value of the bond, the coupon rate gives the annual interest income.

CPI: Acronym for the Consumer Price Index, maintained by the Bureau of Labor Statistics, which measures the changes in the cost of a specified group of consumer products relative to a base period. Because it represents the rate of inflation, the CPI can be used as a general benchmark for gauging the maintenance of purchasing power.

Currency: A nation's paper notes, once redeemable but not now.

Currency risk: Possibility that foreign currency an investor holds may fall in value relative to the investor's home currency, thus devaluing overseas investments.

Current return on equity (ROE): A ratio that measures profitability as the return on common stockholders' equity. It is calculated by dividing the reported earnings per share for the latest 12-month period by the book value per share.

Current yield: A bond's annual interest payment as a percentage of its current market price. The current yield is calculated by dividing the annual coupon interest for a bond by the current market price. The coupon rate and the current yield on a bond are equal when the bond is selling at par. Thus, a $1,000 bond with a coupon of 10 percent that is currently selling at $1,000 will have a current yield of 10.0 percent. However, if the bond's price drops to $800, the current yield becomes 12.5 percent.

Deviation: Movement of an instrument or asset class away from the expected direction. In investment terminology, most often associated with asset class analysis.

Dissimilar price movement: The process whereby different asset classes and markets move in different directions.

Diversification: Most of us understand the simplified concept of diversification: "Don't put all your eggs in one basket." However, no matter how sophisticated we try to be, it's easy to get caught up in favoring one particular basket. Many investors have a disproportionate percentage of their investment portfolio in one asset class. The true measure of diversification is *not* how many different investments you have, per se, but how *negatively* correlated they are to each other. Investments that move in the same direction will tend to increase portfolio risk and reduce predictability. When investments are combined that move differently in time, in proportion, and/or in direction (dissimilar price movement), you have the basis for *effective* diversification. This protects investors from having all their investments go down at the same time, thereby reducing risk.

Dividend: The payment from a company's earnings normally paid on common shares declared by a company's board of directors to be distributed pro rata among the shares outstanding.

Dollar cost averaging: A system of buying stock or mutual funds at regular intervals with a fixed dollar amount. Under this system an investor buys by the dollar's worth rather than by the number of shares.

Dow Jones Industrial Average (DJIA): A price-weighted average of 30 leading blue-chip industrial stocks, calculated by adding the prices of the 30 stocks and adjusting by a divisor, which reflects any stock dividends or splits. The Dow Jones Industrial Average is the most widely quoted index of the stock market, but it is not widely used as a benchmark for evaluating performance. The S&P 500 Index, which is more representative of the market, is the benchmark most widely used by performance measurement services.

Efficient frontier: A two-dimensional graph that shows the highest potential return from a diversified portfolio for a given level of risk that an investor is willing to assume—the point where the maximum amount of risk an investor is willing to tolerate intersects with the maximum amount of reward that can potentially be generated.

Efficient market theory: The theory holds that stocks are always correctly priced since everything that is publicly known about the stock is reflected in its market price. A concept that proposes that all information about a security is available to all interested parties, and that the market price of the security factors in all of that information; hence, the true value of a security is the current market price.

Emerging growth fund: This applies to new companies that may be relatively small in size with the potential to grow much larger. Here, a mutual fund manager is looking for industries and companies whose growth rates are likely to be both rapid and independent of the overall stock market. *Emerging*, of course, means new. Such stocks are generally much more volatile than the stock market in general and require constant close attention to developments.

EPS (earnings per share) growth: The annualized rate of growth in reported earnings per share of stock.

Equities: Stocks. Equity mutual funds are made up of many individual stocks. A stock is a right of ownership in a corporation. The shorthand name for stocks, bonds, and mutual funds is equities.

ETFs (exchange traded funds): These are designed so you can trade index funds. Not recommended.

Excellent/un-excellent companies: Companies with either high (excellent) or low (un-excellent) stock market performances.

Exchange privilege: A shareholder's right to switch from one mutual fund to another within one fund family. This is often done at no additional charge. This enables investors to put their money in an aggressive growth-stock fund, for example, when they expect the market to turn up strongly, then switch to a money market fund when they anticipate a downturn.

Execution price: The negotiated price at which a security is purchased or sold.

Expected risk-adjusted return: Calculated as the weighted average of possible returns, where the weights are the corresponding probability for each return.

Expenses: Cost of maintaining an invested portfolio.

Fee-based: The charges of a manager, advisor, or broker whose charges are based on a set amount rather than transaction charges.

Fee-only: The charges of an advisor who charges an investor a preset amount for services.

Fixed-income mutual funds: Fixed-income mutual fund managers invest money in bonds, notes, and other debt instruments. They have a broad range of styles, involving market timing, swapping to gain quality or yield, setting up maturity ladders, etc.

Forecasts: Predictions of analysts usually associated with stock picking and active money management, T-bills, and Treasury bonds. If these funds own any stocks at all, these are usually preferred shares.

Front-end load: A fee charged when an investor buys a mutual fund or a variable annuity.

Fund ratings: Evaluation of the performance of invested money pools, often mutual funds, by such entities as Chicago-based Morningstar.

Fund shares: Shares in a mutual fund.

Fundamentals: A marketing term referring to the financial statistics that traditional analysts and many Wall Street analysis use. Fundamental data include stock, earnings, dividends, assets and liabilities, inventories, debt, etc. Fundamental data are in contrast to items used in technical analysis—such as price momentum, volume trends, and short sales statistics.

Hot tip: Slang for an individual investment, often a stock, that is apparently poised to rise (but never does).

Income growth mutual fund: A marketing term that describes a mutual fund that is supposed to select securities to achieve a yield significantly higher than that of the S&P 500. These portfolios may own more utilities and less high tech and may own convertible preferreds and convertible bonds.

Index fund: A passively managed portfolio designed to replicate the performance of a certain index, such as the S&P 500. In general, such mutual funds have performance within a few basis points of the target index. The most popular index mutual funds are those that track the S&P 500, but special index funds, such as those based on the Russell 1000 or the Wilshire 5000, are also available.

Individually managed account: An actively managed investment account where the portfolio manager buys securities specifically for the *individual*; whereas, in a mutual fund, the portfolio manager buys securities specifically for the *fund*.

Inflation: A monetary phenomenon generated by an overexpansion of credit that drives up prices of assets while diminishing the worth of paper currency.

Interest: The rate a borrower pays a lender.

Intrinsic value: The theoretical valuation or price for a stock. The valuation is determined using a valuation theory or model. The resulting value is compared with the current market price. If the intrinsic value is greater than the market price, the stock is considered undervalued.

Invest: Disciplined process of placing money in financial instruments so as to gain a return. Given the emergence of valid academic research regarding asset class investment methods, an individual who depends mostly on active management and stock picking may come to be considered a speculator rather than investor.

Investment discipline: A specific money strategy one espouses.

Investment objective: The money goals one wishes to reach.

Investment policy: An investment policy statement forces the investor to confront risk tolerance, return objectives, time horizon, liquidity needs, the amount of funds available for investment, and the investment methodology to be followed.

Investment pornography: Extreme examples of investment pandering.

Investor discomfort: Realization that risk is not appropriate and reward is not predictable in a given portfolio.

IPOs (initial public offerings): The sale of stock in a company going public for the first time.

Know Your Customer Rule: The New York Stock Exchange rule that requires brokers to know their clients' investment objectives and financial conditions before making investment recommendations. The National Association of Security Dealers has a similar rule.

Liquidity: Ability to generate cash on demand when necessary.

Load fund: A mutual fund that is sold for a sales charge (load) by a brokerage firm or other sales representative. Such funds may be stock, bond, or commodity funds, with conservative or aggressive objectives. The stated advantage of a load fund is that the salesperson will explain the fund to the customer and advise him or her when it is appropriate to sell as well as when to buy more shares.

Management fee: Charge against investor assets for managing the portfolio of an open- or closed-end mutual fund as well as for such services as shareholder relations or administration. The fee, as disclosed in the prospectus, is a fixed percentage of the fund's asset value, typically 1 percent or less per year.

Margin account: A margin account allows an investor to use the value of securities held in the account as collateral against a cash loan that can be used to purchase additional securities. *A first time investor has no business going on margin.* You give up your right to be called an investor, you are now a speculator.

Margin call: When the ratio of equity to the total of equity plus margin debt falls below a certain level, the brokerage firm requires the investor to bring the ratio back up. This is done by putting more cash for securities into the account or by selling some of the securities in the account. Here's an example of what can happen: Mr. K agrees to open a margin account with his broker. They buy 10,000 shares of stock valued at $20 a share. The total value of the stock is now $200,000, so Mr. K basically has leverage. To meet the Regulation T requirement, Mr. K is asked to put up $100,000. So Mr. K has a margin loan, called a *debt balance,* of $100,000 on which he has to pay interest. On his equity portion of the $100,000 of securities, monthly interest is added to the debt balance. There are different requirements, one of which is that the firm has a margin requirement for stock, and for an active account it's 35 percent of the market value of the stocks. The NASD and NYSE minimum requirements are 25 percent. This means that if Mr. K's equity falls below 35 percent of the total of the sum of his equity and his debt balance, he needs to put up more cash or other securities— or face liquidation of his positions. So, let's say a year later his debt balance has risen to $105,000 and the value of his stock has fallen down to $150,000. He now has an equity of $45,000 and a total equity plus debt balance of $150,000. His ratio of equity plus debt is right at 35 percent. Let's say the stock falls lower. Now Mr. K faces a margin call. The margin call is made at the end of the trading day when the securities are valued at the current market price. The process is called *making to the market.* Either you make that margin call the next trading day, or your position is liquidated. These are speculative processes that investors use: borrowing money from a brokerage to buy more securities. And this kind of leverage can be really dangerous and wipe you out.

Market: In investing terms, a place where securities are traded. Formerly meant a physical location but now may refer to an electronic one as well.

Market capitalization, The current value of a company, determined by multiplying the latest available number of outstanding common shares by the current market price of a share. Market cap is also an indication of the trading liquidity of a particular issue.

Market timing: The attempt to base investment decisions on the expected direction of the market.

Market value: The market or liquidation value of a given security or of an entire pool of assets.

Maturity: Applies to bonds, the date at which a borrower must redeem the capital portion of his or her loan.

Model portfolio: A theoretical construct of an investment or series of investments.

Modern Portfolio Theory: In 1950, Professor Harry Markowitz started to build an investment strategy that took more than 30 years to develop and be recognized as Modern Portfolio Theory. He won the Nobel Prize for his work in 1990.

Money market fund: Money market fund managers invest in short-term fixed instruments and cash equivalents. These instruments make up the portfolio and the objective is to maximize principal protection. Even though these accounts have short-term (one-day) liquidity, they typically pay more like 90- to 180-day CDs versus passbook or one-week CDs.

Municipal bonds: Fixed-income securities issued by governmental agencies.

Mutual fund: An investment company that continually offers new shares, buys existing shares back at the request of the shareholder, and uses its capital to invest in diversified securities of other companies.

Mutual fund families: A mutual fund sponsor or company usually offers a number of funds with different investment objectives within its family of funds. For example, a mutual fund family may include a money market fund, a government bond fund, a corporate bond fund, a blue chip stock fund, and a more speculative stock fund. If an investor buys a fund in the family, he or she is allowed to exchange that fund for another in the same family.

National Association of Securities Dealers, Inc. (NASD): The principal association of over-the-counter (OTC) brokers and dealers that establishes legal and ethical standards of conduct for its members. NASD was established in 1939 to regulate the OTC market in much the same manner as organized exchanges monitor actions of their members.

Net asset value (NAV): The market value of each share of a mutual fund. This figure is derived by taking a fund's total assets (securities, cash, and receivables), deducting liabilities, and then dividing that total by the number of shares outstanding.

Net trade: Generally, an over-the-counter trade involving no explicit commission. The investment advisor's compensation is in the spread between the cost of the security and the price paid by the customer. Also, a trade in which shares are exchanged directly with the issuer.

No-load fund: Mutual fund offered by an open-end investment company that imposes no sales charge (load) on its shareholders. Investors buy shares in no-load funds directly from the fund companies, rather than through a broker, as is done in load funds. Because no broker is used, no advice is given on when to buy or sell.

Nominal return: The actual current dollar growth in an asset's value over a given period. See also **Total return** and **Real return.**

Nonqualified contract: An annuity that is not used as part of or in connection with a qualified retirement plan.

Operating expenses: Costs associated with running a fund or portfolio.

Optimization: A process whereby a portfolio, invested using valid academic theory in various asset classes, is analyzed to ensure that risk/reward parameters have not drifted from stated goals.

Outperform: Any given market that exceeds expectations or historical performance.

Over-the-counter: A market made between securities dealers who act either as principal or broker for their clients. This is the principal market for U.S. government and municipal bonds.

Packaged products: Specific types of products underwritten and packaged by manufacturing companies that can be bought and sold directly through those companies. Packaged products are not required to go through a clearing process. Packaged products include mutual funds, unit investment trusts (UITs), limited partnership interests, and annuities.

Passive management: The practice of buying a portfolio that is a proxy for the market as a whole on the theory that it is so difficult to outperform the market that it is cheaper and less risky to just buy the market.

Penny stock: A stock that trades for under a dollar per share. Penny stocks are highly risky; they do not trade on the exchange but rather on the pink sheets or over-the-counter broker-to-broker marketplace.

Percentage points: Used to describe the difference between two readings that are percentages. For example, if a portfolio's performance was 18.2 percent versus the S&P 500's 14.65, it outperformed the S&P by 3.6 percentage points.

Portfolio: A group of investments held by an investor, investment company, or financial institution.

Portfolio turnover: Removing funds from one financial instrument to place in another. This process can be costly.

Price/earnings (P/E) ratio: The current price divided by reported earnings per share of stock for the latest 12-month period. For example, a stock with earnings per share during the trailing year of $5 and currently selling at $50 per share has a price/earnings ratio of 10. (It's also the percentage of investors wetting their pants as the market keeps crashing.)

Principal: The original dollar amount invested.

Prospectus: The document required by the Securities and Exchange Commission that accompanies the sale of a mutual fund or annuity outlining risks associated with certain types of funds or securities, fees, and management. At the core of the prospectus is a description of the fund's investment objectives and the portfolio manager's philosophy.

Put: A put gives the investor the right to sell a security at a preset price within a specified time.

R-squared: A measure of how closely the return characteristics of a security or portfolio match those of a particular market index. R-squared is a measure of a scale from 1 to 100, with 100 being closest to the market index in question. In order to understand the meaning of investment data, you need to know how closely they correlate to the comparative index by measuring the R-squared.

Random walk theory: One element of the efficient market theory. It states that stock price variations are not predictable.

Rate of return: The profits earned by a security as measured as a percentage of earned interest and/or dividends and/or appreciation.

Ratings: Performance and creditworthiness measurements of funds and corporations generated by Lipper, Moody's, Morningstar, and others. These ratings, when used to evaluate active fund managers, may be misleading since past performance is no guarantee of future success.

Real return: The inflation-adjusted return on an asset. Inflation-adjusted returns are calculated by subtracting the rate of inflation from an asset's apparent, or nominal, return. For example, if common stocks earn a total return of 10.3 percent over a period of time, but inflation during that period is 3.1 percent, the real return is the difference: 7.2 percent.

Rebalancing: A process whereby funds are shifted within asset classes and between asset classes to insure the maintenance of the efficient frontier. See **Optimization**.

Reinvested dividends: Dividends paid by a particular mutual fund that are reinvested in that same mutual fund. Some mutual funds offer automatic dividend reinvestment programs. In the complex equation theoretically used to determine the performance of the S&P 500, each company's dividend is reinvested in the stock of that company.

Relative return: The return of a stock or a mutual fund portfolio compared with some index, usually the S&P 500. For example, in 1989, American Brands had a total return of 12.2 percent in *absolute* terms. In isolation, that sounds good. After all, the historical annualized return on common stocks has been 10.3 percent. But because the S&P 500 had a return of 31.7 percent in 1989, American Brands underperformed the index in *relative* terms by 19.5 percentage points. Thus, its relative return was −19.5 percentage points.

Risk: Risk is nothing more than the uncertainty of future rates of return, which includes the possibility of loss. This variability or uncertainty causes "rational" investors to expect higher returns on investments where the actual timing or amount of payoffs is not guaranteed.

Risk-free rate of return: The return on an asset that is considered virtually riskless. U.S. government Treasury bills are typically used as the risk-free asset because of their short time horizon and the low probability of default.

Risk premium: The excess investment return above the risk-free return on an investment an investor hopes to obtain in exchange for taking investment risk.

Risk systematic: Potential for predictable, quantifiable loss of funds through the application of valid academic research to the process of disciplined asset class investing.

Risk tolerance: Investors' innate ability to deal with the potential of losing money without abandoning the investment process.

Risk unsystematic: Associated with investment in an undiversified portfolio of individual instruments through active management.

ROI (return on investment): The amount of money generated over time by placement of funds in specific financial instruments.

S&P 500: The performance benchmark most widely used by sponsors, managers, and performance measurement services. This index includes 400 industrial stocks, 20 transportation stocks, 40 financial stocks, and 40 public utilities. Performance is measured on a capitalization-weighted basis. The index is maintained by Standard & Poor's Corporation, a subsidiary of the McGraw-Hill Companies.

S&P common stock rankings: The S&P rankings measure historical growth and stability of earnings and dividends. The system includes nine rankings:

A+, A, and A−:	Above average
B+:	Average
B, B−, and C:	Below average
NR:	Insufficient historical data or not amenable to the ranking process. As a matter of policy, S&P does not rank the stocks of foreign companies, investment companies, and certain finance-oriented companies.

Securities: A tradable financial instrument.

Securities and Exchange Commission (SEC): The keystone law in the regulation of securities markets. It governs exchanges, over-the-counter markets, broker-dealers, the conduct of secondary markets, extension of credit in securities transactions, the conduct of corporate insiders, and principally the prohibition of fraud and manipulation in securities transactions. It also outlines the powers of the Securities and Exchange Commission to interpret, supervise, and enforce the securities laws of the United States.

Securities Investor Protection Corporation (SIPC): A government-sponsored organization created in 1970 to insure investor accounts at brokerage firms in the event of the brokerage firm's insolvency and liquidation. The maximum insurance of $500,000, including a maximum of $100,000 in cash assets per account, covers customer losses due to brokerage house insolvency, not customer losses caused by security price fluctuations. SIPC coverage is conceptually similar to Federal Deposit Insurance Corporation coverage of customer accounts at commercial banks.

Security selection: Process of picking securities, especially stocks for investment purposes.

Separately managed account (aka, individually managed account): A professionally managed investment account where the portfolio manager buys securities specifically for the *individual*; whereas, in a mutual fund, the portfolio manager buys securities specifically for the *fund*. They still are active managers.

Share: Specific portion of tradable equity, a share of stock. Generally refers to common or preferred stocks.

Sharpe ratio: Measure of an investment risk-adjusted return using investment return minus the risk-free return as the numerator and the investment standard deviation as the denominator.

Solicited/unsolicited order: A *solicited order* is a security transaction that results from a broker's recommendation. An *unsolicited order* results from an investor's request.

Sophisticated investor: Under SEC guidelines, an investor is defined as sophisticated if he or she meets certain income and net worth requirements.

Speculator: One who uses an active management style to invest.

Standard deviation: Volatility can be statistically measured using standard deviation. Standard deviation describes how far from the mean historic performance has been, either higher or lower. Mean is simply the middle point between the two historic extremes of the performance of the investment you are examining. The standard deviation measurement helps explain what the distribution of returns likely will be. The greater the range of returns, the greater the risk. The lower the risk, the lower the return expected.

Stock: A contract signifying ownership of a portion of a public or private company.

Stock picker: Someone who is actively trying to select companies whose equity may rise in the short or long term. Valid academic research shows this process is unworkable and results are no better than random.

Subaccount: That portion of the variable annuities separate account that invests in shares of the funds' portfolios.

Time horizon: The amount of time someone can wait to generate or take profits from an investment.

Time-weighted rate of return: The rate at which a dollar invested at the beginning of a period would grow if no additional capital were invested and no cash withdrawals were made. It provides an indication of value added by the investment manager, and allows comparisons to the performance of other investment managers and market indexes.

Total return: A standard measure of performance or return including both capital appreciation (or depreciation) and dividends or other income received. For example, Stock A is priced at $60 at the start of a year and pays an annual dividend of $4. If the stock moves up to $70 in price, the appreciation component is 16.7 percent, the yield component is 6.7 percent, and the total return is 23.4 percent. That oversimplification does not take into account any earnings on the reinvested dividends.

Trading costs: Fees or commissions paid to move money from one financial instrument to another.

Transaction costs: Another term for execution costs. Total transaction costs (or the cost of buying and selling stocks) have three components: (1) the actual dollars paid in commissions, (2) the market impact—that is, the impact a manager's trade has on the market price for the stock (this varies with the size of the trade and the skill of the trader), and (3) the opportunity cost of the return (positive or negative) given up by not executing the trade instantaneously.

Treasury bills: U.S. financial securities issued by Federal Reserve banks for the Treasury as a means of borrowing money for short periods of time. They are sold at a discount from their maturity value, pay no coupons, and have maturities of up to one year. Because they are a direct obligation of the federal government they are free of default risk. Most Treasury bills are purchased by commercial banks and held as part of their secondary reserves. T-bills regulate the liquidity base of the banking system in order to control the money supply. For example, if the authorities wish to expand the money supply they can buy Treasury bills, which increases the reserves of the banking system and induces a multiple expansion of bank deposits.

Turnover: The volume or percentage of buying or selling activity within a mutual fund portfolio relative to the mutual fund portfolio's size.

Underperformers: Securities or markets that do not meet expectations.

Value stocks: Stocks with high book to market valuations—that is, companies doing poorly in the market that may have the potential to do better.

Volatility: The extent to which market values and investment returns are uncertain or fluctuate. Another word for risk, volatility is gauged using such measures as beta, mean absolute deviation, and standard deviation.

Weighting: A term usually associated with proportions of assets invested in a particular region or securities index to generate a specific risk/reward profile.

Wrap fee: A single, all-encompassing fee based on a percentage of assets under management. This fee covers all charges, including advisor costs, commissions and other transaction charges, and reporting. It includes identification of and help in the selection of appropriate money managers, account monitoring, analyzing and reporting on a manager's performance, custodianship of securities, execution of transactions, and consulting.

Yield (current yield): For stocks, yield is the percentage return paid in dividends on a common or preferred stock, calculated by dividing the indicated annual dividend by the market price of the stock. For example, if a stock sells for $40 and pays a dividend of $2 per share, it has a yield of 5 percent (i.e., $2 divided by $40). For bonds, the coupon rate of interest divided by the market price is called **current yield**. For example, a bond selling for $1,000 with a 10 percent coupon offers a 10 percent current yield. If the same bond were selling for $500, it would offer a 20 percent yield to an investor who bought it for $500. (As a bond's price falls, its yield rises, and vice versa.)

Yield curve: A chart or graph showing the price of securities (usually fixed income) through time. A flat or inverted yield curve of fixed-income instruments is thought by many to be an indicator of recession. This is because those who borrow at the far end of the curve usually pay more for their money than those who borrow for only a little while. When the yield curve is flat or inverted this means there is little demand for long-term money and this can be interpreted as a signal that there is little demand in the economy for the products that long-term borrowing would generate.

Yield to maturity: The discount rate that equates the present value of the bond's cash flows with the market price. The yield to maturity will actually be earned if (1) the investor holds the bond to maturity and (2) the investor is able to reinvest all coupon payments at a rate equal to the yield to maturity. When a bond is selling at par, the yield to maturity and the coupon rate are equal.

BIBLIOGRAPHY

For some of the better books around on investing, consult these listed in order of recommended reading:

1. Charles Ellis, *Investment Policy, How to Win the Loser's Game* (Homewood, IL: Dow Jones-Irwin, 1993).

2. Daniel R. Solin, *Does Your Broker Owe You Money?* (Alpha Books, 2002).

3. Dale Rogers and Craig Rogers, *How to Build, Protect, and Maintain Your 401(k) Plan* (Columbia, MD: Marketplace Books, 2004).

4. Benjamin Graham, *The Intelligent Investor*, rev. ed. (New York: HarperBusiness, 2003).

5. Burton G. Malkiel, *A Random Walk Down Wall Street* (New York: W.W. Norton & Co., 1996).

6. Joe John Duran with Larry Chambers, *The First Time Investor Workbook* (New York: McGraw-Hill, 2001).

7. Jane Bryant Quinn, *Making the Most of Your Money* (New York: Simon & Schuster, 1997).

8. Gerald Lobe, *The Battle for Investment* (New York: HarperCollins, 1997).

9. Harry S. Dent, *The Roaring 2000s* (New York: Simon & Schuster, 1998).

10. Mary Rowland, *Best Practices for Financial Advisors* (New York: Bloomberg, 1997).

11. Eric Tyson, *Personal Finance for Dummies* (IDG Books, 1996).

RECOMMENDED READING ABOUT ASSET CLASS INVESTING

1. Larry Swedroe, *The Only Guide to a Winning Investment Strategy* (New York: Dutton, 1998).

2. John J. Bowen, Jr. and Dan Goldie, *The Prudent Investor's Guide to Beating Wall Street at Its Own Game*, 2nd Ed. (New York: McGraw-Hill, 1998).

3. Roger C. Gibson, *Balancing Financial Risk* (New York: Irwin, 1996).

JOURNALS

1. William F. Sharpe, "Are Gains Likely from Market Timing," *Financial Analysts Journal* (March/April 1975), as adapted in a position paper, "The Asset Allocation Decision," *SEI Research Report*, SEI Capital Resources, April 1992.
2. "Active versus Passive Investing," *The Journal of Investing* 2(1) (Spring 1993).
3. Robert H. Jeffrey, "The Folly of Stock Market Timing," *Harvard Business Review* (July–August 1984).
4 Article by Gary P. Brinson, L. Randolph Hood, and Gilbert L. Beebower, *Financial Analysts Journal* (July–August 1986): 39–44.
5. Maurice G. Kendall, "The Analysis of Time Series, Part I: Prices," *Journal of the Royal Statistical Society* 96 (1953): 11–25.

MUTUAL FUNDS

For information on mutual funds, *Morningstar Mutual Funds* is the absolute best—it costs about $400+ per year. For more information, call 800-735-0700, or you can write to Morningstar at 225 West Wacker Drive, Chicago, IL 60606; or visit their Web site: www.morningstar.net.com. It is published every two weeks, and it itemizes each mutual fund, performance, risk, portfolio operating history, and distribution information. It offers interviews with fund managers and gives advice on buying or avoiding particular funds.

INNOVATIONS IN FINANCE

1950   *Conventional Wisdom:* Analyze securities one by one. Focus on picking winners. Concentrate holdings to maximize returns.

1952   *Diversification and Portfolio Risk:* Harry Markowitz, Nobel Prize in Economics, 1990—Diversification reduces risk. Portfolio risk versus security risk. Assets evaluated by their effect on portfolio. An optimal portfolio can be constructed to maximize return for a given standard deviation.

1958   *The Role of Stocks:* James Tobin, Nobel Prize in Economics, 1981—Separation Theorem: (1) Form portfolio of risky assets; (2) Temper risk by lending and borrowing. Shifts focus from stock selection to portfolio structure.

1961   *Investments and Capital Structure:* Merton Miller and Franco Modigliana, Nobel Prizes in Economics, 1985 and 1990—A firm's value is unrelated to its dividend policy. Dividend policy is an unreliable guide for stock selection.

1964   *Single-Factor Asset Pricing Risk/Return Model:* William Sharpe, Nobel Prize in Economics, 1990—Capital Asset Pricing Model: Theoretical model defines risk as volatility relative to market. A stock's cost of capital (the investor's expected return) is proportional to the stock's risk relative to the entire stock universe. Theoretical model for evaluating the risk and expected return of securities and portfolios.

1965   *Behavior of Securities Prices:* Paul Samuelson, MIT, Nobel Prize in Economics, 1970—Market prices are the best estimates of value. Price changes follow random patterns. Future stock prices are unpredictable.

1966   *Efficient Market Hypothesis:* Eugene Fama, University of Chicago—Efficient Market Hypothesis asserts that prices reflect values and information accurately and quickly. It is difficult if not impossible to capture returns in excess of market returns without taking greater than market levels of risk. Investors cannot identify superior stocks using fundamental information or price patterns.

1968   *First Major Study of Manager Performance:* Michael Jensen,
1965; A.G. Becker Corporation, 1968—First studies showing
that investment professionals fail to outperform market
indexes.

1973   *Random Prices and Practical Investing:* John McQuown, Rex
Sinquefield—The birth of index funds: American National
Bank (Sinquefield); Wells Fargo Bank (McQuown). Banks
develop the first passive S&P 500 Index funds. Years later,
Sinquefield chairs Dimensional and McQuown sits on its
board.

1977   *Database of Securities Prices Since 1926:* Roger Ibbotson, Rex
Sinquefield—Stocks, Bonds, Bills, and Inflation—An extensive
returns database for multiple asset classes is first developed
and will become one of the most widely used investment
databases. The first extensive, empirical basis for making
asset allocation decisions changes the way investors build
portfolios.

1990   *Nobel Prize Recognizes Modern Finance:* Recognition of
economists who shaped the way we invest, emphasizing the
role of science in finance—William Sharpe for the Capital
Asset Pricing Model, beta, and relative risk; Harry Markowitz
for the theory of portfolio choice; and Merton Miller for
work on the effect of firms' capital structure and dividend
policy on their prices.

1992   *Multifactor Asset Pricing Model and Value Effect:* Eugene
Fama and Kenneth French, The University of Chicago—
Improved on the single-factor asset pricing model (CAPM).
Identified market, size, and "value" factors in returns.
Developed the three-factor asset pricing model, an invaluable
asset allocation and portfolio analysis tool. Recognized the
way we construct and analyze portfolios by identifying
independent sources of risk and return. Introduced first
concentrated, empirical value strategies. Led to similar
findings internationally.

INDEX

ABOUT THE AUTHORS

Larry Chambers is the author of over 900 magazine articles and 36 professional business books. Two of his books remain specialty bestsellers and five have found their way into book-of-the-month clubs. *The First Time Investor* was named one of the top five books for "investing on a shoestring" by Chuck Myers, Knight Ridder, Washington Bureau, and another became the basis of a History Channel special.

Chambers has recently been chosen as Business and Economics columnist for the Honor Society of Phi Kappa Phi Forum. He has been an online columnist for *Financial Planning Interactive,* an advisory board member for the *Journal of Retirement Planning,* associate editor for the *Journal of Investing,* and on the Board of Advisors for *Personal Financial Planning Monthly.*

Dale Rogers is the founder and CEO of the Rogers Companies, located in Fort Worth, Texas. The Rogers Companies serve over 50,000 401(k) plan participants in over 300 plans. Corporate clients encompass all areas of business including manufacturing, law firms, medical and dental practices, construction companies, architectural firms, service companies, automobile dealers, and consulting practices as well as many nonprofit organizations and governmental entities. In addition, over 350 individual clients are provided investment advisory services.

Rogers Capital Management Inc. is a fee-only registered investment advisor providing institutional investment strategies for corporations, foundations, trusts, and qualified individuals as well as investment selection, monitoring, and education for 401(k) plan participants. Rogers has been an investment professional since 1970.

Rogers and Associates is a fee-only firm of Certified Pension Consultants providing consulting, administration, and actuarial services. Serving a national clientele, Rogers founded the firm in 1973.

Rogers is a frequent lecturer, speaking to thousands of employees of client companies each year as well as to professional groups. He is the author of *How to Build, Protect, and Maintain Your 401(k) Plan* and has written articles for various professional journals and trade magazines. Rogers is a Certified Pension Consultant and a member of the American Society of Pension Actuaries and Consultants and the ESOP Association.

The authors' investment philosophy is based on Nobel Prize–winning academic research and empirical evidence that leads us to believe that capital markets are efficiently priced and that asset allocation is the key determinate of investor returns.

Contact information:
Dale Rogers
Rogers Capital Management, Inc.
1330 Summit Avenue
Fort Worth, TX 76102
Telephone: 817-334-0351
Fax: 817-334-0387
E-mail: dcrogers@rogersco.com